THE PILL
THAT STEALS
LIVES

Katinka Blackford Newman is an award-winning documentary film director and journalist. She trained at the BBC, where she worked in News and Current Affairs and Documentary Features. She has made a number of critically acclaimed films for all the terrestrial channels. She is inspired by extraordinary stories of ordinary people. She lives in Harlesden, North-West London, with her two children, Lily and Oscar

Praise for *The Pill That Steals Lives*:

'If you think this case is exceptional think again. Katinka Blackford Newman vividly and eloquently describes a medical horror coming your way soon' – **Professor David Healy**, psychiatrist, psychopharmacologist, scientist and author, and a leading authority on the contribution of antidepressants to suicide

'This book describes in vivid detail how ordinary people can become murderers if they take antidepressant drugs and how psychiatry can destroy people. It is a catching personal testimony about what is wrong with psychiatry, its love affair with unscientific diagnoses and harmful drugs, and its blindness towards the fact that what look like psychiatric diseases are often side effects of psychiatric drugs' – **Professor Peter C. Gøtzsche**, the Nordic Cochrane Centre

KATINKA BLACKFORD NEWMAN

THE PILL THAT STEALS LIVES

ONE WOMAN'S TERRIFYING JOURNEY TO DISCOVER THE TRUTH ABOUT ANTIDEPRESSANTS

JOHN BLAKE

Published by John Blake Publishing Limited,
3 Bramber Court, 2 Bramber Road,
London W14 9PB, England

www.johnblakebooks.com

www.facebook.com/johnblakebooks 🅵
twitter.com/jblakebooks 🆃

First published in paperback in 2016

ISBN: 978-1-78606-133-1

British Library Cataloguing-in-Publication Data:
A catalogue record for this book is available from the British Library.

Design by www.envydesign.co.uk

Printed in Great Britain by CPI Group (UK) Ltd

1 3 5 7 9 10 8 6 4 2

Papers used by John Blake Publishing are natural, recyclable products made
from wood grown in sustainable forests. The manufacturing processes
conform to the environmental regulations of the country of origin.

Every attempt has been made to contact the relevant copyright-holders, but
some were unobtainable. We would be grateful if the appropriate people
could contact us.

For Lily and Oscar. I'm so very sorry I was stolen from you for a year. I'll never leave you again, unless, of course, somebody pins me down and forcibly injects me with Prozac. And thank you, my darlings, for sharing your story to stop other lives being stolen – I dedicate this book to you.

CONTENTS

PART II: OTHER STOLEN LIVES

ACKNOWLEDGEMENTS

I would like to thank the following:

First, my family and friends who looked on in despair and bewilderment as I disappeared into a distant land of medication induced insanity for an entire year where none of you could reach me.

Special thanks to all of you who visited me while I shuffled around in an old dressing gown, dribbling and not making much sense, but particularly to every one of my siblings, their spouses, my niece Sarah, and the following friends – Lesa Green, Helen Richards, Helen Edwards, Gabriel Kemlo, Juliette Brown and Andrea Madarasz.

Thank you to the staff of St Charles Hospital for having the insight to take me off all the drugs that caused my illness.

Thank you to every single contributor to this book, and especially to Joanna Moncrieff, Peter Gøtzsche, Luke Montagu, James Davies, Professor Tim Kendall, director of the National Collaborating Centre for Mental Health, Joanne Werb, Olga

THE PILL THAT STEALS LIVES

Leclerq, Brian from AntiDepaware, Bob Fiddaman, David Carmichael, Andy Vickery, Blair Hamrick, Darren Hanison, Heather McCarthy, Wendy Dolin, Ellen Le Brun, Tim Tobin, Kim Crespi, Selma Eikelenboom, Richard McCann, Douglas De Coninck, and Professor Dinesh Bhugra, President of the World Psychiatric Association.

Also to those of you who have shared your stories under a different name because you are too wary of the consequences of being identified.

Thanks also to Caroline Scott for writing about my story in the *Daily Mail*. It gave me the courage to begin a much bigger journey.

To the members of my film production team for having faith in the pilot for the documentary I know we will make – Steve Standen, Tim Watts, Iain Mitchell and Allen Charlton.

To Tony Joyce, an old friend who wandered back into my life after twenty years, read every chapter of my book and became a cheerleader on the many occasions I doubted myself.

To Rebekah Beddoe, whose book *Dying for a Cure* provided such comfort and knowledge to my kids and me as we grappled to understand what had happened to me. Thank you for having me to stay with your lovely family in Melbourne. I will always have a special bond with you for our shared experience and the promise we made to each other that we will use our experience to help others.

To Yolande Lucire for your hospitality in Sydney and your patience as you drip fed me the knowledge you have gathered over many years as a psychiatrist.

To my publisher John Blake for having faith in me as a new author. And my editor, Toby Buchan, for his support and enthusiasm.

ACKNOWLEDGEMENTS

There are two people without whom this book would never have happened.

Professor David Healy, words will never express the gratitude and admiration I have for you. Your work saves lives, and your courage and integrity in continuously standing up for what is right rather than what is convenient is a beacon to many of us who have been harmed by drugs that you have tried to warn the world about. Thank you for your patience in explaining things to me very, very slowly indeed and sometimes several times over, as I floundered in a world of science I was unfamiliar with. You have been there at every stage of my journey, from the very beginning when I woke up from my drug-induced, year-long nightmare, to the completion of this book, which you kindly read and corrected. Your reassurance that I wasn't mad but that the madness lies elsewhere has been a guiding light.

I would never, ever have considered writing a book were it not for the serendipitous meeting with the man who became my agent, Adrian Sington. When you suggested I write a book, I laughed and said the most I'd ever written was a cheque. Your persuasion that I should write just one chapter turned into several, and six weeks later became this book.

And finally, the force that shapes our destiny chose to smile on me and determine that I was one that got away. It's a debt I know I must repay. It meant that only one year of my life was stolen, whereas others' lives are stolen permanently. And this is something for which I say a prayer of gratitude every single day.

Thank you.

KATINKA BLACKFORD NEWMAN

PROLOGUE

Before you read my story, you need to know an incredible fact: antidepressant drugs can cause ordinary people with no history of suicide, mental illness or violence to suddenly, and inexplicably, want to self-harm, or even kill themselves or other people. Yes, I know that seems to be an outrageous claim but if you don't believe me, just look at the packaging inserts that come with the drugs. Suicidal thoughts, psychosis and hallucinations are listed amongst many other unfortunate side effects, the most remarkable of which is... depression. And no, that's not a misprint. Sort of like an aspirin giving you a headache, isn't it?

Talking of headaches, I'm guessing that's exactly what the chief execs of Eli Lilly and Company must have had following the launch of their wonderdrug Prozac in 1988. Suddenly there were an awful lot of claims that the drug was turning people into killers. These included the sensational case of a forty-seven-year-old man, Joseph T. Wesbecker, who walked into his workplace, a printing plant, one month after taking a course of Prozac. On the morning of 14 September 1989 he opened fire with an AK-47 semi-assault rifle in Louisville, Kentucky, killing eight people and wounding twelve others before turning the gun on himself.

By the time the case against the makers of Prozac, Eli Lilly, came to court, in 1994, there were already a further 160 claims against them. And since then drug companies have paid out billions in settlements involving homicides, suicides and also birth defects allegedly caused by their antidepressants. We don't get to hear much about them because many of the claims are settled silently.

Fluoxetine (better known by its trade name Prozac) is only one of the eight serotonin reuptake inhibitor antidepressant drugs that are prescribed in the West. The others are sertraline (Zoloft, Lustral), paroxetine (Seroxat, Paxil), escitalopram (Lexapro, Cipralex), citalopram (Celexa, Cipramil), venlafaxine (Effexor), desvenlafaxine (Pristiq) and duloxetine (Cymbalta). They all work in the same way, and there have been cases involving all of them.

SSRI stands for Selective Serotonin Reuptake Inhibitors. It's thought they act by boosting serotonin in the brain by increasing the availability of existing serotonin. SSRIs have become the most commonly prescribed medication in the world and not just for depression but all sorts of other conditions, notably OCD (obsessive-compulsive disorder), eating disorders and phobias. They have largely replaced the older tricyclic antidepressants such as amitriptyline and imipramine, which have also been linked to suicides, but at nothing like the same rate as the newer drugs.

I'm a documentary maker but it's not as a journalist that I came across this story. In 2012 something happened to me that was so utterly terrifying and shocking that my kids and I decided no matter what, we had to tell our story.

While going through a divorce I took a pill (escitalopram, or Lexapro as it's known in the US) and went into a four-day toxic delirium. I started hallucinating wildly, thought I'd killed the kids and in fact took a knife and lacerated my arm. It was pure luck I didn't kill myself or someone else as I had no sense of reality… In fact I thought I was in a dream.

In the course of my research for this book and the film I'm hoping to make I talked to experts who believe people going temporarily insane on these drugs have caused some of the worst mass killings of our time. Cases like James Holmes, known as the '*Batman* killer', because he went into a cinema in Aurora and opened fire, killing twelve and injuring seventy cinema-goers as they innocently watched a midnight premiere of *The Dark Knight Rises* on 20 July 2012.[1] Psychiatrists who interviewed him, and whom I have since spoken to, believe like me, he was in an antidepressant induced psychosis, where he was unable to distinguish between dreams and reality. However, the case that moved me most was the Sierre (Switzerland) Bus Crash of 13 March 2012, in which a group of 28 people, 22 Belgian and Dutch schoolchildren and their teachers, were killed in one of the country's worst national tragedies.[2] The parents are demanding an investigation because the driver was in withdrawal from the antidepressant Seroxat. Forensic experts – the Dutch-based forensic agency Independent Forensic Services (IFS), part of an American parent company – commissioned by the parents to carry out an investigation, have recreated the crash and say it looks as if the driver killed himself on purpose by driving into the wall of a tunnel. Their report concludes: 'The evidence so far supports the hypothesis that Geert Michiels committed suicide while in a toxic delirium caused by fluctuating levels of paroxetine (Seroxat).'

Before my experience, I would have placed these stories in the same category as conspiracy theories and claims the world is ruled by lizards but now I know what a drug-induced psychosis is like. My main memory from that time was that I thought I was in a video game or a dream so that's why I was capable of anything. There are many people who end up in prison because of this and my testimony has been used in various criminal cases to persuade judges and juries that these drugs can actually make you go temporarily insane. One of these was a Court of Appeal case in 2015 in which a thirty-eight-year-old-former hotel worker, Paul Stones, killed his mum while on antidepressants and hoped to have his conviction overturned. Another was a young man, with no history of violence, who attacked a stranger with a crowbar but then remembered nothing afterwards.

My story didn't end with the psychotic episode. After four days of being delusional, I was better once I came off the Lexapro (escitalopram). However, the doctors didn't realise it was the pill that made me ill and so they diagnosed psychotic depression, kept me in hospital and put me on a lot more drugs – five altogether, not just antidepressants but also antipsychotics. Over the next year, I became so ill I couldn't leave the house, needed a 24-hour carer and couldn't wash or dress myself. The kids were nine and ten years old at the time and lost their mum for a year. Luckily my ex stepped in and looked after them. But by the end of it, they had resigned themselves to the fact they had lost me forever.

I came to know from first-hand experience of the other side effect of these drugs: they really can cause you to feel suicidal.

It's hard for me to admit it, but at the close of that year I was about to end it all. The drugs had taken away everything. I was a stranger to my children; the emotional blunting meant I no longer enjoyed anything. Now I wandered around in a stained dressing gown, and the old me had disappeared. I had the beginnings of brain damage, where my mouth was drooping and my speech was slurred. I didn't know where to turn but by luck I made a decision that saved my life: Our private insurance ran out, and in desperation I got myself to an NHS hospital and they took me off all the drugs.

After four weeks of agonising withdrawal I was 100 per cent better. I got a job, a house, and started training for a half marathon – all within weeks. There is no other plausible explanation for my remarkable recovery except that it was the drugs themselves that made me ill. That was three years ago that my ordeal ended, in the autumn of 2013 and I haven't taken a single antidepressant medication since, and I never will again.

My children and I began an extraordinary journey of discovery. We met others less fortunate than us and realised that this happens to many people.

There are two things people say when I tell them all of this. How do you know it's the drugs that made these people suicidal and violent and not their depression?

There is a world of difference. Like many of us, I've had some pretty bad things happen in my life. Far worse than what led to me taking the antidepressants. I've cried, I've seen therapists, I've bored my friends rigid and I've even rung the Samaritans. But suicide is something I would never,

ever consider. With the pills, it was different. The chemical effect of these drugs on people who can't tolerate them is indescribable. It's hard to believe until you experience it for yourself, but these pills flip a switch in your brain to make you do things you would never have dreamt of doing before. And it can happen literally within hours of starting them, changing dosage or coming off them altogether. Overnight, people with no history of self-harm or violence slit their wrists, try to hang themselves, jump under trains, attack others, drive into walls or go on murderous rampages. Usually there is no rationale. It's as if a monster suddenly takes you over while you are on the pills and leaves if you are lucky enough to get off them.

Further proof is an experiment in 1999 carried out by one of the world's leading experts on this subject, Professor David Healy, who took twenty healthy volunteers who had been screened for psychiatric illnesses, put them on the antidepressant Zoloft and two of them became suicidal. By the end of the second week, one of the volunteers went into a sort of trance and decided she was going to go out and throw herself under a bus or a train. It was pure luck that prevented her – she was on her way out the door to kill herself when the phone rang and it jolted her to her senses.[3]

This happens on the drug trials too with tragic results. An example is the case of Traci Johnson, a nineteen-year-old student who volunteered to try out the new antidepressant drug duloxetine, marketed under the brand name Cymbalta.[4] Over the trial weekend at the company's laboratory in February 2004, she hanged herself, having had no previous history of mental illness. Deaths like hers go unreported because the drug companies are under no obligation to do so. A recent review by the Nordic Cochrane Centre showed that during trials four deaths went unreported by a pharmaceutical company, including one patient who strangled himself, but because he survived for five days he was excluded from the results because it was claimed he was no longer on the trial while dying in hospital.[5]

The second thing people say is, yes, that's all very well, but think of all those whose lives are saved. Yes, there are people with proper clinical depression and real mental illnesses who may benefit from medication, but these are a small percentage of the 5 million in the UK on antidepressants and others on psychiatric medication. In fact there are around 10 million people in the UK taking medication for a whole host of disorders we are now persuaded we are suffering from. And around 400 million worldwide. In 1950, 1 in 100 people had a mental illness, now it's 1 in 4.[6] While depression, the illness I was supposed to be suffering from, used to happen to very few people, now doctors are dishing out antidepressants to ordinary people like me, who seem to be having normal reactions to difficult life events such as divorce, death of a loved one or even their beloved pet dying. Talking of which, Prozac is also prescribed for dogs and cats so it's not just us humans who are apparently becoming more depressed.[7] Then there are cases of children as young as a year old being prescribed them.[8]

There is a whole range of so-called conditions that both adults and children alike are being prescribed medication for. This is particularly prevalent in the US, where good old-fashioned shyness is now 'social anxiety phobia' and my penchant for coffee could receive a diagnosis of 'caffeine withdrawal disorder'. 'Oppositional defiant disorder', a pattern of angry moods in a child lasting six months (i.e. your average two-year-old), is something else you can now get a pill for. It raises the question of whether we are really becoming more mentally ill, or if the madness lies elsewhere. [9]

And let's think for a while about who is profiting from this huge increase in supposed diseases. In the UK we are consuming four times as many antidepressants as we were two decades ago, and 53 million antidepressant prescriptions were issued in 2013, while in America $11 billion was spent on them, a rise of 400 per cent since the 1980s. [10]

Professor Dinesh Bhugra is president of the World Psychiatric Association and he too is worried about the drug companies making money out of convincing us we are sick. He told me how a major pharmaceutical company took one of their pills that used to be sold for depression, and then rebranded it as a panacea for 'social phobia'.

'Aren't we allowed to be shy anymore?' was his question.

He too is concerned that we need to differentiate between normal sadness and depression, and that the trend towards medication is worrying.

'There has been a massive increase in prescribing antidepressants. A pill seems to be an easy answer, but it might be that you need to look at the world in a different way,' he says.[11]

I had a particularly bad reaction to antidepressants and of course not everyone becomes suicidal or homicidal on these pills although it's more common than you might think – it's estimated 1 in 100 people are affected.[12] And in the latest report by Nordic Cochrane Centre, the biggest-ever review which was published in January 2016, it was found antidepressants doubled the risk of suicide and aggression in the under-eighteens.[13]

The question is, do they help the rest of us? Like me, you may perhaps want to believe that when the going gets really tough, there will be a magic pill that will help you out. Well, after two years of meeting experts and people who have taken antidepressants, I'm not convinced that for most of us there is. At this point I'm not going to explain why for two reasons: first, you won't read the rest of my book and second, for the same reason I decided not to tell my kids that Father Christmas and fairies don't exist in the same week, but here are the views of just some of the people who have contributed to this book.

Professor Tim Kendall is one of the most influential people in healthcare in the UK. That's because, as director of NCCMH (National Collaborating Centre for Mental Health), he and his researchers look at all the available evidence and advise the NHS on their guidelines. I was staggered when he told me that not only can the drugs have serious side effects but previously unpublished trials show they are no more effective than a placebo in treating mild to moderate depression, he told me. This means people who were given a drug-free pill without knowing what it was, did almost as well as those given an antidepressant. As a result of these discoveries, the NHS guidelines now state antidepressants should only be used as a last resort, and that psychological therapies should be the first-line treatment. Despite this, more and more people are being prescribed antidepressants, with the NHS spending £282 million in 2013 a rise of over 30 per cent in a year.[14]

Professor Kendall went on to tell me: 'Some people have very, very bad reactions to these drugs. All are associated with withdrawal symptoms and many patients are finding that two years down the line they can't get off them.'[15]

THE PILL THAT STEALS LIVES

I went on to discover that even for the small percentage who get a supposedly positive result, critics argue this is only a temporary respite, an emotional blunting that doesn't address the real problem, much like drink or illicit drugs. As Professor David Healy says:

> Twenty-five years ago no one would have believed that a drug less effective for nerves or melancholia than heroin, alcohol or older and cheaper antidepressants could have been brought on the market and that almost as a matter of national policy people would be encouraged to take it for life.[16]

The most alarming thing is that these drugs are only tested for 6–8 weeks and the drug companies themselves largely do this. They only need to produce two positive trials to get their drugs approved by the FDA (US Food and Drug Administration) and are under no obligation to report the trials that don't prove positive or indeed any adverse effects that come about.[17]

During our interview Professor Dinesh Bhugra of the World Psychiatric Association told me how he once witnessed at first hand how drug companies hide their data. As part of a larger trial he was asked to test an antipsychotic drug on twenty patients. When the results showed it was no more effective than a placebo, the drug company failed to publish his results.[18]

In September 2015 my teenage kids and I decided to publicise our story. Lily, Oscar and I appeared in the *Daily Mail* and I self-funded a filmed pilot, which we are in the process of trying to get commissioned.[19] It features our story and others, and this book is partly about that process and the discoveries we made along the way.

We discussed the implications of their involvement in all of this. My philosophy with my kids is to give them the facts and let them make up their own minds. On this, I had to say I hadn't a clue what the consequences could be. Maybe the other kids at school would tease them, saying their mum is a nutcase. Who knows? They thought long and hard about this. It took them around ten seconds before they gave a unanimous 'yes' for two reasons: first, if it stops this happening to others and saves lives, then it's worth it. And second, because they want an iPhone and surely that should be their reward?

I had no idea that the journey I began in September 2015 would end six weeks later in an extraordinary personal discovery that has changed my view of myself and has ramifications for many people who think that depression runs through the family. The drugs I was prescribed stole a year out of the lives of me and my kids but it's nothing compared to the people I've met and the stories I've heard of others whose lives have been permanently stolen. Even those I've met who benefit from the drugs have experienced some devastating side effects and pretty dubious long-term effects. There are people in this book who may well have started out feeling 'better than well', as Prozac first promised. Only now, over twenty-five years later, we are seeing the neurological damage these drugs can do, and are faced with people who can't get off them and will have to take them for the rest of their lives.

With over 100 million worldwide taking antidepressants, of course there are many who are helped and undoubtedly some whose lives may even be saved by them. But for a significant number things can go badly wrong. And surely it's vital that those prescribing them and those taking them need to know how to spot this so that the treatment can be stopped or changed at the first sign of it. As Joseph Glenmullen from Harvard Medical School says in his book, *Prozac Backlash*:

> As the more dangerous side effects of the Prozac group come into view, perhaps we will be able to see not only the dark side of these latest miracle cures but also the liability of any potent, synthetic drug targeting the brain. Future generations may well look back on the last years of these drugs as a frightening human experiment.[20]

I am someone who has inadvertently been a participant in that experiment and if my own experience is anything to go by, it really can be a very frightening experiment. And for many the consequences of that experiment continue after they have tried to get off the drugs, because, as the trials are only short term, we are in fact the long-term studies.

So I'm not convinced that for most of us, it's worth it. But that's just my belief. It's the purpose of this book to give you the facts and let you make up your own mind.

This is our story.

PART I

THE YEAR MY LIFE WAS STOLEN

'Medicine sometimes snatches away health
and sometimes gives it' – Ovid

Chapter 1

SATURDAY, 22 SEPTEMBER 2012

It's 7 a.m. and for some reason I'm in my ex-husband's flat in West Hampstead. We've been separated for eight months, and all of that time we've barely been on speaking terms. It's not at all clear to me how I've ended up sleeping on the bottom bunk bed in the children's room in his flat with our daughter, Lily, then aged eleven, on the top bed. Only I haven't had any sleep at all. All night I've been lying awake with terrible heart palpitations, an unnamed anxiety, a feeling of inexorable doom. By morning, I'm terrified: I know something unspeakably awful is about to unfold.

I've been feeling strange for two days now, ever since I went to see a psychiatrist near Harley Street. I visited him in desperation after I hit a wall of gloom on realising we had to sell our five-bedroom Victorian family home in Queen's Park, north-west London. It was one of the few moments in my life when I felt totally out of control. When I broke up with my

3

husband, I hadn't mentioned to the children that we might have to sell up and move – I suppose I had naively presumed he would let me keep the house. How was I going to break the news to them that we would have to move away from all their friends and from the home they'd grown up in? As a filmmaker, I craft stories. But this story didn't have a happy ending and I felt like I'd let the kids down badly.

I never drink, but I started having a glass of wine when I came home from work. I had some zopiclone sleeping tablets that I used to take for jet lag and I began taking those too. But none of that helped, because nothing took me away from the inexorable fact of having to sell the house. Looking back, I realise those first steps that were meant to take me away from the problem were my nemesis. I should have had the sleepless nights; I should have felt the pain, the anxiety of losing the house. It would have been fleeting and we all would have adjusted, as indeed we have done many years down the line. My attempts to run away from the problem, albeit in a small way, were the start of a descent that took on its own life.

By the time I visited the private psychiatrist I was in a right state. Already I'd been to my GP, who rightly said he couldn't do anything. But I'm very impatient and when things don't go my way, I am prepared to pay for a solution. Someone out there must have a solution to the horrible feelings I was now faced with, I believed.

The elderly man in the book-lined office just off Euston Square looked at me sternly and asked if I had been crying a lot. The answer was undoubtedly 'yes'. He asked me how I'd been sleeping and whether I'd stopped enjoying things I used to enjoy. Our twenty-minute interview ended with him pronouncing that I was depressed. He wrote out a prescription for an antidepressant drug I'd never heard of called escitalopram (brand names Lexapro or Cipralex), and another called mirtazapine, and told me to come back in a week.

I never saw him again.

I wasn't sure if I agreed with his diagnosis but now I'd spent a few hundred pounds on my appointment and he seemed to know what he was talking about.

Escitalopram (Lexapro) is an SSRI antidepressant like Prozac, sertraline (Zoloft), paroxetine (Paxil, Seroxat) and citalopram (Celexa). This new group of drugs was introduced to replace the older drugs and they were regarded as safer because it's harder to overdose on them and also you can take them in one dose.

SSRI stands for Selective Serotonin Reuptake Inhibitors and it's thought they act by boosting serotonin in the brain. They do this by increasing the availability of existing serotonin. This is a complex process but a simplified version is that they interfere with the normal process whereby a brain cell cleans up unused serotonin in a process called reuptake. The result is an excess of serotonin left in the synapses of the brain. That probably sounds like a good thing to you, because if you're like me, you think having more serotonin makes you feel better. Sounds good, doesn't it? Well, it would be if it was true but unfortunately, it's a bit more complicated than that.

While I hadn't heard of escitalopram, of course I'd heard of its cousin – Prozac, the wonderdrug that everyone was talking about in the nineties. Publicised in a book by Peter Kramer called *Listening to Prozac,*[1] It became a cure-all not just for depression but for all sorts of other things like low self-esteem, jealousy, fear of rejection, perfectionism, nail biting, headaches, sexual addictions and upset stomachs.

The drug made people feel 'better than well' and could alter their personality: 'Since you only live once, why not do it as a blonde?' And it was seen as completely safe: 'There is no unhappy ending to this story… the patient recovers and pays no price for the recovery.'

Prozac and the drugs that followed promoted the idea that depressed people have low levels of serotonin and that their pills act as a top-up.

So now I'm going to tell you what you may well refuse to believe. Because, like me, you will think you know that this is a fact. The idea that depression is caused by a chemical imbalance, or low serotonin, is not true: it is, in fact, a myth.

Scientists will tell you that you can't measure serotonin in a living brain and there is no scientific proof that depressed people have any more or any less serotonin than anyone else. The idea that the more serotonin you have, the better you feel came not from science but from the pharmaceutical industry as a marketing tool to sell their drugs. In the US where it's permitted to advertise drugs, ads appear featuring bored-looking housewives with the slogan 'Prozac Mood Brightener'.

Not just that, but another ploy was when Merck marketed the concept of depression along with amitriptyline 'by buying and distributing 50,000 copies of Frank Ayd's book on recognising and treating depression in general medical settings'.[2] As well as normal ads, the drug companies send out leaflets and promotional material to doctors.

There is one such mailing sent out by Eli Lilly and Company with the headline: 'Like diabetes or arthritis, depression is a physical illness. When serotonin is in short supply, you may suffer from depression. When you have enough serotonin, symptoms of depression may lift.'

Professor Tim Kendall, who advises the National Institute for Health and Care Excellence (NICE), describes the serotonin theory as 'complete bunkum'. He believes that it's just a way for the drug companies who make SSRIs to sell their products. NHS Choices (www.nhs.uk), the website which advises patients, also states: 'It would be too simplistic to say that depression and related mental health conditions are caused by low serotonin levels but a rise in serotonin levels can improve symptoms.' Professor Sir Simon Wessely, president of the Royal College of Psychiatrists, says: 'Most researchers have long since moved on from the old serotonin model.'[3]

Yet somehow, four years ago, if you'd told me that low serotonin had nothing to do with depression, you might as well have told me that the earth was flat. It was simply one of the things I knew. If you were feeling low then antidepressants like Prozac kind of topped you up with serotonin, along with possibly sex, chocolate and sunshine.

Neither sex nor sunshine was on offer when I stepped out of the psychiatrist's office into the September evening and joined commuters as I headed back to the kids in Queen's Park so it was either chocolate or the Prozac-like pills I was clutching a prescription for. I'd already tried chocolate as a cure for depression as a child. My mum had introduced the idea – if I was sad, like many Jewish mothers, the cure was food. I would soon learn the side effects of her particular panacea, which were, of course, to get what she called 'puppy fat' but what the rest of the world called 'just plain fat', with the short-term benefits soon outweighed by being teased mercilessly at school. And now as being single was part of the reason for my distress, stuffing my face with chocolate didn't seem a particularly sensible idea. All this went through my head as I entered the chemist's, clutching a prescription written out by a man with many letters after his name, who had told me with all due certainty that I was suffering from a medical condition.

I can't remember how long it was after taking the first Lexapro (escitalopram) pill that I started behaving oddly but it was a matter of hours. One of the first symptoms was that I became very withdrawn and was unable to sit still. I now know that I was suffering one of the well-known side effects of antidepressant poisoning called 'akathisia' – where quite literally you are so anxious, you have to continually walk around. Below is *Wikipedia*'s definition of akathisia, and it's a word I'm going to keep coming back to, because if only people would recognise it, then without doubt, lives could be saved. It's a sign of drug toxicity. In short, if someone is walking around like a demented animal, unable to keep still, then they are in lethal danger of harming themselves or others and should stop taking whatever they've just taken. Just to give you an idea of how excruciating this condition can be, there was a woman called Sandra Sorg, a nurse in Madison, Wisconsin, who suffered from it so badly, that she asked to be put in a straitjacket. [4] Eventually, in 1989, she hanged herself with a sheet; even more tragically, she remained in a coma for some years before she died.

> **Akathisia**, or acathisia (from Greek καθίζειν *kathízein* – 'to sit', *a*- indicating negation or absence, lit. 'inability to sit') is a movement disorder characterised by a feeling of inner restlessness and a compelling need to be in constant motion, as well as by actions such as rocking while standing or sitting, lifting the feet as if marching on the spot, and crossing and uncrossing the

legs while sitting. People with akathisia are unable to sit or keep still, complain of restlessness, fidget, rock from foot to foot, and pace …

Akathisia may range in intensity from a sense of disquiet or anxiety, to excruciating discomfort, particularly in the knees…

Akathisia is frequently associated with the use of dopamine receptor antagonist antipsychotic drugs … Another major cause of the syndrome is the withdrawal observed in dependent individuals. …

Antidepressants can also induce the appearance of akathisia …

This *Wikipedia* entry goes on to give a table of drugs that can induce akathisia, giving categories and examples of each with some of their most common trade names. Among these are:

Antipsychotics: Haloperidol (Haldol), droperidol, pimozide, trifluoperazine, amisulpride, risperidone, aripiprazole (Abilify), lurasidone (Latuda), ziprasidone (Geodon), and asenapine (Saphris)

SSRIs: Fluoxetine (Prozac), paroxetine (Paxil), citalopram (Celexa)

Antidepressants: Venlafaxine (Effexor), tricyclics, trazodone (Desyrel), and mirtazapine (Remeron).[5]

Everything is a bit of a blur but I don't think I slept at all on that Thursday night. The children recall hearing footsteps throughout the night and my recollection was that I was wandering aimlessly around the house, and that the zopiclone sleeping tablets I already had weren't having an effect. Around that time one of my best friends, Juliette, came over and found me behaving very oddly. It was as if I was in a trance and I kept telling her that I had to kill myself, she recalls. She would ask me why but I didn't have an explanation. I just kept on saying it over and over again. She says my daughter Lily kept trying to snap me out of it but it was as if she had become invisible to me.

This sort of adverse reaction, the thoughts that came out of nowhere about killing myself, was identical to those that appeared in an article that came to light soon after Prozac came on the market. In 1990 a report appeared in *The American Journal of Psychiatry* on 'The Emergence of Intense Suicidal Preoccupation During Fluoxetine Treatment'.[6] Two Harvard psychiatrists describe how patients developed serious preoccupations with suicide soon after being given Prozac: 'We were especially surprised to witness the emergence of intense, obsessive and violent suicidal thoughts in these patients. Two patients fantasised for the first time about killing themselves with a gun and one patient actually placed a loaded gun to her head. One patient needed to be physically restrained to prevent self-mutilation.' Once off the drugs, they returned to normal.[7]

Later, I was to come across countless examples of people like me, who had never considered suicide, suddenly being gripped by an inexplicable urge to kill themselves. One such person was Stewart Dolin, whose widow Wendy has now set up The Medication-Induced Suicide Prevention and Education Foundation in Memory of Stewart Dolin (http://missd.co). A senior partner in a law firm, he enjoyed travel, skiing, dining, and was in a happy marriage. In 2010 he developed some anxiety regarding work and was prescribed paroxetine (Paxil). Within days his anxiety grew worse, he was feeling restless and was having trouble sleeping. Six days after beginning the medication, following a regular lunch with a business associate, he left his office and walked to a nearby train platform. Someone saw him on the platform pacing back and forth, looking very agitated. As the train approached, this happy, wealthy, dedicated husband and father took his own life, leaving no note and without any logical reason as to why he would suddenly want to end it all. So that is the power of akathisia, an acute inner restlessness that drives people to suicide.[8]

To return to my story… All day Friday I was behaving oddly and by the afternoon it was time to pick up my son Oscar, who was ten at the time, from school and drop him off for an overnight trip organised by his school to the Science Museum, London, where kids have a group sleepover. By now I seemed to have lost the power of speech. It was as if something else was taking over my mind and body. By now the children knew something was wrong and they phoned Robert, my ex, to tell him Mummy was behaving oddly, would he please come round. We had barely spoken in the last few months. I suppose it was odd seeing him, but this paled into insignificance given the oddness of the way I was feeling.

Robert came home early so we could pick up Oscar from school. I was in the passenger seat and by now I had gone into a sort of trance. I remember Lily trying to talk to me but it was as if my mind was shutting down. My ex guessed correctly that I wasn't capable of looking after the children on my own that night and so after dropping Oscar, the three of us went back to the flat in West Hampstead he had rented when he moved out earlier in the year. Robert ordered in pizzas, but I couldn't eat – I was pacing up and down, crying, unable to talk or engage.

But that Friday was nothing compared to what was about to unfold.

On the Saturday morning I got out of the bottom bunk bed and my head started to spin. Robert knew I had to take these pills and so he gave me the escitalopram (Lexapro) and insisted I take it. At that point my vision started to blur and my auditory senses began to close down. It's as if someone has turned off the soundtrack in a film. My heart was pounding and I was sweating but soon I started to have clarity of vision that was terrifying. I was filled with a certainty that today was my last day alive and that somehow God had ordained it. I was now convinced that my ex was part of a plot to poison me with the pill he had just fed me. Lily kept asking me what was wrong but by now the hallucinations had started. Everything was starting to appear in bright colours like a Van Gogh painting – but that was just the beginning.

We drive back to our old house in Dundonald Road. I don't remember much about the journey except that by now I'm getting higher and higher.

By the time we pull up outside the house, the delusions about being filmed have started. Some of the neighbours have come out to say hello to Robert. After all, it's the first time he's been back at the house for ages. In my warped imagination, I believe there are hidden film cameras there to capture the fact that they prefer him to me.

I run into the house. I haven't had a shower since the first visit to the psychiatrist and so I go upstairs to the old bedroom and get into the en suite shower. My conviction that there is a film crew waiting outside continues and I'm now too frightened to leave the house.

It's still warm and I put on an old white linen long dress. It's then that the hallucinations worsen; I think I've stabbed myself in the stomach. I have a clear image of my bloodstained dress, but it's not from the view of looking down but as if I'm out of my body, as if I'm a camera above my head looking on. I then have an image of me being taken away from the house by police, with my white dress stained with blood.

Now everything becomes a series of disjointed images that don't make sense. One moment I know I'm downstairs and I have a very clear recollection of my brain tripping into a different realm where I start to believe that everything is now a video game, or a dream, so nothing really matters.

At some stage I know my brother Richard and my sister Amy have come to the house; I guess because my ex is so concerned at my mental state. I remember turning to one of them and saying, 'Is this reality?' Suddenly and inexplicably I have a sense I can do anything because we're all going to wake up soon.

Next up, we're in the garden sitting with my brother, sister, my ex and Lily. I hallucinate that I have a knife and stab myself in the stomach again. I can still see the image of Lily's shocked face, which at the time I found hilariously funny. Of course, none of this ever happened. What did happen, and what I have no recollection of, was that I did take a kitchen knife and lacerated the upper side of my left arm. But I don't remember that, and I still don't know what time of day it happened.

By early evening the hallucinations took on a different tone. Now convinced I'd stabbed the children, I became frantic: I *had* to find them. I ventured out of the house towards Queen's Park to look for them. Of course in my mentally altered state there were film cameras following me but now it wasn't just film cameras on the doorstep, they were everywhere, in a *Truman Show*-like capacity, and everything I was doing was being broadcast on national TV. The show I was on was a show about the worst mother in the world, the one who had stabbed her children. Everyone was watching my every move.

As I walked down to Queen's Park, knowing that the entire nation was watching my every move, my visual senses had by now gone absolutely crazy. The sky had gone very dark in keeping with my apocalyptic vision. At this stage, though, I was very, very calm.

Things didn't follow a sequential pattern but I know I didn't find the children in the park. I remember knocking on neighbours' doors trying to find them.

I remember being back in our marital home and switching on the TV. I saw news reports about me, and there were interviews with friends, people I'd dated, all saying what a shallow person I was, and what a terrible mother I was. After a while I couldn't bear to watch the TV and also I thought there were cameras filming me watching the TV so I turned it off.

My ex was in the garden, sweeping the patio. Convinced the show was about what a terrible wife I was, and how he did all the work, I was now worried about what the viewers were thinking of me.

At some point we go over the road to our neighbour John, who has cooked dinner for all of us. I sit with the kids in the living room with the TV while my ex and he are in the kitchen. John works as an assistant director in film, and of course I am now convinced that he is in on the plot, that he is helping to direct the team of hidden cameras around his house capturing the moments that showed me to be a terrible person.

Knowing that everything I said was being broadcast around

the nation, I sat with my kids and his kids. I desperately wanted my son Oscar to come over and cuddle me so that the viewers would know that the children loved me. But he wouldn't come anywhere near me because he was so frightened of the person I'd become.

When we leave their house to go across the road, I know there are more hidden cameras in our house and that still everything I do is being broadcast live around the nation. It's a game show now, where viewers have to vote as to who the children should go to, who is the better parent. My ex is winning hands down. All our friends and even my friends who have been interviewed say that he is the best parent, and that I'm useless – well, after all, I have stabbed the children.

I think but don't know that I took another of the pills that evening. I know I became so psychotic that I became aware of how dangerous a state I was in. At some point I asked to be taken to hospital. This whole scene was still being broadcast on national TV as far as I was concerned and viewers were now applauding the fact that my ex would have the children while I was carted off to hospital.

Then later that evening my sister and her husband came round. We got into her car and she told me we were going to a private hospital in central London (we had health insurance and they would cover it). As we drove to the hospital, I still thought we were being filmed. On arrival, they asked me to sign a form saying I consented to taking any drugs. They sedated me that night, took me to a private room and I fell into a deep sleep for the first time in two days.

Chapter 2

WHY I WAS LUCKY TO SURVIVE

I bet you're thinking golly gosh, what an extraordinary story. Well, I'm afraid it's not: it's all too common. The extraordinary thing is that I survived without harming myself or others – because that's what happens a lot of the time.

Although on the pill packet I took it says escitalopram (brand name Lexapro) may cause violence, and hallucinations in 1 in 1,000 cases, most cases go unreported and Professor David Healy, a world expert on this subject, puts it at much higher, more like 1 in 100. But even if we take the drug company figure, that is still a large number. If 50 million people have taken Prozac, then that may equate to 50,000 suicides.

Professor Healy estimates that 'there are probably between 1,000–1,500 extra suicides in the US each year, triggered by an antidepressant –an extra 2000–2,500 in Europe. The data is similar for violence. There are probably between 1,000–1,500 extra episodes of violence in the US annually that would not have happened without antidepressant input and between 2,000–2,500 extra episodes in Europe. Some of these will include school or other mass shootings, which were unheard of 25 years ago.'[1]

Of course all drugs can have adverse side effects but when it goes wrong with antidepressants and some other serotonin-boosting drugs, it goes *really* wrong. Far worse, it would seem, than with recreational drugs. If people become delirious from cannabis, they can become euphoric or paranoid. If it's LSD, they have visual hallucinations. With mescaline, they become religious. But with serotonin-boosting drugs, they become obsessed with death, dying, suicide, knives and guns.

The first cause célèbre involving antidepressants was the test case of Joseph T. Wesbecker, as described earlier in the Prologue to this book (page 00). John Cornwell's book, *The Power to Harm*, provides a fascinating insight into this. The mass murder and suicide has all the hallmarks of an adverse drug reaction. Wesbecker's wife Brenda seemed to be describing akathisia as she said to the police: 'There has been a change in him since the drug started.' According to the police report, 'She stated they sleep in separate rooms because of Joe's mental condition and the medicine that he takes causes him to be fidgety and occasionally he gets up in the middle of the night and walks around.'[2] When the print worker went into his factory and carried out the mass killing, one of the survivors who was shot in the lower abdomen describes him as completely psychotic – 'He looked like he didn't have any blood in his body at all.'[3]

The surviving victims took manufacturers Eli Lilly to court for damages, claiming Prozac had caused Wesbecker to kill. The ensuing trial in 1994 shows how adept pharmaceutical companies are at defending their drugs and why the potentially lethal side effects are hidden from the general public. At first it appeared that Eli Lilly had won but then the judge found they had rigged the trial. In order to withhold damaging evidence they secretly paid the victims what their attorney described as a 'tremendous amount of money. It boggles the mind.'[4] When the judge, John W Potter discovered this had happened, he moved to re-examine the trial. Three years later, Eli Lilly agreed to the verdicts being quietly corrected to 'dismissed as settled'. By then, just a few years after Prozac's launch, there were already 160 other lawsuits against the drug and it was imperative to Eli Lilly's survival that the reputation of their blockbuster drug wasn't damaged. In an internal document in 1990 one executive states that if Prozac was to be taken off the market the company 'would go down the tubes'.

It was also revealed in the initial trial that before Prozac came to the market, the drug company's own trials had shown it caused agitation and 'excessive stimulation' in 38 per cent of patients. When this happened, instead of withdrawing participants from the trial and counting them as someone who didn't agree with it, they gave them a tranquilliser.[5] The company subsequently withheld this study and never gave it to the German drug regulatory agency, the BGA (Bundesgesundheitsamt) or the FDA. (Food and Drink Administration USA).

Other documents from the initial trial reveal that a 1985 in-house analysis found twelve suicide attempts in the Prozac group and only one each in the control group and the comparison drug, a tricyclic antidepressant. Again, the company withheld this information from the regulatory authorities.[6]

It's still not known how much the drug company paid the victims of the Wesbecker case. And many of the 160 cases linking Prozac with homicides, violence and suicide were settled with cash and a gagging clause.[7] An exception was the Forsyth case in 1994. William Forsyth from California suffered anxiety. He'd never been suicidal, and he'd never been seriously depressed. He was given Prozac, felt terrible and asked to be admitted to hospital. When he came out, his son arrived at the family home to find his parents lying in a pool of blood. William had stabbed his wife, June, fifteen times, then fixed a serrated kitchen knife to a chair and impaled himself on it. As in many antidepressant-related cases, there was no note, and no rationale.

The case against Eli Lilly was lost, but in the process a number of documents were revealed, which showed the extent of how they kept this information away from the public. There was evidence that the company had drafted but later abandoned a package insert stating 'Mania and psychosis may be precipitated in susceptible patients by antidepressant therapy'. Then there was a memo dated 2 October 1990 referring to an upcoming Prozac symposium: 'The question is what to do with the "big" numbers on suicides,' the memo states. 'If the report numbers are shown next to those for nausea they seem small.'[8]

Given the secrecy surrounding compensation settlements and the fact that side effects are deliberately hidden, it's in internet chat rooms where you see the real human tragedies behind antidepressants. They are teeming with tales of suicide and violence involving every single one of the antidepressants. One site, SSRI Stories (http://ssristories.org), has since 2011 collated over 6,000 stories of cases linked to prescription drugs and violence. Here is a sample from 15 March 2015: '14 year old Suicide Causes Coroner to Question if Prozac was the real Trigger', then there is the case, reported in the *Oxford Mail*, of Jed Allen who in May 2015 murdered three people before hanging himself. He was taking antidepressants and had 'told psychologists he had dark thoughts about hurting people who had wronged him'. And finally 'Antidepressant gets blame for bank robbery' from the *Winnipeg Sun* (24 February 2015) tells how a judge agreed a man was suffering delirium after weaning himself off Effexor (venlafaxine).

Most of these cases will go completely unrecorded and unrecognised as having anything to do with an adverse drug reaction. And if people had told me in the past that they were to do with antidepressants, I would have thought that was completely ridiculous. It's only when you've experienced something similar or if you happen to be an expert in the field that you start to recognise the symptoms.

First, the switch in your brain that causes you to be violent also causes you to be suicidal – so many of these cases involve people killing others and then themselves. Then there is the akathisia, the inner restlessness, the mental turmoil and the inability to keep still. Another factor is emotional numbing: you have absolutely no empathy, which comes with a disinhibition, so that you lose anxiety and contemplate extraordinary things you wouldn't usually do. And finally some people hallucinate, a common experience is to hear the voice of God telling them to kill. Often the hallucinations involve death, knives, dying.

The similarities are extraordinary. Here is an extract I found on a website called the International Coalition for Drug Awareness (drugawareness.org), which is almost identical to mine. The man took Lexapro, the same drug that I took, but that's a coincidence. All of the SSRI antidepressants work by the same mechanism, of boosting serotonin in the brain.

I took the pill, I lay down to sleep, and I woke up in hell. Eight hours after taking one 10mg Lexapro pill I woke to thoughts of murder and a bizarre desire to repeatedly stab my neighbor to death. I was having a severe adverse reaction to the Lexapro often described as homicidal Ideation, very closely related to Suicidal Ideation, and brought on by elevated serotonin levels. These thoughts and desires lasted for approximately 3 days. Those 3 days after ingesting the SSRI are the only 3 days in my life of 43 years that I have experienced anything remotely similar to this. I have no history of violence.

I wasn't trying to think about anything, the thoughts just came into my mind. It was as if I was being instructed. The thoughts were graphic and specific. According to the thoughts, using a large kitchen knife, I was to repeatedly and deeply stab my neighbor until he was dead. I felt an eerie desire to have warm blood all over my body. Later, in my thoughts my dead neighbor would still be alive afterwards and we would laugh together as he bled. I would see images and it was a bit like thinking about a movie I had watched.

These extremely violent thoughts were enmeshed with comforting sensations similar to satisfying hunger and were emerging without any instigation on my part. It didn't feel like rage, it was more like a strong urge. It was as if I was half dreaming. More accurately, it was like drifting in and out of sleep while allowing the dream to take hold.

When I had these thoughts they scared me so much I would scream and run into my bedroom. After the first day, I wasn't as scared and just tried to think about anything else. I called my brother and asked him to remove all the guns and knives from my house immediately. I knew the drug had caused a major brain malfunction and I thoroughly believed/feared that if I told anyone I would be locked away and tortured with more brain drugs. I decided to wait and hoped that I might heal or that the drug would leave my system. I drank a lot of water.

The thoughts were in my mind but the thoughts weren't mine. I didn't generate those thoughts. I only had these thoughts for 3 days because I discontinued the drug after the first pill. But it seemed so real that I wondered some days if it had already happened and I was remembering it. Then I would see my neighbor and feel relieved. That is how disconnected from reality I was at the time.

This experience gave me deep insight into why some people on SSRIs might commit the unbelievable acts they do. Mass shootings, baby killings, suicides and all of the bizarre acts in the news are often attributed to insanity or even demon possession.[9]

Often the drugs are so powerful that people have no recollection of what happened. Take the case of sixteen-year-old Corey Baadsgaard, who woke up in a juvenile detention centre. He had no recollection of the fact he had taken his classmates hostage with a gun. Corey was taking Paxil and for months had been hallucinating but somehow didn't realise it was the drug.[10]

Eighteen months after my recovery, in 2015, I got a phone call from a leading barrister, David Martin-Sperry, who had read about my case on the RxISK website. He was taking the case of a man who had killed his mother to the Court of Appeal. Paul Stones claimed that he didn't know what he was doing because he went into a psychosis caused by taking antidepressants. The barrister asked me if he could use me as a witness and I agreed. However, the judges felt the original trial was fair and so didn't overturn the conviction. In the same year I was approached by another barrister and was asked to be a witness in the case of a twenty-year-old undergraduate student in the UK. .

He had been prescribed citalopram after he had broken up with his girlfriend. When he came home, his parents thought they were seeing the symptoms of depression rather than those of an adverse drug reaction: he had intense nightmares, couldn't sleep and became a totally different person. He would sit in the corner crying, or just be pacing up and down. A few months after being prescribed the antidepressant, he did something totally out of character. One evening, he went out with a crowbar and attacked a stranger many times, even after he had fallen to the floor. When he woke up in a police cell, he had no recollection of what he had done. He had never shown any aggression before and the court recognised that the drug had made him violent. Because the medical evidence was so compelling, he received a lesser charge. He was fortunate enough to be seen by an expert who recognised it was the drugs rather than depression that were making him ill. He came off the antidepressants and to his family's relief became well again He's now fully recovered and is getting on with his life and trying to put the trauma behind him.

There are many cases involving kids, particularly suicides. Half a million children in the US are prescribed antidepressants, and many thousands in the UK. The marketing of antidepressants is the fastest-growing market even though repeated studies show they are no more effective in children and adolescents than placebos.[11] And that the risk of suicide is doubled. Antidepressants are dished out for all sorts of conditions, including shyness, pre-exam nerves, and eating disorders. In 2004 children aged five and under were America's fastest-growing segment of the non-adult population using antidepressants.[12] In the UK, there have been cases of children aged one taking them.[13]

In a number of cases, this has resulted in tragedy. There are certain characteristics shared by people who kill themselves from antidepressants. Suicides tend to involve jumping under a train, hanging or shooting themselves, often taking others with them. Because it's thought that the antidepressants take a few weeks to have a therapeutic effect,[14] these cases also get overlooked. In fact, as in my case, you can experience an adverse side effect literally within hours of taking your first pill, or from changing a dosage, or withdrawing from an antidepressant.

When it all goes wrong, the drug companies leap to the defence of their product and argue that it is the condition rather than the drug that is to blame. A startling example of this is the case of Matt Miller.[15] He was thirteen when he changed schools, and was nervous about it. His doctor gave him Zoloft (sertraline) and within a week he hanged himself. He was found kneeling, because, as David Healy points out in his lecture 'Hearts and Minds – Psychotropic Drugs and Violence',[16] many antidepressant suicides begin by people putting a noose around their neck and trying it out. Then they slip forward. The response of not just the drug company but also the regulators was that it may not be the drug, with one expert arguing it could be due to auto-erotic asphyxiation.[17] Yes, in a thirteen-year-old!

Professor Healy goes on to point out that historically drug companies and regulators have not protected us from drugs with devastating side effects. Thalidomide is a case in point. It was hailed as a wonderdrug for insomnia and morning sickness in the 1950s and is still on the market in some countries and even after many cases of babies being born without limbs, both the regulators and the drug companies argue that what may have happened is that the drug may not have caused this, but in fact it just prevented spontaneous miscarriages. Professor Healy concludes if you are waiting for the US Food and Drug Administration (FDA) or the Medicines and Healthcare Products Regulatory Agency (MHRA) in the UK to say a drug isn't safe, then you could be waiting for a very long time. And actually, let's remember that an awful lot of drugs that we now regard as positively dangerous were once used by psychiatrists and took years to be banned. As Gwen Olsen says in her book *Confessions of an Rx Drug Pusher*: 'History reminds us that it took 20 years after Eli Lilly and Parke-Davis introduced LSD and PCP in the United States before the government declared them illegal.'[18]

Eli Lilly first produced and marketed LSD in the 1960s as an aid to psychoanalysis, a cure for alcoholism and a way to clear up mental disorders. Parke-Davis promoted 'angel dust' or phencyclidine (PCP) as an analgesic and anaesthetic. Of

THE PILL THAT STEALS LIVES

course, Dr Sigmund Freud was one of the strongest supporters of the medicinal use of cocaine in psychiatry before he himself became addicted. More and more, all of these drugs act on the brain by increasing serotonin levels. It would be fair to conclude that psychiatry has given us some of the most addictive, destructive drugs in history.

Is history repeating itself?

One of the biggest problems in all of this is that cases of antidepressant suicide and violence are not being recognised. Often patients are misdiagnosed with a mental illness and given more of the drugs to which they reacted badly in the first place. For example, the case of a thirty-five-year-old woman from Australia, who took the antidepressant nortriptyline, one of the older tricyclic antidepressants, along with the herbal tablet valerian. She was being treated for distress because her husband drank.

> I didn't sleep for two nights, dreamt, then slept maybe three hours, felt awful. I dreamt that my daughter had dark teeth and I saw a black halo around her head, a spear hanging over it. I felt like a zombie. I believed I had to help my daughter, that a bad spirit possessed her. I picked up a knife and stabbed her and woke up. I was not myself. I was looking on from the outside, controlled by dark forces.
>
> She said: 'Mum, what are you doing here?'
>
> I realised what I'd done.
>
> I asked my husband to kill me. He called the police. I felt better in the police cells without the pills, but the pills started again and thoughts of killing myself returned.[19]

So this woman, with no history of mental illness or violence, killed her teenage daughter. She pleaded mental illness, was misdiagnosed with schizophrenia and is now being prescribed more drugs, which are making her violent and suicidal. This is what often happens.

If you have an adverse drug reaction, the chances are you're not going to be believed... as I myself was about to find out.

Chapter 3

SUNDAY, 23 SEPTEMBER 2012

I wake up in a small room on the ground floor of one of London's most expensive private hospitals.

The violent hallucinations have gone, along with the sense that everything is in bright colours and that the soundtrack has been turned off. I have total clarity of mind; I know with absolute certainty that everything I do is being broadcast across the nation on live TV. There are cameras in the ceiling right now, this room and the entire hospital is rigged up with secret cameras to capture my every move. It's like *Big Brother*, only I'm the only participant. And the show is about what a terrible person I am, but more importantly, that I'm the worst mother in the world. At the end everyone is going to vote as to whether I lose the children or my ex gets to keep them.

I try to keep calm in the knowledge that every move I'm making is being monitored by the secret cameras above my bed; I've got to get out of here, but I don't know how. I'm wearing a pair of White Company pyjamas and there are a few clothes in a small overnight bag that someone must have packed for me last night. Yes, it's coming back to me. I think I said I had to go to hospital and now I remember Lily's worried face, rummaging around my wardrobe in our bedroom at Dundonald Road, asking me what I needed to be packed.

In the corner of the room, I can see my pink handbag. I'm reluctant to get up, knowing that now the whole nation is going to see me in a pair of not-very-flattering pyjamas and that the drawstring of the trousers is broken and there is a danger they might fall down. But I have to get to my bag, to see if my purse is there: it may provide a means for me to get out of here.

I rummage around and find my purse has got some credit cards and a bit of money in it. More importantly, my mobile phone is there too. I take out my phone and frantically look for the number for Queen's Park Taxis. I've got my credit card out, ready to pay for a taxi to get me out of here. The thought goes through my head that the audience that is watching me across the nation is now going to hate me more. It's going to confirm the view that they probably already have of me that I just throw money at problems.

But I never get through to the taxi company because then there is a knock at the door. A nurse comes in with a plastic container with a pill and a glass of water on a tray. She tells me she's giving me the pill that I have been taking, the escitalopram, or Lexapro as it's known in the States, that the private psychiatrist gave me a few days ago. Apparently when I was admitted the night before my sister Amy brought those pills with her.

I tell her I want to leave and when can I do that? She tells me that I can't do anything until a doctor comes to see me, which will be later in the day. Do I want any breakfast? No, I've no appetite whatsoever. I can't even think of food. I'm on a high, with an almost manic energy and drive to get myself out of there and back to the children. Food is the last thing on my mind.

She insists I take the pill in front of her. A few moments after she's left, I can feel my head starting to spin and my heart is palpitating again. There is a sort of whoosh that goes through my entire body, and I can feel my vision once more blurring and the colours in the room are getting brighter.

Christ, I know there is something in that pill – I know it! Someone is trying to poison me. There is an en-suite bathroom so I rush in there, pretty sure it's the only place in the hospital where there are no secret cameras. I'm not a great fan of reality TV, but I've watched a few episodes of *Big Brother* and I know it would be an invasion of privacy to have cameras in the loo so I'm sure the producers of this show, which, after all, is being broadcast right now to the entire nation, surely wouldn't have been allowed to put cameras in the bathroom.

I rush in there, stick my fingers down my throat and retch as much of the water and the pill as I can manage. Almost instantly the room seems more normal, the colours less bright, and the palpitations fewer. Jesus, I'm now coming to realise what's really going on! Someone is poisoning me with an acid tablet that is making me hallucinate so that the children will be taken away from me.

I daren't go out in the corridor. There are bars on the window and I look out onto a side road. It's a Sunday morning and I wonder about the kids, about my ex, and think to myself, what the hell is happening? I look down and for the first time

I notice my arm is bandaged up. When I slip the bandage off, I see a cut about six inches long on my left forearm. I'm not sure how the cut got there but somehow I seem to know that I did it to myself with a kitchen knife. I have a distant recollection of this but I can't recall where and I certainly can't recall why. Was it at Robert's West Hampstead flat, or did it happen at Dundonald Road? I think it was in the middle of the night but I'm not at all sure.

Sometime during that morning a doctor with a foreign accent comes in. I'm anxious because I want to make a good impression so I can get out. I ask him if I can go home and he replies that it's not his decision and the man who makes the decisions is another of the doctors, who will be in later to see me. It doesn't take me long to ascertain that the doctor with the foreign accent is a liar and he is in on the plot. He pretends he doesn't know that there are hidden cameras in the ceiling and feigns surprise when I tell him.

After he's scribbled down a few notes, he goes off into the corridor, where I know for certain that he will be interviewed by the second unit film crew. I'm annoyed with myself that I didn't do better – he didn't seem to like me very much and I'm pretty sure the interview he is going to give about me isn't going to be very flattering. I'm losing; the audience are going to hate me.

Later on in the morning there is a knock on the door and a nurse tells me my ex, Lily and Oscar are here. Am I well enough to see them? My feelings are mixed. More than anything I want to see the kids but I'm really worried how I'm going to come out on the live TV show, which I know will be broadcasting the whole event. I just want some private time with them away from the cameras so I can explain to them what is happening, that I love them, that everything we do is being broadcast and that someone has poisoned me with an acid tablet to make me look awful so that their Dad can have them forever. I need to explain to them that whatever they do, to please behave well because if this meeting goes badly, the audience will vote for Robert to have them forever.

Before I can think all this through, all three of them arrive in the small private room. Lily, you will remember, is aged eleven and Oscar is ten. They went back to school the week before, after the long summer break. It's a warm September day and Lily is wearing shorts. She is just hitting puberty and I'd been about to buy her first bra and give her a talk about periods. That hadn't happened and in fact it never was to happen because it was another year before I was able to have a normal conversation with her, by which time she had already started her periods and bras were a regular feature in her wardrobe.

Lily's pale face is full of concern. She has gathered together some things she thought I would want – some make-up, some extra clothes. Oscar is looking scared; he looks down at the floor and his eyes won't meet mine. He doesn't try to greet me; already I've become a different person to the one he's known. In just five days he's seen his mother go into a trance-like state, wander incessantly round the house, and then inexplicably attack herself with a knife. No wonder he is scared.

My ex is on crutches and I remember now that eight months of no contact had recently come to an end when he rang me to say he had broken his toe. He had the kids at his West Hampstead flat, and I got a call from him on a Saturday morning three weeks earlier when I was running from Queen's

Park to Regent's Park on my first 15K run in training for the Royal Parks Half Marathon I was going to do in the October. He was yelling in agony because he'd walked into the bed; he had the kids and couldn't get hold of his parents, who would usually have stepped in. Feeling sorry for him, I headed back for the car and took him and the kids to hospital, where he had been bandaged up and given crutches.

The fact that Robert is on crutches gives me further cause for concern. He is now going to seem all the more sympathetic to the national audience, who will now see that even on crutches he is doing a better job of parenting than me.

I'm frozen with fear as the three of them arrive. Lily looks puzzled, she can't work out why I haven't run to her and cuddled her. There is a tray of uneaten food by the bed and she asks me why I haven't touched it. Her beautiful face is now in an expression which is a mix of compassion and confusion. I can see she wants to reach out and touch me but like Oscar, she's scared.

I know that the cameras are capturing all of this and it's not looking good so I decide I have to appeal to Robert's better nature. He knows what's going on, he's in on the secret, and I've got to get him to help me. I've got to get this message to him without the cameras catching it. I'm not sure how the room is rigged for sound but I take a gamble.

'Rob,' I whisper, 'come here.' I beckon for him to come over to me. He looks confused. 'Rob, please, I'll do anything you want. Please. You've got to get us out of here, quick. I'm sorry. I'll do whatever it takes, just get us out of here,' I continue.

He pretends he doesn't know what's going on. I can't believe he's doing this to me. Twelve years of marriage and he's prepared to let the nation believe that I'm a terrible mother and they're going to let him take the kids away from me. I'm beginning to get hysterical now. I can't contain my rising panic and the whisper turns to a shout. Soon, I'm screaming at him to get us out of here. I'm imploring him from the bottom of my heart, whatever it takes, please get us out.

Two nurses appear at the door, alarmed by my screams. They quickly assess the scene and see my distress. Then they turn to Robert and tell him firmly to leave immediately. I can see Lily's eyes welling up with tears as the nurses usher them out of the room. Begging the nurses to let the children stay, I run to the door. Oscar can't look at me; he just wants to get out as quickly as possible. Robert is being very English and very polite and doing exactly what the nurses are asking him to do. As the three of them are herded out of the room, I rush to the door, shouting and screaming, begging the nurses to let them back in again.

As the two nurses try to calm me down, another nurse rushes in with a glass of water and a blue pill. They tell me I have to take it. Immediately I feel calmer but it's not long before the anxiety kicks back in again, as I think back to the scene with the children. If this carries on I'm going to lose them forever. Right now the audience can be in no doubt that Robert is the better parent.

I don't have a clear recollection of exact times that day but I do know I didn't dare venture out of my room. And I know at some point my sister Amy visited, and I think it was late afternoon or early evening. I asked her why I was there and she told me that late Saturday night I had asked to go to hospital and that this was being paid for by Robert's private insurance.

While she was there, there was a knock on the door and

one of the doctors came in. I knew that he was the one person who had the ultimate power in determining whether or not I could leave the hospital. I was determined to make a good impression.

He sat on the chair at the bottom of my bed while my sister sat by my side. I was huddled beneath the bedclothes, still in my White Company pyjamas. Immediately, I liked him. He was slim, good-looking, and had a kind face. His eyes twinkled behind steel-rimmed spectacles revealing a sense of humour that I saw many times in the following year as he tried desperately to rescue me to the shores of sanity. Little did he know, and probably doesn't even believe now, that the remedies prescribed by him and his colleagues were to become the cause of my illness, the poison that nearly cost me my life.

Immaculately turned out, he wears a waistcoat and a tie. He takes out a notebook and a smart-looking fountain pen. That fountain pen and others like it were going to write prescription after prescription over the next year, for a host of drugs that I now know are at best ineffective for many, and at worst, downright dangerous. Little did I know this as he sat there at the end of my bed.

My first question to him is when can I leave? He gently replies that he'd like to conduct an interview and then he'll decide. It may be tomorrow, it may be a few days' time. 'Let's see,' he says.

He starts asking questions. For some time now, ever since that first pill, I seem to have lost the power of speech. My sister answers for me – she tells him how I've been going through a divorce, how recently I've started crying a lot, how I've been having sleepless nights, etc. As she's talking, I start to think about the cameras that are of course broadcasting this live to the whole nation. This is my interview, I should be doing the talking, and it's my chance to redress the bad impression the audience will have gained of me after the children's visit. So I interrupt her and say I'll answer the doctor's questions.

But I have great difficulty talking so I try to explain this to the doctor, who is doing his best to disguise his frustration as I attempt to string sentences together. I remember telling him that somehow it felt like I had locked-in syndrome, that I couldn't express myself. I noticed him writing the word 'aphasia' down in his notes with his smart fountain pen.

I summoned all of my will power to express to him the reason I was there. At last the words arrived. I looked him in the eye and for the first time in nearly five days was able to construct a proper explanation, a whole row of sentences.

'I've got a suicide pact with God,' I tell him.

To say that this mild-mannered doctor raised an eyebrow would be an understatement. 'Are you religious?' he asks.

'No, but I'm going to kill myself on 25 September. It's been decided. So that Robert can have the children.' He asks if I've been hearing voices. 'Sort of,' I reply, before adding imploringly, 'Can I leave soon?' A look of concern comes across his lightly tanned face. He says gently, 'You're not leaving yet. Just stay with us for a bit, you're not quite well enough to leave.'

He puts the lid back on his pen. 'The nurses told me you don't want to take the antidepressant you came in with. That's fine but I've prescribed some other pills for you, and some sleeping tablets. And I'll come in tomorrow and we'll have a further chat.'

He nods to my sister, who is now looking concerned, and

asks if he can have a chat with her outside the room. She leaves and I can hear them talking to each other in the corridor. They sound concerned but I can't make out what they are saying.

After five minutes, she comes in. Now my sister never loses it; she's always calm, logical, unflappable, whatever happens. True to form, she returns to the room as if everything is OK. Somehow she is managing to smile even though her baby sister has overnight turned into a knife-wielding maniac with a suicide pact with God.

'So,' she says matter-of-factly, 'I have to leave quite soon, so what are you going to do this evening?' She notices I am looking frantically at my mobile phone and asks what I'm doing.

'I'm checking the news,' I reply.

'What for?' she wants to know.

'For the news reports about me attacking the children – I know I'm all over the news, aren't I?'

I'm surprised she doesn't know why I'm checking my phone. It's obvious I'm going to be worried about the news coverage.

For the first time, her unruffled exterior reveals a chink of worry as her voice wavers with concern.

'Tinks, darling, please relax. You're not on the news. You haven't attacked the children. Why don't you just watch TV tonight and take it easy?'

Christ, she's annoying me now because she is so obtuse! Of course I can't put the TV on – it's full of stuff about me.

She puts her arms around me and kisses me. 'I'll see you tomorrow, darling. Love you.'

With that, she leaves. As dusk turns to night, I lie on my bed in the hospital. The dinner the nurses have brought in stays untouched. I stare at the TV that is on the wall opposite my bed and I see interviews with friends, and people I have dated. It's the same stuff – how shallow I am, what a bad mother I am. Robert is in our old family home with the kids. I'm in a mental hospital being filmed on a programme that is being livestreamed to the nation and my friends have turned against me.

A nurse comes in at some time with some tablets I don't recognise and a sleeping tablet. Now there is a nurse posted by the door, watching me the whole time.

I learn later that this is because I'm on suicide watch.

Soon after taking the sleeping tablet, I fall asleep.

Chapter 4

MONDAY, 24 SEPTEMBER 2012

When I wake up after my second night at the private hospital I feel an enormous sense of relief: there is no film crew. I don't know how I know this, but I know it, and I know that the cameras that were in my room recording everything and transmitting it live across the nation are no longer there.

But the initial sense of relief is almost immediately displaced with anxiety. If the film crew isn't here, where the hell are they? I conclude that they have now gone to Lily and Oscar's school in Chiswick; that they are interviewing the teachers about what a lousy mother I am. This thought is interrupted when a nurse comes in with a tray with tablets, this time around four of them. I've no idea what they are, but I know she's not going to leave until I take them all.

I look at my phone and again decide not to log onto the news because I can't face seeing more reports about how I tried to kill the children. Instead I log onto my calendar and see that I have an appointment with the psychotherapist Suzanna Goodheart whom I had started seeing three weeks ago. It was in fact her suggestion that I saw the psychiatrist who gave me the antidepressant escitalopram (Lexapro).

I recalled how it had been August, the end of the children's summer holidays, when I'd gone to her at a friend's suggestion, and sat tearful and crumpled on her large brown velour sofa in the panelled drawing room of her Victorian house in Hampstead. She'd looked at me with concern etched all over her kind, middle-aged face, gently probing, trying to get a handle on why it was now, eight months after my separation, that I was suddenly upset, unable to cope, sleep, think straight. And I remember that in the three sessions I had with her, I was unable to explain to her or indeed myself what it was.

Yes, why was it that eight months after Robert moved out an icy fear descended on me, paralysing me to the point where I was almost unable to function? It was most definitely a feeling of being alone in the knowledge that not only were Robert and I no longer on the same team, but we were in opposition now. And I remember the day war broke out.

It was January 2012. We were sitting on a couch, this time a different one: the couch of a relationship therapist. It was a last-ditch attempt to see if we could set sail again from a ship that was slowly sinking and nearly sunk. Even though my mind was made up, I'd gone along with it. It wasn't the episodes of *Coast*, it wasn't the fact he preferred to spend Sundays cycling in Richmond or polishing his Cannondale to spending them with me, or that somehow we never did get round to going out for dinner *à deux*, or going on that mini break to Barcelona or even just a country house hotel – none of that. It was a gut feeling, something I couldn't find the words for then, and took me some time to work out.

The best I can do to describe it was that it didn't feel like love; that our marriage was as deceptive as the façade of our Victorian house in Queen's Park. Yes, we looked the part, Robert and I. We dutifully gave each other birthday presents and Christmas presents that always amounted to £300 almost exactly, taken from our personal allowances. For me, this was usually a Prada handbag; for him, a couple of cycling tops from Wiggle. We gave sumptuous suppers and made a formidable couple at parents' evenings, him the clever lawyer, me the witty creative. We hosted parties, we could razzle, we could dazzle, fooling the world and probably ourselves. And just as the edifice of our smart-looking house hid a stash of cheap IKEA furniture and things that didn't work, so our relationship was not quite what the world saw. That over the years, not only had the longueurs in our communication become longer, but also our attention had turned very much away from what was best for the other to very much what was best for ourselves.

And in fact was it ever different?

Even in the opening salvo of our glossy courtship that danced its way through the streets of Notting Hill and Golborne Road in that hottest of summers in 1999, did I ever consider what I might be for Robert rather than what he might be for me?

I cast my mind back to our first meeting. It was the summer of 1999 and I was living in Golborne Road and he was living in a flat in nearby Westbourne Park Villas. Only his flat had recently suffered a house fire and was under renovation. A mutual Australian friend, Mark, had introduced us at the Cobden Club, which at that time was the hangout of Notting Hill trustafarians and moneyed bohemians. But Robert was neither of these: he was a tall, good-looking, middle-class English lawyer from Watford, who was a bit shy but had a manner that oozed kindness and generosity. And despite the fact he wasn't my type (at 5 foot 3 inches I usually go for shorter, stockier, Mediterranean-looking men), those qualities were the things that made me fall for him.

Shortly into our courtship we went to Portofino in Italy with Mark and a group of other friends. I remember I began a terrier-type interrogation in which I managed to extrapolate from him that actually he preferred taller, skinnier women, who, in fact, looked just like his ex-girlfriend. Even I, with my can-do attitude, realised that there was nothing I could do to make myself taller so I focused my efforts on the latter, and in our twelve years of marriage, I flitted between the Atkins Diet, the Scarsdale Diet, the South Beach Diet, Carol Vorderman's Detox for Life and pretty much any other diet that was on the market, culminating in a liquid-only diet of our nanny Andrea's Herbalife meal-replacement shakes.

All of these activities meant I was too busy to notice things: lots of things. Things like he didn't look that happy. That the 14-hour days he was working to keep us all going were giving him a greyness, a look of resignation, and that he only seemed truly happy when he was heading out the door on one of his carbon-fibre bikes.

Was that love? I wondered as I sat on the therapist's couch, in a dark basement just off Lisson Grove in early January 2012, as I thought back to the early days of our courtship, the wonderful wedding at a fort in Cornwall, the births of our two beautiful children, the holidays, the birthdays, the Christmases, the house moves, to all of the many, many life events we had shared for twelve years. Yes, we had shared a lot, but was that love? Was it? And as we sat there huddled in that basement flat on Lisson Grove, I felt strangely cold even though there was a heater blowing air at us, and it was then I mentioned a word that so far neither of us had dared to utter: divorce.

There was a shocked silence as the word left my lips. Even the therapist was silent. Robert, usually unruffled and pretty much always kind, turned to me in a moment that will always remain in my memory and said: 'If you try to divorce me, I'll make mincemeat out of you.' Later, I'd made light of it and asked him if he meant mincemeat or minced meat. But joking aside, although I knew that I was neither going to end up in a jar and be presented at Christmas, or in a shepherd's pie, yes, I did know that. I also knew in that moment that things were on a different level, that while we had been at one against the world, a team, now we were going to be opponents.

My only experience of being in opposition to Robert was when we played chess. We first started playing on our honeymoon to Venezuela. As this was just seven months after we'd met, it was indeed the very first time that we spent time together without the distraction of our friends and those all-night parties on Golborne Road. Chess became the thing that distracted us from the realisation that we didn't have an awful lot in common, really. And we played continuously, the difference being that while we were evenly matched, if I started to lose I'd throw in the towel, whereas if he was losing, he'd continue doggedly even if he just had one pawn left. And it was this image that stuck with me as we headed out into the night air after that therapy session on Lisson Grove, a mixture of anger and fear rendering us incapable of even looking into each other's eyes, as we scuttled off to confide in our now-different camps of friends.

Yes, that was the night war broke out.

And looking back, I can well imagine the welter of emotions that lay behind Robert's uncharacteristically malicious response. Divorce was a far more frightening prospect for him than me. A creature of habit, he was addicted to the predictable. He grew up in a family that had an apple-pie like stability about it, his dad a university lecturer, his mum staying at home to look after him and his brother, both parents only leaving their house in a village near Watford to work, attend Rotary Club meetings, the Women's Institute and to rattle tins for charity outside supermarkets. Rob emulated this stability by staying in the same law firm for twenty years, despite the fact it was the other side of town, and despite the fact he could probably get a higher paid job somewhere else. He hated change, and when I said the 'D' word to him, he would have found himself staring into an abyss where he was about to lose everything he had worked for – the house, our friends, the nanny, the Burmese cats, the Audi, the holidays, maybe even the kids.

All of this would have been much harder for him. However, I'd grown up with change. I'd lost my dad when I was twelve, attended various boarding schools, lost the family home, lived in different places, and my work as a freelance film director took me from job to job every four months. My life had started out difficult, unpredictable. I was used to change, and when I didn't have it, I created it, living on the edge wherever possible, taking risks, seeking adventure. Robert was a stranger to change, growing up as he had on the shores of stability in that picture-perfect English village. How different was that from my background – my mum a single working parent, a journalist who had no choice but to leave me because my father's death when I was twelve catapulted us into being broke and so she had to fly off to various parts of the world to pay the school fees. And so, like many others who have trodden the same path when those fundamental things are under threat, the most important being shelter and your kids, Robert went into survival mode. He was no longer going to be nice, or even kind: he was frightened. And actually he wasn't the only one.

And as I sat on the therapist Suzanna Goodheart's leather couch in Hampstead, I struggled to explain exactly what it was that had brought me to this point. After that night in January, I'd decided if war was going to break out, I needed to enlist the cavalry. I'd been recommended a solicitor who was reassuringly described on an Internet site as the country's third-best divorce lawyer. As long as Robert hasn't found the first or the second, I mused, then that should be OK. Much later on, when I became ill, I was to discover that what wasn't mentioned on their website was that Jeremy Levison might only be the country's third-best divorce lawyer, but without doubt he is top of the league as the country's most sympathetic.

But that's another story and they didn't have a league table for that.

As I arrived at the offices of Levison, Meltzer, Pigott in Holborn my heart was doing somersaults at the idea that this was costing £500 per hour. I'd never spent that amount; the big finances in our marriage were down to Robert. I prayed that if I spoke very fast indeed then we could get our first meeting down to under an hour – I was terrified about what Robert would say when he looked at the joint bank accounts.

Our finances were pretty straightforward and in less than an hour – fifty-five minutes actually, because I was monitoring this very closely – Jeremy Levison, with thirty-five years of divorce law practice behind him, was able to tell me that unless Robert kindly decided to give me the house, then a judge would order it should be sold and the proceeds split.

This idea filled me with horror. The one thing I'd promised myself was that I would give my children the idyllic family home I didn't have – or at least I only had it until I was twelve. I could never forget the trauma of selling our white five-bedroom painted house in Leatherhead's plushest road, Givons Grove, and having to dispense with my rabbits, my guinea pig, my two cats, everything as we packed up and headed off to a place I'd never heard of called Torquay, where my older brother David and my dad, now horribly ill from a stroke and subsequent depression, had decided to buy a hotel.

It was an attempt to rescue the family finances that had taken a downward and near-disastrous tumble since my father's illness that had forced him to sell up and leave his property business. The next two years had been odd: while my peers at boarding school had gone home at weekends and holidays to their country houses, in pretty English villages, I was going to a hotel in Torquay, where my brother, then twenty-one, presided with a group of friends whom he gave jobs to. My mother would occasionally visit from London, where she was working. Now she barely bothered to disguise the fact her relationship with her husband had disintegrated to nothing, and then there was my father, a man who was destroyed, who had lost everything – his health, his wealth, his wife – and sat impotent in a room all day contemplating the ruins in which his life now lay.

And so at some point I'd promised myself this would never happen to Lily and Oscar; that I would give them an apple-pie childhood. That even if it was apple pie minus Daddy, it was still going to be apple pie, loads of it, preferably topped with ice cream (organic, of course) to make up for the fact that Daddy wasn't there. And now, as I sat in the offices of Levison, Meltzer, Pigott, that apple-pie promise was precariously perched on Robert's whim, on whether he would turn round and say, 'OK, you keep the fuck-off house, with the nanny and the Burmese cats, I'll just scuttle off and live in a bedsit. As long as I've got somewhere to put my three bikes, sweetheart, then that will be fine.' So the growing realisation as summer drew to a close that we would have to sell the house was most definitely and absolutely the thing that took me tearfully to Suzanna Goodheart's leather sofa in late August 2012.

The other factor was that my secret desire was that by now I would have met someone else. Not just for companionship, but someone who could rescue me from the borders of a land I had no wish to enter. I was poised there on the precipice of being plunged into a world of house sales, mortgages, PEPs, ISAs and pensions... All the things Robert had dealt with, and which I felt frightened of.

And as the leaves turned orange, as we shopped in John Lewis for new school shoes and pencil cases, I realised the hope that a knight in shining armour would appear from the Internet sites of Match.com or Guardian Soulmates was fast diminishing. Time was running out as the letters from Robert's solicitor told me that it was really rather unlikely that he was going to accept a bedsit even if he had plenty of space for his bikes – very unlikely indeed.

By my third visit to Suzanna Goodheart, I had begun a descent down a slippery slope which I now know was the beginning of my downfall. Instead of facing the problem head-on, I'd tried to run. The biggest lesson I've learnt out of all of this is that anxiety and sleepless nights are invaluable. They're a signal that things aren't OK and acknowledging this will give you the key to solve whatever the problem is. Modern psychiatry teaches that these things must be quelled, that they are a result of modern stresses and a scourge to be extinguished. Anxiety is now an illness with an array of pills to combat it. Sleeplessness is to be avoided at all costs. But they're not; they're the keys to our happiness. Only I didn't know that then…

On my third visit to Suzanna Goodheart, she made a suggestion that was to determine the course of the next year, and who knows, maybe the course of my career and whole life. When I complained that I still couldn't sleep, that I felt desperate, empty, lonely, isolated, longing for love, she suggested I visit a psychiatrist she knew. And that's what I did a few days later.

As I sat in bed at the private hospital on that Monday morning, in September 2012, two days after I'd checked in, looking at the calendar on my phone, I saw that I had an appointment scheduled that day with Suzanna Goodheart.

There was no doubt in my head that the film crew would have gone to interview Suzanna about what a shallow, awful person I was. Even though I'd only seen her for three sessions, she'd be a good interviewee for them. She'd be able to give them lots of stuff about how superficial I am, how I wanted to be rescued by someone, how I couldn't cope without a man in my life. Yes, I could picture it all now. So I sent a text to her saying I couldn't make it.

For the rest of the day, I had an entourage of visitors: my brothers , David and Richard, and my closest friend Jim, who had, unconventionally, been best man at my wedding. It was odd because all of them told me there was no film crew and I wasn't on the national news. I couldn't understand why they were lying to me and then I had a terrible thought. Maybe they were in on the plot, maybe they'd betrayed me and had been filmed by the other side, Robert's team, and had given interviews about what an awful person I was. So during their visits I was completely silent, huddled in my bed, not knowing if I could trust them. But I'd been silent anyway since I'd arrived – it was as if the power of speech had completely left me.

Things changed by the evening when my friend Juliette came. I'd called her two days before when I was first taken to the private hospital when there were cameras everywhere and had told her she had to get me out of there. She had no idea where I was, though. When she came round that evening, the nurses had just left me with yet more pills they insisted I take. Suddenly my mood had changed completely. I was no longer worried about the film crew and in fact I may have even forgotten their existence. Suddenly euphoric, I was absolutely manic, regaling her with all the things I was going to do when I left hospital. She even took a video of me on her phone.

By Monday night, even though I'd been there two full nights, I still hadn't left my room on the ground floor of the hospital. That night, once again, I was sedated with yet more pills to get me off to sleep.

Chapter 5

TUESDAY, 25 SEPTEMBER 2012

I wake up and I'm relieved. Not only is there no film crew in the hospital, there's no film crew anywhere – and there never was. I'm confused. Was all of that a dream? No, it can't be, because I'm lying in bed in a mental hospital, albeit a posh private one, but yes, it's a mental hospital so some of what I remembered must have happened. I'm really confused now. So I look at my left arm, and when I look under the large bandage, there is a huge cut.

I get up and for the first time open the door to my room. Immediately outside my door there is a nurse sitting there. I later learn there has been someone sitting there since my arrival, on suicide watch.

I'm not allowed, I'm told, to leave my room. Not until I'm seen by a doctor. A nurse brings a tray of breakfast and for the first time since my arrival, I eat – I'm actually starving and consume the contents of the breakfast tray.

For the first time I notice my surroundings. Until now all I've seen has been the TV on the wall opposite my bed, where I've been watching news reports about myself. Now I notice there is an abstract painting above my bed, a sink with a mirror beside a wardrobe. The room has the appearance of a faded seventies hotel, the only difference being there are bars on the window.

When I look in the mirror, I look totally bedraggled – my hair unwashed, my eyes bloodshot. I realise I haven't washed, or even brushed my hair for I don't know how long. There are a few clothes in the wardrobe and so I decide to have a shower and get out of the pyjamas I've been wearing since my arrival.

Once dressed and showered, I feel better. I'm still disorientated, confused, though. What the hell happened? I'm wondering. Never mind the past, I think, let's just focus on now. What I know is that I'm in hospital, Robert is now back at Dundonald with the kids, and there was some doctor, wasn't there, who interviewed me and told me I couldn't leave? Christ, what was it I told him? It's all coming back, thoughts crowding my head, trying desperately to make sense of what happened to me.

A nurse comes in with some pills. Somehow I know instinctively I mustn't take them. I tell her. She tells me I have to; I've signed a piece of paper apparently, when I first came to the hospital, saying I consent to take any drugs. I should talk to the doctor, she says, when I see him later today.

I catch sight of a piece of a notepad and pen on the chest of drawers beneath the TV and decide to write down some notes to try and help me piece together what happened. This all started with that pill, didn't it? Yes, I'm sure it did. Wasn't that a pill that Robert gave me? OK, now I'm wondering.

THE PILL THAT STEALS LIVES

Could it be that Robert gave me an acid tablet instead of the antidepressant? Would he have done that? Why? Some sort of set-up to get the kids, would he actually do that? Right now I'm so confused. I'm not sure whether that idea too is completely deluded.

So I start to write some scribbled notes: action plan – tell the doctor it was the pill, tell him I mustn't take any more pills, phone the kids, and get out of here.

It's the afternoon before I see one of the doctors again. He looks pleasantly surprised when he enters the room and sees me dressed and showered. I haven't tidied up and I feel embarrassed when he has to remove a pink bra from the chair at the end of the bed. As he makes a joke of it, I notice for the first time, this man has a rather lovely sense of humour and a bedside manner that would almost in itself justify the exorbitant fees of this private hospital that thankfully was covered by Robert's private health insurance.

I attempt to be measured and calm as I try to explain to him my thesis as to why just two days ago in my last meeting with him I was insistent that there was a suicide pact with God, that killing myself was preordained. I notice I'm able to talk properly for the first time since I've got there, but not fluently, not like before, and in any case I'm nervous, really tentative about how I deliver this piece of news that even I don't fully understand.

'It was the pill, I took,' I say, 'the one that was given to me before I got here, the escitalopram, I think, unless someone gave me something else. It made me go crazy. I thought everything was a game, I thought I was being filmed, I was kind of hearing voices … I know there isn't really a suicide pact with God – yes, I really know that, I promise. I'm OK now, and please, please can you let me out of here so I can go home to Lily and Oscar.'

And I realise that by the end of this speech my voice is starting to rise, and I'm sounding slightly desperate, slightly hysterical.

Calm down, I tell myself. I've got to convince this man who is taking notes again with his smart fountain pen that I'm sane. He, and he alone, is the keeper of the keys at this £6,000-per-week glorified prison.

And he smiles at me kindly. 'It really doesn't matter what happened in the past now, does it? Let's just focus on the present. How's your mood today? Have you eaten? You're dressed, that's good.'

I can tell he doesn't believe me. OK, I'm going to have to get firm now. 'I've decided I want to leave. Now. Thanks for your help, but I'm off.' 'That's not going to happen,' he says, with a firmness in his voice that makes me realise he can stop me if he wants to. 'Can you stop me?' I ask. 'Yes,' he replies, 'if I have to, I can.' He nods towards the cut on my arm, something neither of us has mentioned yet. I'd rather hoped if I didn't mention it, he would have forgotten it. With a feeling of despondency I realise he hasn't. It's not looking good. I don't know much about the Mental Health Act, but I know enough to know that someone who comes in talking about a suicide pact with God, and has lacerated her left arm for no particular reason, can be detained – I think 'sectioned' is the word for it. I look at his smart fountain pen scribbling notes on a pad of A4 paper and I realise that today I don't have a hope in hell of getting out of the private hospital where there is still a nurse on suicide watch at my door, monitoring my every move. I have no doubt there are strict security measures throughout the hospital making it impossible for me to leave until I can persuade the doctors to write something very different to what he is no doubt writing now with his smart fountain pen.

And so I decide that I must play the game, whatever that is. And that is the last mention I make of the pill and my belief that it caused me to go psychotic. I shut up about it, fearful that if I mention it again, people will take it as a sign I'm still nuts. Maybe I did imagine it – I'm not sure. And so I don't talk about it again for an entire year.

Chapter 6

DISCOVERING I GOT
OFF LIGHTLY

Looking back, it seems quite bizarre to me that I was in one of London's top private hospitals, yet no one clocked the fact that I'd had a severe adverse drug reaction. But since then I've come across many cases of the same and worse. And it seems to happen across the board, in both private and NHS hospitals.

Claire's son has always suffered from Asperger's. He was extraordinarily bright, very gifted at chemistry but also a bit of a social loner. At twenty-five he was prescribed a higher dose of Prozac and became acutely psychotic. He locked himself in a room and Claire and her husband could hear him shouting to himself. He then hurtled down the stairs, shrieking and screaming in terror. The family, having no idea what was going on, dialled 999 and soon the police and ambulance turned up. A doctor prescribed diazepam (a tranquillising, muscle-relaxing drug used to treat anxiety) and soon a crisis team arrived and he was admitted to hospital, where he was put on their acute ward. Two weeks later, he was diagnosed with schizophrenia and instead of the Prozac he was put on narcoleptics also known as antipsychotics.

He tries to come off the meds and the withdrawal is so bad, he goes into psychosis which the professionals now perceive as proof he needs more medication that is clearly toxic to him. He has started dribbling now and has lost all hand-to-mouth coordination, and the meds caused him to have disfiguring facial movements. There was a long battle getting him out of hospital. He is now home, and needs full-time care. Permanent brain damage caused by meds is shown by his difficulty in thinking straight, abnormal tongue movements and memory loss. He hears voices all his waking hours. But he can't come off the drugs completely because he will go into tardive psychosis. His mum worries about how this may affect his life expectancy.[1]

It's not just the antidepressants – there are over 100 drugs that act in the same way, causing suicidality and violence. Recently, I've heard from the wife of a major who was prescribed an anti-malarial drug. Like me, he became psychotic, the doctors refuse to believe it was the drug and even now he is incarcerated in a mental hospital, being given antipsychotics despite several independent experts offering the view that these are causing him brain damage.[2]

Another tragic case is that of O'Shea McCarthy, a young man entering his sophomore year of college in Chicago. He was given a strong antibiotic, Levaquin, following a routine operation and had a severe reaction, which included panic attacks and depression. He knew it was the Levaquin but doctors didn't believe him, decided to treat him for bipolar and gave him a cocktail of drugs instead. After two years of a horrendous decline, his life ended tragically with him jumping from a second-storey window of his family's home in a state of panic and agitation, driving off and colliding with a cement wall. His mother, Heather, is determined to publicise his case because the important thing in all of these cases, including mine, is that doctors recognise when people are suffering the potentially lethal side effects of these drugs.[3]

Chapter 7

SUNDAY, 30 SEPTEMBER 2012

It's been a week since I was admitted to the hospital. Since Tuesday, I've been OK. I even ventured out beyond my room and into the restaurant and on one occasion I was allowed out, accompanied by a nurse to the Tesco supermarket directly opposite.

As I suspected it's impossible to leave unless you have permission. There are nurses here monitoring your every move, and a woman at reception who will only buzz you out if the nurses have told her in advance.

The other patients vary in age and gender, but the one thing they share in common is that they've got money, or at least enough to afford private health insurance, and if not, they're very rich indeed so that they are able to pay the exorbitant fees. It boasts a host of celebrities, including many actors and pop stars. There is a medley of patients, for a range of different conditions. I quickly learn the most interesting ones are on the top floor – that's the addiction floor and it is peopled by cokeheads and smack addicts. Then there are some stick-thin people wandering about who are being treated for eating disorders. At meal times they have to eat at one table, where they are being supervised by a member of staff, and some look as young as fifteen.

Everyone here seems to smoke, and the small terrace by the cafeteria is the main meeting point.

Unusually for me, I've kept myself to myself, only striking up the briefest of conversations before scuttling back to my room. It's because I can't account for why I'm here. I don't have a simple back story, particularly why there is a huge gash on my left arm. If it was on the undersides of my wrists, people would assume this was a suicide attempt, and I would have fitted in here perfectly because there are a fair share of those who have either self-harmed or even tried to kill themselves. But it's not, and I have trouble explaining to people why the hell I'm here. So in the end I mumble something about divorce and depression and hope they won't notice the cut.

And actually this is no lie. One of the doctors, on his second visit towards the end of the week, has pronounced it thus. He says I've been very, very ill, and though better, I am still ill. Not only have I had depression, I've had *psychotic* depression, he says with an air of absolute authority, emphasising the word 'psychotic' as if it might be a word I've never heard of before. I have heard of the word 'psychotic' and the word 'depression', but I'd never heard the two words conjoined in that way. Some time down the line, when I had formed the opinion that possibly not everything that the doctors said was strictly accurate, I learnt that psychotic depression is extremely rare and mainly happens to old people. Also, it doesn't tend to emerge out of nowhere for precisely four days, then magically disappear overnight never to return again.

From the off, I doubted this diagnosis. I still had in mind the pill I'd taken. But by now I'd decided my best strategy was to keep shtum. True, the addicts on the third floor may be fun to hang out with, no doubt the stick-thin anorexics could give me some good dieting tips, and I'm betting there are a load of people with a whole host of unusual disorders that could well give me ideas for a documentary. All that may be true, but my mind is firmly fixed on getting the hell out of here as quickly as possible and back to Lily and Oscar in Dundonald Road, where Robert no doubt will be back in our old marital bedroom, possibly even having moved his bikes back in, and now issuing new carb-loaded meal plans to our nanny Andrea in my absence.

Andrea was our Hungarian nanny, who had been with us for two years. In her early thirties, she resided in the self-contained nanny flat at the top of the house. As soon as I met her, I gave her the job because of her sunny disposition and can-do attitude. Andrea cleverly juggled her job with us so that she could indulge her real passion, which was fitness and selling healthcare products. She did this after taking the kids to school and before the evening when she cooked us all a meal and helped the kids with their homework. But she was much more than a nanny to all of us.

She was super-smart, Andrea, and super-kind. She had a natural wisdom, in some part borne of the fact she came to England ten years ago with no money and no qualifications and got herself a job first as a cleaner, then an au pair and now a fully-fledged nanny. Her life experience gave her wisdom, which meant she could become my confidante as she witnessed the initial crumble and then the final disintegration of the domestic ménage that she'd first been hired into. She was a shoulder to cry on when I looked into the abyss of first separation, then divorce. When Robert moved out, we were all soothed by her positivity and home-cooked meals as we adapted to life without him. And she held my hand as I trod timorously into the previously unknown world of Internet dating, helping me choose photos and insisting that I tell her exactly where I was going as a safety precaution for those first few dates.

Without Robert we developed a girlie camaraderie akin to two flat sharers rather than employer and employee, as we borrowed each other's clothes and exchanged stories of dating disasters. She told me firmly that it was absolutely de rigueur I should get a Brazilian just in case one of those dates developed into something more intimate than a series of flirty texts and cocktails in bars I'd never heard of. And I'd have her in stitches as she ladled up sweet potato soup in the kitchen while I pontificated as to whether in Brazil they have Brazilians, or do they go to their beauticians to have an English?

And so, in the cold months immediately after Robert's departure, Andrea, or 'Banny', or 'Banny Boo Boo', as the kids adoringly called her, was the light that lit up our otherwise darker lives, the glue that held us back together when each one of us had our private moments of upset. Yes, each of us at some time ran upstairs for comfort to the top floor, where Banny Boo Boo offered words of wisdom and hugs in a room jam-packed with Herbalife shakes and skincare products.

In the run-up to the pill incident, Andrea was concerned when she saw me teetering on the edge and had done everything to try and calm me down. I suppose in retrospect, the prospect of losing the house was also linked to the prospect of losing her, because it would be unlikely we could afford a house that had enough room for a nanny. But she'd gone to Barcelona for a long weekend when I became psychotic and ended up in hospital. When she came back on the Sunday night, I imagine she would have been astonished to find Robert and not me at the house.

She'd visited me in hospital after the pill had worn off and brought me clothes and photos of the children while radiating concern. As happened many times, I was unable to explain to her what had taken place. I know this sounds strange, but the psychotic incident was so vivid that I almost believed it was reality and so therefore other people must have somehow witnessed what occurred in my head.

As far as she was concerned, I guess, I had just asked to be admitted to hospital and asked Robert to come and look after the kids. She knew about the cut on the arm, and she knew I wasn't allowed to leave the hospital, but we never talked about it. And actually I never talked about it with any of the many friends and family who visited me either at the hospital or in the weeks ahead. I honestly don't know what the hell they thought I was doing incarcerated in a £6,000-per-week mental hospital with a 6-inch self-inflicted knife wound on my left arm.

Anyway, it had become obvious to me that the doctors weren't going to let me leave the hospital for the foreseeable future. I'd pleaded with them but they were having none of it. In fact, they said that it was a sign of how ill I was that I wanted to go home and didn't recognise the benefits of being in hospital. Even though I recognised this as being a ridiculous piece of reverse psychology, I realised that I was going to have to play by their rules. But I didn't really understand the game. What was their agenda, I thought to myself. Do they really think I'm at risk? I've now had four days of being normal, they can see that, surely? I've even been to the gym here.

In our session before the weekend one of the doctors announces his plans for me. After the weekend I'm to start a treatment programme involving group therapy sessions. CBT (Cognitive Behavioural Therapy), IPT (Interpersonal Therapy), yoga, mindfulness, art therapy. It's all there, on a timetable posted in the corridor, and I'm free to choose which sessions I go to, but I have to attend all day, every day. And the nurses are going to make sure I go. I gulp at the prospect of having to face a load of strangers and having to explain why I'm here. Now I've one last hope.

'What about the insurance?' I ask. 'Won't it have run out?' I hold my breath.

No, the doctor has thought that one through: he's already applied to extend my stay. So far it's extended to next week, and then we'll see. Later, I discover that the insurance will generally cover you for up to four weeks at a stretch, and it was exactly at that point that the doctors pronounced in their very professional opinion I was ready to go home. But I didn't know that then and I was hopeful at the very least I'd be allowed home by the end of the following week.

Then there was the question of the pills. When one of the doctors pronounced that I was very ill indeed with psychotic depression, he also told me that I would have to continue taking the pills the nurses had already started giving me – the antidepressant mirtazapine and an antipsychotic medication called risperidone.

'For how long?' I asked.

'A year,' he replied.

'A year?'

'Yes, a year.'

Because I had been very ill indeed – with *psychotic* depression.

I knew that this was not the time to argue with the doctor. And I knew that the nurses were going to make absolutely sure I took the little pills that were brought round on a tray, not just to me but as far as I could see to pretty much every single patient at the private hospital , whether they were there for eating disorders, stress, bereavement or addictions to drink, drugs, glue, sex, whatever. In the minds of the doctors at this hospital, and many other hospitals in the country, not just private but also NHS, all of these ailments are treatable with a pill of one kind or another.

I learnt later that depression, the illness I was supposed to have, used to be incredibly rare. It was once known as 'melancholia' and was a condition where people for no apparent reason couldn't get out of bed. Psychiatrists only used to see about two or three cases per year. In the sixties and seventies, people like me going through a difficult life event would have been diagnosed with 'nerves' and given tranquillisers such as benzodiazepines. Once the addictive properties of these drugs became known, along with the ensuing lawsuits against the doctors who had prescribed them, a new pill was needed. But in order to have a new pill, you need a new condition or disease. Drug companies now set about persuading those who previously had 'nerves' or anxiety that they were in fact depressed and needed an antidepressant.

Edward Shorter describes this process in his book, *How Everyone Became Depressed*.[1] In the past, the notion of nerves suggested that patients had an illness of the entire body that spa treatments, for example, could correct. Today, with the ubiquity of the diagnosis of depression, we have the idea that low mood and an inability to experience pleasure are our main problems; we see ourselves as having a mood disorder situation solely in the brain, which antidepressants can correct. But, he argues, this is not science, it is pharmaceutical advertising. Meanwhile the serious melancholic depressions are missed. The consequence is many suicides that might otherwise have been prevented and a population taking antidepressants as though they were over-the-counter antacids and getting all the side effects and few of the imagined benefits of these medications.

Right now, psychotic depression was the label the doctors had given me and nothing was going to persuade them otherwise. And they had a cure. Now that they had given me another course of pills, I was about to experience for the second time just how dangerous those pills can be.

But right now, as I waited on the Sunday morning for Robert and the kids to arrive, I felt OK. Not brilliant, but OK.

Normal.

Chapter 8

SEEING LILY AND OSCAR AGAIN

It was the first time I'd seen the kids properly since my return to sanity.

And it was the first time I was allowed to properly leave the hospital. We had decided we would all go to Regent's Park. As I waited for my family to arrive, peering through the bars of the window in my room, I remembered that today was the day I was supposed to be running my first-ever half marathon, the Royal Parks Half Marathon.

I feel depressed. Christ, no, don't even think that word here – they'll never let you leave! No, I feel annoyed. Pissed off. Fucking pissed off, I think, as I contemplate Robert now gathering up the children in the house I'd been living at in Dundonald Road to visit their mother, who is now locked up in a mental hospital.

He's still on crutches from his broken toe. Lily has brought some flowers, which she tentatively gives me. She's not sure about me, yet – she can still remember the craziness of our last meeting. Clearly traumatised, Oscar still can't look me in the eye. We all walk in silence to nearby Regent's Park. This is the oddest of scenarios. We'd all got used to the disbandment of our family unit. Now we were forced together again in the strangest of scenarios, Robert hobbling around, and me with an unexplained wound on my left arm. And only allowed out for two hours maximum as if I were a prisoner who had committed a heinous crime.

I can't imagine how odd this must have been for Lily and Oscar. In a week, their Mum had become a knife-wielding maniac, their Dad had moved back after eight months away, while Mum was locked up in a posh loony bin that looked like an old people's home with bars at the windows.

We have lunch in the café, and then sit in the warm September sunshine by the lake. But we don't know what to talk about. It's the first time Robert and I have been together for eight months. Without future events to plan, we have nothing to say. And there is a gap between me and my children that I am unable to close. In the past I had promised them complete transparency yet now there was something I couldn't explain. I myself couldn't unravel what the hell had happened to me so I'd no hope of explaining it to them. And so it went unmentioned except for Lily occasionally stroking my arm and saying, 'Poor Mummy.'

We didn't talk about it until a year later – by which time far worse things were to unfold. But we didn't know that then.

Tuesday, 2 October 2012. I'm wearing a pink floral dress, pink lipstick and my room at the hospital is looking immaculate as I lie on the bed, waiting to see the doctor. I'm on a single-minded mission to play the game and get out of here. Claudia, the young nurse from Chile, had advised me just to take the medication and attend all the classes.

For the last two days I'd flitted between classes of CBT, IPT (Interpersonal Therapy), mindfulness and yoga. I'd sat with anorexics, bulimics, depressives, manic depressives, agoraphobics, claustrophobics and people suffering grief, stress and social anxiety. And those who were there like me, for depression.

By now I'd accepted that this was the label that had been given to me, and while I was there, I wasn't going to challenge it. But it didn't ring true. I knew about depression: my father had suffered it and I remembered, when we moved to that hotel in Torquay, how he would sit in a room in the small family flat on the second floor and do nothing all day. That was depression, I thought, as I sat in sessions, listening to people's stories. How could that be me? A month ago I was playing tennis, hosting suppers for my new friends. There had been a house party in Sweden. I was training for my first half marathon, making a film about Tourette's syndrome, packing everything into the finale of my first summer holiday as a single mum with the kids. It bore no resemblance to the disease that stole my father and had him sitting in a room all day, talking of ending his life.

But I played the game as best I could. Desperately I struggled to dredge up something I could talk about. I was supposed to be depressed about divorce, wasn't I? So I'd mutter something about loneliness, about being a single mum. But it was all an act. I had to maintain it as every single movement and interaction was monitored throughout the day by therapists and nurses whose scribbled notes went back to the man who held the keys, the keys to this very expensive prison.

As he arrives, I notice he's wearing yet another bow tie, this time yellow with purple spots. Flashing him a smile, I comment on it. Now I know the rule that I can't mention I want to go home so instead maybe I can flirt my way out of here.

He begins to tell me he wants to change my medication, something about prolactin levels being high. He has done a blood test and apparently prolactin is a hormone that increases if you are reacting badly to a drug. But I don't take much notice of what he is saying. I vaguely hear him telling me he's switching from risperidone to aripiprazole (or is that the other way round?) I haven't heard of either of these drugs. Only later do I learn that they are very powerful antipsychotics with a host of debilitating side effects even worse than antidepressants.

This is to be a longer session; he's going to interview me. It doesn't take him long to get round to my childhood and my dad. He nods knowingly as I reluctantly hand over the pieces of the jigsaw I know he's going to make. As I give him the final piece, that my dad committed suicide when I was twelve, he looks sympathetic.

'About the age of your daughter,' he murmurs, his scribbles becoming more purposeful.

'Yes, I suppose so,' I say, bewilderedly.

I'm glad when we move on because I don't talk much about my dad's death – I never have. In fact, halfway through the autumn term after it happened, I hadn't told a single one of my friends. My house mistress called me in. The nights were drawing in as I sat in one of the dormitories and tried to find the words to explain to a select group of friends what had happened in the summer holidays.

THE PILL THAT STEALS LIVES

Could they tell other people, please?

'Oh, and by the way, I'm completely fine about it.'

The doctor now has all the information he needs to conclude that his diagnosis is correct. That I'm suffering from a disease that, as we all know, is genetically handed down.

Well, we all know that, don't we?

Chapter 9

FINAL WEEK AT THE PRIVATE HOSPITAL, OCTOBER 2012

By the end of that second week I was ill again. The medication had worked its way into my system. On top of the antidepressants and antipsychotics, they were giving me zopiclone sleeping tablets, and the interaction of this and the other medication would have increased the toxic overload in my system, as I was to learn later.

Sometimes I feel overwhelmed by being spaced out. But the main thing is the akathisia, this appalling inner turmoil, a crushing anxiety, together with the inability to stay still. It's so bad that in a group therapy session despite the fact I know that I have to be on my very best behaviour, I am unable to keep still and ask to be taken out by a nurse. I tell her I feel very anxious. She gives me a blue pill, a Valium. It works for a bit, but not for long.

I remember in the evenings pacing round and round the

corridor like a caged animal. The other patients are looking at me as if I'm some deranged animal. I can't engage in conversation with them. I'm trying desperately to hide these symptoms from the doctors and the nurses. Whenever they come by, I do my best to keep still but it's agony. I'm allowed out to attend a parents' evening at Lily's school. Robert asks me why I keep pacing up and down. I've got a bad back, I lie. I've no idea what is going on in my body but whatever it is I'm suffering, I feel that I must hide it so I can get released from the hospital.

The kids come and visit me but I can't talk to them anymore. I don't know why, my mind just seems to have blanked out. And once again I'm losing the power of speech. I remember a doctor sitting them down in front of me and explaining to them the reason for my incarceration.

'Your mother is very ill,' he says. 'She has a chemical imbalance in her brain but we're giving her some pills to correct it.'

I've no idea whether he believes the chemical imbalance theory. And I have heard many cases of other people being told the same by doctors and psychiatrists.

David Healy is an expert on the history of antidepressant drugs and in his book, *Let Them Eat Prozac*,[1] he tells how the serotonin theory is not a story of science but pseudo-science used by the drug industry to sell drugs claiming to boost our serotonin levels.

It came about in the early 1960s when a scientist in Edinburgh, George Ashcroft, was studying serotonin. He found low levels of the main serotonin metabolite in the cerebrospinal fluid (CSF) of depressed subjects and created the hypothesis that lower levels of serotonin could be the cause of depression.

No one took any notice at the time. Everyone was much more interested in another neurotransmitter, noradrenaline but by the end of the 1960s lowered levels of serotonin or noradrenaline had been dismissed by pretty much all of the experts, including Ashcroft.

The idea came up again in the 1990s, this time in the marketing departments of companies selling SSRIs. They couldn't get an academic psychiatrist to support it – no self-respecting academic would – and so they used patients, journalists and advertisements to promote the idea and did so astonishingly successfully.

'This key myth still flourishes in popular consciousness almost forty years later,' says David Healy.[2] And he's right. Most people believe that depression is caused by low serotonin, which can be topped up by a drug, much in the way that a diabetic can be treated with insulin. Yet some antidepressants actually lower serotonin. Indeed the serotonin deficiency myth is so strong in our culture that David Healy tells how he can bring chat shows to a crashing halt when he says there is no truth in it.

Interestingly, both Lily and Oscar told me later that they were always sceptical about the doctors' claims that I had a chemical imbalance.

Meanwhile, the drugs began to take their grip on my body for the second time.

There is a moment that encapsulates the beginning of what I believe to be the most frightening descent into hell a human being can experience. It's a known side effect of antidepressants – emotional blunting or the loss of empathy.

One of the doctors is sitting in the chair opposite me. There's a form I need him to sign. Robert has asked for it, something to do with the health insurance. If he signs it, he's going to be late for his evening appointment. He's a music lover and he's going to a concert with his wife. There's a voice in my head, I can hear it now: it's saying words I've never heard except when I've been angry with someone.

'I don't give a fuck about whether you're late,' it's saying.

And I heard it when the nurses would come in and clear up my room. I'd make no effort to engage – I didn't care how much mess I'd made. I'm not interested in them, not one jot.

And it wasn't long before I didn't give a fuck about anything – the kids, my family, myself, life itself.

I suppose the doctor wasn't completely wrong. By then, I did have a chemical imbalance in my brain – but caused by the pills that I had been prescribed.

And it was about to get far, far worse.

Chapter 10

FRIDAY, 12 OCTOBER 2012

Today, I'm being discharged from the hospital. I should be happy, but I'm not. I'm properly ill now, but I don't know where it's come from: there are seeds of doubt.

Yesterday, I'd gone onto my computer and I'd googled the drugs I'm on.

There it was, the side effects: increased depression, anxiety, feelings of hopelessness. When the nurse came round, I refused to take the pills. One of the doctors was on the phone.

'I've read up on the side effects,' I say. 'I think I've got them.'

His voice is very stern: 'You've been very ill with *psychotic* depression. You have to take those pills.'

I was frightened. Scared he might not let me out if I refused to take them, then scared because he was a doctor and maybe he knew best.

A few days earlier, I'd phoned Robert. We'd hardly spoken

since I'd been in hospital. I know I can't look after the kids. My body is racked with involuntary movements, a bit like Parkinson's disease. I can't think straight.

Would he move in while I get better?

And so I move back to Dundonald Road mid-October 2012 but he never moves out.

Because I don't get better.

And this is why – because by now I really do have a chemical imbalance in my brain. It's what experts have recognised as Prozac backlash – the brain's reaction to intruding chemicals.

> When a drug boosts serotonin in the brain, the brain's chemical balance is upset. The result is artificially induced fluctuations not only of serotonin but also of the many other chemicals that act in concert with it.[1]

And that is why even if these drugs started out making you feel better than well, the end can be rather different. Because the result of this altered brain chemistry can be neurological damage and a whole host of side effects including Parkinsonism, agitation, muscle spasm and tics.

You get these side effects from taking one drug. Mid-October 2012, I left the hospital on two and as I inevitably grew worse, I was given more and more until a year later I was on five drugs, including antipsychotics and mood stabilisers.

For the next year, I began a slow but steady descent into a hell that I know I won't have the words to describe. By the end, the agony of the toxic harm wrought on my mind and body was to take me to a state where I no longer wanted to live. I would have ended it all, had it not been that fate took a hand.

One week after my discharge, it's half term. The kids huddled on the sofa, watching TV. I used to take them out, didn't I? They're not allowed to watch TV during the day. They were afraid of this stranger who had once been their mother. We didn't talk, I just paced up and down. Akathisia, that inner turmoil, the inability to sit still: the condition that drives people to suicide.

I have to get over this. My friend Anita has invited Lily and me over for lunch. But I can't talk; I can't sit still.

The look of confusion on her face; we can't converse. It is excruciating.

Anita tries to get through to me, but she can't. Later she told me how distressing it was for her.

Lily begged me never to go out with her again.

Two weeks later, it's Halloween. Everyone is out on our street, Dundonald Road, dressed up. Too frightened to go downstairs and meet people, I huddle upstairs in the bedroom with the cheap IKEA blinds. I ring my sister Amy, crying. How can I explain? I can't see people because I've lost the power of speech. And not just that: I've also lost the ability to feel so I simply can't relate to them. I'm so alone.

What the hell has happened to me?

Amy tries to calm me down. 'Tinks, darling, please just go downstairs and join in the fun. The kids want you there, so do your friends. It's trick or treat, it's no big deal!' But somehow I cannot do this simple thing of going downstairs and joining the assembled throng of people whom I'd been close to just a few months ago. I simply can't and don't know why.

In November, the doctors had a 'cure'. They increased aripiprazole to 20 mg and added 50 mg sertraline. Oh, and some diazepam for good measure. When I complained of restlessness, they said, 'Oh yes, that's akathisia – a side effect of the aripiprazole.' They replace it with 20 mg olanzapine, one of THE most powerful antipsychotics. Linked to unexplained deaths, strokes and diabetes, it also causes you to binge eat.

Three bags of popcorn at one sitting, a couple of bags of Liquorice Allsorts... When the children went to school, I'd rush to their rooms looking for sweets, eating any I could find. I'd come down in the middle of the night, stuffing bread with Nutella in my mouth.

The akathisia continues. I just can't sit still.

Before I know it, I'm three stone heavier: I'm wearing an old tracksuit and I've started shuffling now.

The children couldn't reach me; I couldn't reach them.

Soon I was dribbling.

Oscar begs me not to go anywhere near his school.

He starts saying he hates me.

They wanted me out, so Robert would arrange for me to stay at my siblings'. He was at a loss as to what to do.

Still more pacing, dribbling; voracious eating.

I've started to talk about suicide.

By Christmas time I start to drink. I've never drunk more than a couple of glasses of wine before. But I do now – I'm taking bottles of spirits *to bed*.

Where was Santa Claus this year? I hadn't been well enough to do their stockings

Lily's and Oscar's faces are etched with disappointment. It was always Mummy that organised the stockings. And Robert was already overwhelmed with the ever-increasing responsibility of running the household single-handedly and having a dribbling invalid in the house. He hardly had time to breathe, let alone think about Father Christmas.

Boxing Day – I'm on my own in bed with a bottle of whisky. I hadn't bought any presents. Lily and Oscar don't want to spend Christmas with me. My family have begged me to join them but I'm too unwell. I try to sleep all day. By now there is nothing else I can do.

I've started to plan how I'm going to end it all.

My family organise a carer: first Mina, and then Jeanette. They have to wash me and get me dressed – I can't look after myself.

By March 2013 I can't bear to see the children's hatred for me so I move out to a flat in Cornwall Crescent, two miles down the road in Notting Hill leaving them in Dundonald Road with Robert. The doctors from the private hospital respond to my declining state by adding another powerful antidepressant, Zoloft (sertraline) – 200 mg of it. There's no carer now. I've started smoking, the first time I've touched a cigarette for twenty years. I used to be a keep-fit fan, didn't I? I'm smoking maybe up to seventy cigarettes per day. And I do nothing; just eat. I can't even watch the TV. The children cry when they have to visit me. They ring Robert, begging him to pick them up.

I'm trying to make an effort. I want my kids back but I don't know how – I can't reach them. Occasionally I break out of the house to buy things for them and scuttle back. I don't know them these days so I buy them things they don't want.

The drink isn't working.

Nothing works.

I've tried playing the piano. But there's no point – I can't feel the music. I can't feel anything much.

When did I last hug the kids?

In May, I book myself back into the hospital. Desperate, I'll

79

try anything. One of the doctors puts me on lithium – 1,000 mg – and 25 mg lamotrigine and 20 mg Prozac (fluoxetine). That's as well as olanzapine – you know, the antipsychotic that has a suicide rate far higher than antidepressants – during a trial run for which, 12 people out of 2500 killed themselves.[2] At one point they add in another antipsychotic Seroquel (quietapine). Then there's zopiclone to get me to sleep…

I'm there for six weeks – they think I may be bipolar.

The kids don't want to see me now.

When I leave hospital, I'm no better… actually worse.

We need to sort the divorce out so we go to mediation in some very expensive offices in Covent Garden. Over pie charts of how we're going to divide the assets and platters of exotic fruit, I fall asleep.

Oscar cries when I go to his sports day. He tries to pretend the woman dribbling and chain smoking is not his mother. His friends are whispering.

Bills pile up, my teeth are yellow – they're developing cavities but I don't care.

By the end of August there's no way out: I want to kill myself.

I know I've still got the kids, but I've lost everything. Because I can no longer feel and most importantly I can no longer love. And, as I once read, a life without love is no life at all.

And, so you see, for some time now, I've ceased to be human.

I can't escape the pain anymore, the continual pain of having to walk around and around, possessed by this monster that I don't understand. Every night I'm down at a supermarket buying vodka and herbal sleeping tablets to dull the pain. But then I have to wake up at some point.

Or do I?

The pain of seeing the life I had, but couldn't reach. The faces of the children I once loved.

I'm in a bubble – a toxic bubble.

Chapter 11

WHY ANTIDEPRESSANTS MAKE SOME PEOPLE SUICIDAL

So yes, it's true. About six months after being on those pills, I started thinking seriously about ending my life. This is something I have to live with every day. Until then, my view on those who kill themselves who have kids was that it's an appallingly selfish act. All that has changed now I know the power of this medication.

And this is something people simply will not understand: that these drugs can bring the strongest of people to their knees as the chemical effect defeats you. You have no chance against them. And I fought it, yes, how I fought it, and fought it over that year. Every day I'd wake up with a chemically induced feeling of wanting nothing more than to get the hell off this planet, but I was determined to find a way to get back in. I'd think of all the things that used to give me pleasure and I'd try to do them all. Throughout that year I forced myself to play tennis, the piano, to run, to dance, swim, to go to places

I'd been to before that I knew I enjoyed – museums, galleries, friends – and to play the games I used to play with Lily and Oscar. I'd buy a whole wardrobe of clothes now in size 16 to try to make myself feel OK. But none of it worked. Had my opponent been just one drug, defeat might have been on the cards – but I was now on five of them.

The feeling of wanting to kill yourself on these drugs is quite unlike the feelings of despair you might have without. Until then the closest I'd ever felt to despair was when I once rang the Samaritans when I broke up with a boyfriend, with whom I was madly in love. I was thirty years old, the pain was excruciating and I wondered if I would ever stop crying, but six weeks later, I'd found another boyfriend and was trekking in Bali.

Like all of us, I've had some pretty crap things happen in my life but I've never, ever wanted to end it all before. My dad's suicide and subsequent loss of the family home, my best friend dying at the age of eighteen in a freak accident involving a faulty water geyser and carbon monoxide fumes. I've coped with all of them, because there is always hope that things are going to get better. And that is true for almost all life situations: even if you are a prisoner of war, the war may end and you may be set free. And you have other humans to share this.

With drugs, it's a different scenario. The feelings of inexplicable awfulness are inexorable. You're on your own because you no longer have the empathy that connects you to others. Now you're taken hostage. Worst of all, you don't recognise it in yourself. You've been brainwashed into thinking you've got a disease and the drugs are making you better. And this is reinforced if you try to get off them, which

I did at various points. Withdrawal is agony, and most people will go back on. And there is no end. No hope. Nothing.

After I recovered, I struggled with the guilt of how close I'd come to leaving my kids without a mother. I felt it would help to meet others who had similarly contemplated killing themselves because of the chemical horror of these pills.

James's story is far worse than mine.[1] He is a successful businessman and people development professional, who had never suffered from any mental health illnesses. As a result of a very stressful year, including the impact of the financial crash on his business and family, in 2010 he was prescribed citalopram for anxiety. Like me, he had a bad reaction, and they piled on more and more and more. He was on every single one of the antidepressants and when those didn't work, they started giving him the same antipsychotics as they gave me including olanzapine which, as mentioned before, has been shown in trials to have an extremely high suicide risk. He became a very different person – in his wife Sarah's words: 'He turned from a loving and caring husband and father into an unpredictable monster.' Never previously violent in his life, James started attacking his wife and at their GP's suggestion the police became involved.

James put on half his body weight again, and like me, he couldn't wash, couldn't dress, and didn't want to leave the house. At one stage, while in hospital, he became so psychotic that he thought the police were after him for wasting NHS money and he was sectioned. He saw many doctors and psychiatrists, NHS and private, and was given various treatments, including whole courses of Cognitive Behavioural Therapy and ECT (Electroconvulsive Therapy). None made any difference – they just kept changing the medication and dosage levels.

James is lucky to have an incredible wife, who despite everything he put her through, remained supportive. She continually questioned doctors if it could be the medication that was causing the problems, but was brushed aside and told on a number of occasions: 'You must listen to the experts.'

The ending is both tragic and happy. Having been on medication for over two years, and his life having little resemblance to what it used to be, things took another dramatic turn. James doesn't remember a thing about this, but apparently, he told his wife he was going out and never returned. He booked himself into a hotel and took an overdose of all his pills. Twenty-four hours later, he was found and rushed to hospital, where he was in a coma for nearly a week. His family was told if he did live then he might suffer severe organ and brain damage. His wife agreed to normal life-saving procedures, including a full blood transfusion, but as she had always suspected it was the pills that had caused his illness, she insisted they didn't give him more. She was so adamant that she and their daughter kept up twenty-four-hour vigils.

Finally, when he regained full consciousness, James was better. Completely. The old James was back. From his hospital bed, he rang up friends and family whom he'd not wanted to see or speak to during his period of 'illness'. Unfortunately, when he was unconscious, his arm was trapped and now it is nerve damaged, causing him chronic pain, which he will probably have to endure for the rest of his life. It also serves as a continual reminder of what he and his family had to live through but as he said to me: 'It also reminds me I'm lucky to be alive and rebuilding my old life. Ironically, if I hadn't taken the overdose, I would most probably still be on the antidepressants and I dread to think what state my life would be in by now.'

So, meeting him, I feel lucky. And it's some consolation to swap stories with someone who knows. He also told me something I forgot: he's had to have four teeth removed because the medication gave him a dry mouth. I got off lightly with just two. He tells me he too has flashbacks and once had to walk out of a cathedral café because it reminded him of the cafeteria at the mental hospital. And we talk about the guilt, what it did to his family, and if he can forgive himself for trying to kill himself. How he had never, ever in his life considered suicide before.

It has been hard, with professional support, but James has now been able to forgive himself. Can I do the same?

After a year I don't know where to turn. It's September 2013. The akathisia is so bad now that I'm wandering around the streets of Notting Hill like a demented animal.

I'm shaking from the medication. I ring my brother Richard, who is having lunch in the West End. He drops everything and comes over. I tell him I want to go back to the private hospital – I can't think of anything else.

My body is racked with pain from a year of continual poisoning. But not just my body, the drugs cause brain damage. Sometimes permanently, I learn later.

One of the doctors notices something. The side of my mouth is drooping, like a stroke victim. I remember my dad – the same thing happened to him.

My depression is so bad it's become drug resistant, the doctor tells my family. Next up was ECT (Electroconvulsive Therapy), although I didn't know that at the time.

WHY ANTIDEPRESSANTS MAKE SOME PEOPLE SUICIDAL

After a night on suicide watch, I am told I have to leave: the private insurance has run out. I don't have enough money on my credit card to pay. They've already charged me over £2,000. They send me home and refer me to the local health home-treatment team.

I just want out. I'm planning it now: jumping under a train.

Chapter 12

THE DAY MY LIFE WAS SAVED

And that's how that last chapter would have ended. But the fate that seems now to be driving my life stepped in that day – 22 September 2013.

I was going to end my life that day.

I'm back in my flat in Cornwall Crescent under the supervision of Kensington and Chelsea home-treatment team. Their helpers come in every day to make sure I'm taking my medication.

I've planned it after their morning visit: the tube at Ladbroke Grove is where I'm heading.

As the home-treatment worker dispenses the pills, I'm standing there in an old white dressing gown with stains on. I'm shaking from the pills, the drink, and the cigarettes. I haven't washed for many days. I wonder what Lily and Oscar are doing. There's no mention anymore of them visiting. How long is it since I've seen them? Many weeks, I guess, and when they visit, they ring their dad and cry for him to pick them up. Their mum has become a stranger.

I can't be sad about their absence in my life, I really can't, because I have no feelings. There is an emotional anaesthesia which people reading this simply will not understand. Unless you've been through this you can have no idea of what it's like to be chemically lobotomised. Sadness, along with joy and every other shade of emotion has long since disappeared from my life. Oscar is eleven; Lily is now twelve years old.

I was twelve too. In July 1976, I remember all of us were holding hands as we walked into the crematorium in Leatherhead. It was raining. It was a small affair. None of my father's family was there – they blamed my mum for his suicide. The small group of assembled family friends averted their gaze. On an occasion like this people simply do not know what to say.

None of us are crying yet. But then my older brother David does. And then we all do, our hands gripping tighter. There are no eulogies today. My mum is valiantly making an effort. Despite the lipstick, she can't hide from us or anyone else the fact she feels somehow responsible. She only visited Torquay at the weekends; she couldn't cope with his illness. No one could. I remember eavesdropping on secret family meetings. The arguments. He'd just say over and over again he wanted to kill himself. I remember thinking, how come? You haven't tried everything. Why don't you go on holiday? Take up a new hobby? Why do you want to kill yourself? Why? It never made sense to me.

He'd left a short, scribbled note before he'd jumped off the hotel balcony. It began, 'I must now relinquish the reins.' In it he listed a few items he was leaving to each of us: I got a radio/tape recorder. I no longer have the copy of the note I used to have, or the tape recorder. I can't even remember what happened to them.

Since then, I've not thought much about my dad. And I'm not thinking of him now as I contemplate the end of my own life. Though my brain is too addled from the medication for me to actually be able to dress myself, it can just about contemplate the two most important beings in my life.

I have an image of their faces at my funeral. And I catch sight of my own, now bloated with the drugs, my hair unwashed, eyes glazed, and sores around my mouth from the dribbling and the drugs. And that's when I turn to Theresa from the home-treatment team and ask her to take me right then to the local NHS hospital, St Charles. She doesn't argue, she can sense my desperation. The akathisia is so bad by now that I can barely manage to get myself into her car and sit still for the ten-minute drive. And the compulsion to chain smoke to combat the effects of the drugs is so overwhelming that the moment we step out onto the pavement I have to light up.

It's a large Victorian building and the mental health unit is at the far end. When I'm interviewed by the psychiatrist, something makes me say the words, those words – you know, the words that are going to get you detained if you say them in a mental hospital. Not just in a mental hospital but to a psychiatrist in a mental hospital. And it was as if something else was making me say those words. The words that meant there was no chance the psychiatrist could do anything else but keep me there, not just for that day but some considerable time. I looked him in the eye and despite the fact I was shaking from the medication, despite the fact I wasn't able to dress myself that morning, despite all that, I was able to deliver the words with utter clarity. And out they come – those words. Those words that I now know saved my life.

'I want to kill myself,' I say.

Within hours, I regret my decision but it's too late because they've sectioned me. But there's no bed for me, so I have to stay in the lounge all day and at night time I'm carted off to a ward to sleep. They contact my family, and my brother David and my niece Sarah come up from Chichester to sort out the flat and bring some clothes to the hospital. They can't disguise their shock when they see me. The doctors have told them I will be in for some considerable time. I'm told later that Andrea, our nanny, brought Lily. The staff wouldn't let her see me. They said it would be too distressing. Nonetheless, Lily is very determined and told Andrea to bring her every single day after school, and she did her homework in the hospital waiting room. They begged the doctors to be allowed to see me but they rightly said it wasn't a good idea. This is bedlam. What the hell have I done? In no time my personal possessions have been rifled. My iPad gets nicked. There are people with proper mental illnesses here. Or is it the drugs? I don't know, and I'll never find out. All I know is this lot are hearing voices, screaming, shouting at night; saying the police are after them.

'Don't drink the milk,' I'm told. 'There's a guy who's been pissing in it.'

Shit, I'm in a proper loony bin, what the hell have I done? I've got to get out of here. There's some advocate, I think he calls himself. I shouldn't be here. I want to appeal against my section. There's some tribunal. I beg the judge to let me go. Please, I shouldn't be here. Let me out. He looks at me with pity, almost certainly noticing that I haven't been able to dress myself properly because all my clothes are inside out.

My family, I ring them, begging them to get me out of there.

'We can't,' they say. 'You've got yourself sectioned. You told them you were going to kill yourself. There's nothing we can do.'

I'm on the phone to one of the doctors at the private hospital.

'Please get me out of here.'

If I can get the money, I can get transferred back to the private hospital. But where the hell am I going to get the money from – six grand a week? Robert – 'Please, give me the fucking cash! I've got to get the hell out of here. I'll do anything.'

They take me off the drugs. Not just one, the whole lot – all five. I start shaking, I'm now lying on the floor, writhing in agony; I can't sleep, eat, think, anything. I start scratching myself uncontrollably. I've no idea what's happening to me. I start to hallucinate and I'm finding it hard to stand up.

I can't sleep; I'm in pools of sweat. In the middle of the night I ring my older brother David. I'm screaming in agony. He tries to calm me down but neither he nor I understand that now my mind and body are going through indescribable agony from going cold turkey. Later I learnt that coming off from one of these drugs is supposed to be as bad as withdrawing from heroin[1] – and I was coming off five.

'Please, ring the nurse. Tell her to give me something, a Valium, an anti-anxiety drug, *anything*!'

The nurses are sometimes sympathetic, sometimes not. They can't give me any more medication until the morning. There's nothing they can do.

Three weeks later, on 12 October, they let me out for the

day: it's my nephew's wedding. It's like I'm on the set of a horror movie. There's an unnameable fear, a feeling I'm totally separate from humanity. The drugs were bad, but this is worse, far worse. I'm screaming and crying all day. I can't sit still at the ceremony. This is akathisia at its worst. I have to leave. My family take it in turns to sit with me outside the church. 'I just want to kill myself,' is all I would say. Lily and Oscar were there. Nothing could shock them by now. They'd given up; their mother has long since disappeared.

But they, and only they noticed something no one else did.

For the first time in a year, I was crying.

That night I was taken back to St Charles Hospital after the wedding reception, and I imagine my family and all the friends assembled at that wedding would have thought that I would be there for a very long time indeed. They might have concluded that what had started as depression had now gone way beyond that to a mental illness that looked as if it had taken an intractable hold on me. To many, it would have looked as if I would never recover.

But they were wrong. A week later, on Saturday, 19 October, I was better. The mystery illness that had lasted an entire year, that had me homicidal, suicidal; that had flummoxed doctors, therapists, carers, health workers; that had me unwashed, undressed, smoking, drinking, shaking, dribbling, unable to leave the house; that had separated me from my friends, family, and most importantly, my children, it had gone. Disappeared. Vanished completely.

How do I know?

Because Lily and Oscar said so.

It was my birthday and I was allowed out to have dinner

with the family. My recovery must have started the preceding week for me to have organised it, but I don't have a clear recollection. The day was going to start with a shopping trip with my sister Amy and Lily and then Carluccio's for dinner with my family.

And when we went shopping along the King's Road, to Lily's favourite shop, Brandy Melville, I met my daughter again – for the first time in a year. My God, she's changed! She's a young woman now. She's quite beautiful, I think, as I notice her long limbs, her long, golden-brown hair. She now wears a bra, I think. When did that happen?

Yes, we're laughing and smiling again, my daughter and me, as we go shopping that day on the King's Road in the October sunshine – my daughter, Lily Newman, and me. And she suggests we go to my old favourite shop: it's L K Bennett.

'Mummy, buy a new dress. For your birthday party tonight.'

I try on a blue dress. Gosh, I've lost a lot of weight! Just a few weeks ago, I'd been a size 16. Now I'm a size 12.

Yes, the sun is out today. And there are people, aren't there? Mothers, daughters, brothers, sisters, nephews, uncles, cousins… maybe in families, but all related. Yes, all related, not just to each other but to me too. I smile and they smile back. Yes, human warmth in all its splendour, in all its glorious Technicolor, spilling out and lighting up the pavements. Yes, it was there all around me, clasping me in its embrace on that day that was my birthday, on Saturday, 19 October 2013.

I'm wearing the new blue L K Bennett dress when Oscar is dropped off by his dad at Carluccio's on the corner of Westbourne Grove. His eyes won't meet mine. He's lost all hope, last week's wedding being the worst he's ever seen me.

When he sees the dress, the make-up, he looks surprised. But he's still suspicious.

It's a big gathering – my sister Amy, my older brother David, my best friend Jim, his partner, my niece Sarah… I don't know if they know.

But we know, Lily, Oscar and me. Yes, we know, don't we? I think, as I remember Oscar looking at me quizzically from the end of the table, then tentatively coming over to me.

Yes, we do know, don't we? I think, as I remember him putting his arms around me for the first time in a year. We definitely know, don't we? As I drew him into my arms, smelling, touching, stroking and drinking up the smell, touch, sound, sight of my little boy, my son, Oscar Newman, now eleven years old. And I drew him to me so tight, it's lucky he didn't stop breathing.

And for the first time in a year I felt the warmth of tears of joy running down my cheeks.

Yes, we know, don't we, Lily and Oscar, that on that day, 19 October 2013, my forty-eighth birthday, Mummy was back.

Chapter 13

OCTOBER 2013

The doctors at St Charles see I'm getting better but I still have to stay: I'm there for six weeks.

They relax the section and I can come and go as long as I go back there at night. I don't mind this at all. It's now become a refuge to me, a place of safety. My humanity has come back and for the first time I can relate to people. I make friends with patients and nurses. And by now I've got a room – and a bed – of my own.

Lily says that when I got better, it was as if I woke up and couldn't remember anything that had happened. Well, that was pretty true – it really was like waking up out of a coma.

I remember walking back to the flat I'd left that Sunday in Cornwall Crescent. It was as if it had been inhabited by an entirely different person that I didn't recognise as me. My brother David had organised a cleaner, but it still bore the marks of my old life: unpaid bills, the stench of cigarettes, empty bottles of vodka. Who was this person? I wondered, relieved I was still required to go back to that bed in St Charles.

What the hell happened? I muse. And it doesn't take long for my brain, now free from the damage of the drugs, to work it out. I find out about the charity RxISK, which has a website (http://rxisk.org) and publicises the dangers of prescription drugs. It's teaming with stories like mine. I talk to them and tell them about what happened on that first night on escitalopram (Lexapro). For the first time I begin to understand what has happened to me: it wasn't me going nuts, the drugs had caused it. And I soon learn it's happened to people all around the world; most have killed themselves or others.

Sometimes both.

And what about the last year? Yes, the drugs have serious side effects. One of them could have knocked me out. People want to kill themselves just from Prozac. Five? I was lucky, *very* lucky. I look around me, because I know that every single one of my fellow inmates will be taking the very drugs that nearly killed me. I hope to God they don't react to them as badly as me. And I'm still on one of them, venlafaxine (Effexor), which they have kept me on as they gradually take me off the drugs, and then there is another one they keep giving me beginning with 'C'. Clonazepam... is it for anxiety? I make a note to tell them I'm no longer anxious.

I start to look around me and wonder about the other inmates. When I didn't have a bed, I was carted off to the dreaded Shannon ward, the worst of all bedlams. The highest security ward in the hospital, this was most definitely where the maddest of the mad were kept. This lot were raving loonies: they were hearing voices, yelling, their tongues were hanging out, they were shaking, crying, shouting all of that and more.

THE PILL THAT STEALS LIVES

They were the maddest of the mad. And they were all on medication. It wasn't until much later that I was to understand that psychiatric drugs cause long-term neurological damage and a condition called tardive dyskinesia where you have involuntary movements which sometimes never go away. A bit like Parkinson's. But even then I remember looking around me and wondering how many had started out like me. I don't know when I realised that if the hospital had made a different decision, if they'd kept me on the drugs, I would still be there.

I step onto the bed to look at myself in the mirror. My body is unrecognisable. Not just three stone heavier, but there are weals over my skin where I've scratched myself while withdrawing from the drugs.

I start getting fit again. At the beginning I'm just allowed out for half an hour with a nurse so I ask if I can run round Wormwood Scrubs, which is nearby. Later, my best friend Jim is allowed to take me out, and we run to his house in Holland Park together.

I ring up Maggie. She was our very first nanny and was with us for many years, so I have known her since Lily was born. We had and always will have a very special bond. Since leaving us she had become a personal trainer. While ill, I'd contacted her and tried to do some sessions. I was 11 stone, chain smoking and couldn't focus. We never really worked out – I kept on stopping for cigarettes.

'Mags, I don't know what's happened. I want to kill myself.' I told her.

Her face looks bewildered. She's seen me through two childbirths, and the collapse of my marriage. None has resulted in this. What disease, what illness could possibly have caused her former employer and friend to come to this?

When I turn up at Queen's Park from St Charles, she looks at me, astonished.

'Tinks, you're better,' she says, throwing her arms round me, as if I'd just come back from a foreign destination.

'Yes, I am,' I say.

By now, I'd lost a stone, but that wasn't the thing that defined my recovery. And we'd giggled, like before, as she put me through my paces, picking up from the time a year ago when she had been training me for my first half marathon. Once off the drugs, I really don't want to smoke anymore. In just a day, I go from smoking 70 a day to none at all. I came to understand why all mental patients smoke – it must be something to do with the way medication disrupts the chemistry of your brain. After I left hospital, I didn't touch a single cigarette again.

I know I have to find a home by Christmas for me and the kids. What the hell was I thinking of when I moved to Cornwall Crescent, a two-bedroom flat just off Ladbroke Grove? How could this be a home for Lily and Oscar, away from their friends and sharing a bedroom in a damp basement?

Tears are one of the many bodily functions that have now come back into my life. They fill my eyes, as I reflect from my room in St Charles on that decision to leave Dundonald six months into my illness. I wonder what that was like for my children: to lose their mum, both emotionally and then physically.

At the time they wanted me out – the creature I'd become was not their mother. I remember clearly Oscar in the garden.

'I hate you, Mummy! I don't want you here anymore. Please get out!'

This wasn't a temper tantrum because I'd taken away his screen time: he meant it.

And Robert had driven me with three suitcases and a few boxes one Saturday morning to that flat in Cornwall Crescent. That was the last time I was in Dundonald Road.

Yes, I must have a home for the kids and me by Christmas, I think, from my room at St Charles, as I contact every single estate agent in Kensal Rise.

I need a job, too, I decide. I've been called for an interview on a drama documentary. It's at the time I'm still under section so my friend Lesa has to take me there. Every time you leave the hospital, they take a photo of you so if you do a runner, they can give a description to the police. I feel like a criminal as I leave for the interview, hoping they don't want me to start the next day.

It's hard to describe what it was really like recovering from those drugs. My emotions, buried for a year, sometimes overwhelmed me. Once the tears began, they wouldn't stop. I was sometimes overhelmed with gratitude to have survived and to feel alive again. I'd be running by the river, in Chiswick. I'd see the sun hit the Thames and I'd break down, seized by the beauty of the moment. Playing the piano again, for the first time; hearing a piece of music. But of course, the most important thing was looking into Lily and Oscar's eyes and feeling love for them again. And yes, we began a very special love affair, borne out of that very unusual year when I was stolen from them.

Now I'm better, there is one person I can't wait to see: my mum. I'd seen her a few times during my illness. She was now eighty-nine, living in a very posh old people's home in

Oxfordshire. We all knew she didn't have long to live. The doctors told us she was being kept alive by the many pills she was now taking for various medical conditions – heart, diabetes, blood pressure... God knows what they were.

I'd even stayed with her when I was ill, but she couldn't cope. I was a mad, demented animal, walking round and round in her small apartment there; too ill to go into the communal dining room. If I wasn't pacing about with akathisia, I lay on her bed, my body bloated, my mind addled. I bore no resemblance whatsoever to the daughter she'd known. The one thing she was going to make sure of, though, was that I took the medication she knew was going to make me better.

While I'm at St Charles, my sister Amy tells me that Mum's had yet another stroke, this time serious. I arrange to travel by train to the hospital in Oxford on Saturday, 2 November. At 8.30 just after breakfast, I'm sitting in the lounge and I see my sister walking towards me. I'm not expecting her. It's a mirror image of that moment in July 1976 when she and my mother had arrived unexpectedly at my friend's house in Eastbourne to tell me of my dad's death.

She doesn't have to say anything.

A few weeks later, the four of us join hands to walk behind my mum's coffin as we head towards the church in the village of Blewbury, Oxfordshire. It's a beautiful day. We're all sad, but we don't feel regret because my mum lived a long and happy life. True, she might have lived longer, had she chosen a healthier lifestyle. Despite doctors' warnings, she'd insist on eating whatever she wanted. But that was her choice, I reflected, as I remarked on the calm and stillness of that November morning.

She'd been too ill to join us at Carluccio's on my birthday

a few weeks before. My sister had told me she wanted to buy me the blue L K Bennett dress that Lily and I had chosen that day. And that was what I was wearing, as we headed into the church behind my mother's coffin, though by now, I'd changed it for a size 8.

Many of the guests were also at my nephew's wedding a month before. Mum had been too ill to go to that too. I can see the look of astonishment on their faces when they see me – I bear no resemblance to the mad woman they had seen a few weeks ago. And they were even more surprised when I took my turn to stand up and pay tribute to this woman who had played such an important part in my life.

She was a clever woman, my mum – really smart. I'm sure if she'd not been constrained by being a mother to us four, she would have enjoyed a glittering career as a national journalist. And it was her love of words that brought us together, amongst other things. I remember how she'd look over the first articles I wrote in my student years. 'Why do you have to use so many words when far less will do?' she'd say, as she took a pen and crossed them out.

With this in mind, I stand up before the crowd of guests and family, and pay my final tribute to my mum, Nonnie Stanley, wearing the blue LK Bennett dress she bought me for my birthday, which she never saw me in.

I'm including the entire text of my speech, even though she would have put a line through half of it. But I never got the chance to say goodbye and though there may be too many words, this is my own, very special tribute for the very special woman who was my mother.

Nonnie was an amazing mother. When I was twelve, my father, Deryk, died and Non was faced with the challenge of being a single parent. We didn't have much money so she went back to work on the *Nursing Mirror* and persuaded the headmistress of the boarding school I was at to reduce the school fees. She was absolutely determined that my education would not suffer.

Non was never a 'mumsy' type of mother. One of her first decisions as a single parent was that now she didn't have a family to cater for, she was never going to cook again. True to her word, from when I was twelve, she almost never entered the kitchen again except to dish out the odd convenience meal.

When she met my stepfather Leslie, Non stuck to her guns. Despite the fact that he sent her on a Prue Leith cooking course, she remained resolute. In the end poor Leslie was so desperate for a decent meal that he was forced to employ a full-time Hungarian cook.

I have many fond memories of my time living with Non and Leslie in their Chelsea flat. My school friends descended during the holidays and Nonnie was known fondly as 'Mrs Tinks'. She provided a wonderful shoulder to cry on and my friends would often come to her for advice, as did I. Non had remarkable insight into people and relationships and was a wonderful confidante.

Her solutions to life's problems were sometimes as simple as to just go out and buy yourself a new lipstick or a new dress to cheer yourself up. It will come as no surprise that countless rails of nearly-new clothing half-filled her flat at Letcombe and I once counted fifty umbrellas in all different shades and colours.

Non had a very lively mind. Even towards the end of her life, when her eyesight was failing, she still knew everything that was going on in the news. She looked down on anyone who didn't read the *Daily Mail* and made it her business to know everything there was to know, from showbiz gossip to politics.

Non was a wonderful grandmother to all her grandchildren, including Lily and Oscar. She spoilt them rotten to the point where I had to lie to her that Lily and Oscar were diabetic to stop her feeding them so many sweets and treats.

A great friend to many, she was a fantastic mother to David, Richard, Amy and me, and a loving grandmother to Tom, Sarah, Fred, Ellie, Mark, Alex, Lily and Oscar. She will be missed by us all and we will never forget her zest for life, her unerring generosity and her unforgettable sense of humour.

I want to end this tribute on a reading chosen by Nonnie. I think it sums up how she would like us to go on with our lives.

> *If I should go before the rest of you*
> *Break not a flower nor inscribe a stone*
> *Nor when I'm gone speak in a Sunday voice*
> *But be the usual selves that I have known*
> *Weep if you must*
> *Parting is hell*
> *But life goes on*
> *So sing as well.*

And so we all went back to my brother Richard's house to celebrate the end of my mother's happy life. We may have wept a tear or two, but not too many, as we raised glasses of champagne to drink a toast to her. How different an occasion it was to my father's funeral after he committed suicide nearly forty years earlier.

When I left St Charles Hospital in November 2013, I vowed never to take another psychiatric medication again. The doctors told me I had to take venlafaxine (Effexor) for a year. I chucked it away.

Three weeks later, something returned I'd forgotten had disappeared: my libido. I remember my mum confiding in me that my dad was impotent. It was another two years before I realised the significance of this.

PART II

OTHER STOLEN LIVES

'It is difficult to get a man to understand something,
when his salary depends on his not understanding it' –
Upton Sinclair, *I, Candidate for Governor:
And How I Got Licked*

Chapter 14

FRIDAY, 4 SEPTEMBER 2015

I go out to Harlesden High Street, which is a bustle of multi-cultural shops and stalls. I'm going to buy a big fresh salmon to poach for a family party tomorrow to celebrate Lily and Oscar's thirteenth and fourteenth birthday parties.

The sky is bright and it mimics the clarity of vision I have about my life right now.

The fishmonger and I banter about the salmon but I'm only half interested: my mind is on the fact that Iain, my film editor, is arriving at my house soon. He's agreed to spend a day editing some footage that a friend and cameraman, Steve, has shot of the kids and me.

I'm a bit nervous because it's really the first time I've shared with anyone except close friends and family what the kids and me went through almost exactly three years ago.

Armed with my salmon, I go back along the high street,

passing the many mobile phone shops that line the streets of this not very gentrified area.

Iain arrives and I give him the treatment I've written. He knows I want to make a film about antidepressants but he doesn't know I want to tell our story.

The proposal is called 'The Year My Life Was Stolen'.

I wait for him to load the rushes I've shot into his computer as I go to the kitchen and make him a coffee. He starts watching the interviews. The kids are talking about how they lost me for a year, me talking about going psychotic.

'Fucking hell!' he exclaims. 'Did this really happen?'

'Yes, it fucking did,' I say, handing him his coffee.

'Wow!'

And so began a journey that ended six weeks later with a discovery that was to change my view of the world and myself forever.

Chapter 15

SATURDAY, 5 SEPTEMBER 2015

I wake up at 6 a.m. in our grey terraced house in Harlesden, north-west London.

That's a good night's sleep for me. In the last two years I've suffered terrible insomnia and I have no idea whether this is a side effect of the cocktail of drugs I was on.

The children are still asleep. Oscar had his friend Ben over for a sleepover. I'm reminded of the time when the children wouldn't have friends near the house because they were so embarrassed about me.

Lily is still sprawled asleep on my French superking double bed. Her head of long, golden hair is sandwiched between two cushions spelling the word 'Love'. Since my recovery two years ago, the children fight with each other to sleep with me and sometimes it ends with all three of us sleeping together. I know many would disapprove, but I'm lenient because I rationalise they lost me for an entire year of their comparatively short lives and maybe this is why they still cling to me, both physically and emotionally.

Lily is wearing some short silk pyjamas and I gaze admiringly at her long, lithe limbs. She possesses the insouciant beauty of a youngster who has done nothing to earn her looks. Though she's now interested in make-up and fashion, she doesn't need to do anything at all to look absolutely gorgeous. But with Lily it goes beyond the physical: she has an inner beauty and wisdom that shines and touches everyone she meets. I wonder if that is in some part a result of having to grow up so quickly during that stolen year.

'You're very sage,' I often tell her.

'And you're very rosemary,' is her usual reply.

I marvel at the fact both she and Oscar seem to be relatively unscathed.

We've been living in our new house in Harlesden for a year now. Our little home is beautiful. Decorating and furnishing it was a labour of love. The life we've created for ourselves here is a mini version of the married life I had when we lived two miles down the road in the plusher area of Queen's Park. Except of course we're just three. Oh, and three cats too, of course. Our sixteen-year-old moggie, Rocco, and two other cats, Choochee and Precious, we bought to replace Rosie and Charlie, the pedigree Burmese cats that Robert got in the division of spoils. It was the culmination of a divorce battle that would make *Kramer vs. Kramer* look like a romantic comedy.

While our old married home had been a hotchpotch of different styles, never really complementing each other, this house is just me. Without the compromise of having to make decisions to conform to Robert's black and white and minimalist taste, the house is a medley of bright and different colours. Everything is a cacophony of vibrant hues including the bright orange Nespresso machine that whirrs into action and the multi-coloured cups I fill up to take up to my sleeping children.

My bedroom is one of my favourite rooms of the house. I've furnished it in a French baroque style and at the foot there is a large antique chest of drawers, which I'd bought in one of the antique shops on Golborne Road. On top is a big TV and I recall how I'd relished the idea of having a TV in my bedroom, something that had been banned in our marriage. To the side stands a full-length ornate framed mirror. There is a fluffy grey throw on the bed, and grey velvet cushions. The only colour other than grey is the purple velvet pouffe by the bed, and the big mauve fluffy towels in the adjacent bathroom, which has sliding doors opening up into the bedroom. There is a beautiful purple glass vase too, a wedding present – one of the few things in the house that I kept from our marriage.

Above the bed there is a large abstract canvas painting in pinks and purples – one of many that adorn the white walls of the house painted by a guy I'd met on Tinder. Like most of the people I've met in the last two years of Internet dating, it didn't progress beyond a friendship.

It's been two years exactly since I left St Charles Hospital vowing never to take a single antidepressant medication again. Many friends and family still don't know or understand what happened – except the children. From the day of my birthday celebration at Carluccio's, the children knew that I was better. And they knew it was the drugs that had made me ill. I don't know how they knew, but they just did.

We knew it intuitively, but we understood it better when we started reading up on the subject together. One of the first books we came across was *Dying for a Cure* by an Australian called Rebekah Beddoe. The similarities between what happened to Rebekah and me were extraordinary although it started out differently as she was diagnosed with postnatal depression. She now puts that down to a normal reaction to sleepless nights and the stress of having a new baby.

Rebekah was put on the SSRI Zoloft (sertraline) and ten days later was gripped by a panic so severe she thought she must be having a heart attack. A few days later, she took a knife and sliced her arm – she had never self-harmed before. Doctors didn't realise this was a side effect of the medication and two weeks later, she was in a psychiatric hospital. Two weeks later, she swallowed a load of sleeping tablets, the first suicide attempt of three during her two-year descent into madness.

Doctors put her on more and more medication; eventually she was prescribed eight different drugs, including lithium. They were mostly the same as the pills I'd been given. She got worse and, like me, started self-medicating through smoking and drink. Like me, she ended up like a zombie, unable to care for herself. Her moods oscillated from screaming fits to other days when she was so zonked out she could barely lift a coffee cup. Her mum and husband Nigel juggled their jobs and lives to step in to look after Jemima, their baby.

Her saga only ended because she saw a BBC One *Panorama* report called the 'Secrets of Seroxat', which described how another similar SSRI antidepressant, Seroxat (Paxil), can make people suicidal and cause them to self-harm. Without telling the doctors, she gradually weaned herself off the medication and got completely better. She hid this from the doctors, who then took all the credit for making her well again.

In the three years she was 'ill', Rebekah was diagnosed with different disorders – postnatal depression, adjustment disorder, narcissistic personality disorder, personality disorder with borderline traits and bipolar mood disorder.

Her book is a lucid insight into how the drugs hold you in their spell. She didn't realise it was the medication that was making her suicidal until she looked back at an old diary, which confirmed she had started self-harming after she'd taken the drugs.

The message in her book is important: 'To all those reading this who are taking psychiatric medications or have a loved one taking psychiatric medications for chronic depression, bipolar mood disorder, or any other psychiatric disorder, I urge you now to think back: did the crux of the issue develop after the initiation of a psychiatric drug? If so then it just might be that the drug is to blame.'[1]

Sadly, Rebekah has been left with long-term damage from the drugs. Diabetes is a known side effect of olanzapine (sometimes known by the name Zyprexa), and she has it. In fact, Eli Lilly, the manufacturers, have forked out $1.2 billion dollars to settle some 30,000 lawsuits filed by people who claimed the drug caused diabetes or other maladies.[2] I was on it too, but not for as long. Her story was one of many that I have now heard that made me realise how lucky I have been.

So this was just one of the many books that the kids and I read as we snuggled up under the duvet in the attic room of our rented house in Kensal Rise. It helped us all understand the process whereby I had been stolen from them for a year. Now they know more about antidepressants and mental health issues than most adults. It reassured them that unless someone forcibly injects me with Prozac, I won't get ill again.

But it wasn't so clear to the rest of the world. To most people it looked like I'd suffered a catastrophic illness, which had been cured rather than caused by drugs. Trying to tell them it was exactly the opposite that had happened – that the drugs had caused my illness – was like going round telling people the world was flat. Much of the time I was, and still am, faced with pure disbelief.

Antidepressants make people better, don't they? And I was going round trying to tell people they had made me ill. Not just ill, but suicidal. They'd caused the illness they are supposed to cure. What, they cause depression? Are you having a laugh?

Added to that, there was the spectre of the knife-wielding incident when I'd been psychotic and slashed my arm. Some people knew about that, and this would have been proof that I was off my trolley to begin with.

My euphoria after coming off all the drugs at St Charles wouldn't have helped. I came across as unbalanced because in a sense I was: my brain was having to make a massive adjustment to five major mood- and mind-altering drugs leaving my system in just a few weeks. The resulting flood of previously hidden emotions was sometimes overwhelming and when I expressed them, people were understandably wary.

Frequently I'd burst into hysterical laughter or tears. Once, shortly after coming off the drugs, I was so overwhelmed by the beauty of nature, as I went on a morning run by the river, that I posted something to that effect on Facebook. A close friend had visited me just a few weeks before at St Charles when I'd been detoxing from the drugs and was suicidal. He concluded I must be bipolar. I was never able to persuade him I was poisoned, not mentally ill, and this caused such a rift in our friendship that we no longer talk.

Robert too believed that I had a severe mental illness. And who could blame him? After I left the private hospital at the beginning of my illness and he moved back to Dundonald, he did everything he could to nurse me back to health even though there was never a chance of reconciliation. He, more than anyone, witnessed my descent into an appalling illness that no one seemed able to cure. Of course I was unable to work too so he was carrying the financial burden of looking after us all. For some months, he had to keep paying for the flat he'd rented in West Hampstead because moving back was supposed to be only temporary. Each of my family had taken time off to care for me but they all had to work. Robert took countless days off work and when I was too ill to look after myself, he paid for carers to look after me. Whatever our differences now, I will always be grateful to him.

When the effects of the drugs raged through me, I reached out for anything to self-medicate and to quell the monster of akathisia, the terrible restlessness that had now invaded my body, where I literally couldn't keep still for an entire year. This ranged from drinking excessive cups of tea and coffee, chewing gum non-stop, chain-smoking, raiding the children's rooms for sweets, gorging mountains of food, and drinking alcohol when previously I'd been a near teetotaller.

Robert had the invidious job, under the doctors' instructions, of becoming my keeper, of trying to stop this deranged woman who was still in law his wife from this inexplicable descent into self-destruction. This led to a bizarre imbalance in our relationship. At one point, everyone, including the kids and our nanny, Andrea, were instructed to lock away the tea and the coffee, and all the money in the house was hidden away so I couldn't go the shops to buy Diet Coke and chewing gum. But my urge to self-medicate against the effects of the drugs was unstoppable. In the middle of the day, when the kids were at school and Robert was at work, I'd call on a neighbour and beg them for some coins so I could go to the corner shop for my fix.

Every week I had to visit the doctors at the private hospital and Robert would come along, listening intently to their latest panacea. It was always along the lines of 'Well, if we increase the Prozac, and decrease the olanzapine, level out the lamotrigine, then top it up with some lithium, then Katinka is sure to get well within a few weeks.' I'm applying poetic licence to this, but it's not a huge exaggeration, as you'll see from the list of the final medication I was on: lithium 1,000 mg, Prozac (fluoxetine) 20 mg, olanzapine 10 mg, lamotrigine 25 mg morning and 50 mg night, zopiclone 7.5 mg, promethazine 24–40 mg at night and thiamine 50 mg.

One of the many reasons I moved out of Dundonald Road to a two-bedroom flat at the height of my illness was because I couldn't bear the regime of not being able to get my fix of whatever it was – Diet Coke, chewing gum, and later cigarettes. The other reason was that even in my medicated state, it was too much to see the look of hatred and disdain on the children's faces. Oscar has allowed me to include the fact here, that on many occasions he would shout with tears streaming down his face: 'I *hate* you, Mummy! Please move out.' And so one day, six months into my illness, I had managed to dress myself and get a bus down Ladbroke Grove. This was no small achievement as by then, I was hardly able to leave the house without getting lost. I saw a flat in an estate agent's window, got them to show it to me that day, and put down a deposit. It was an impulse decision which I regretted immediately afterwards, but by then the children were begging me to move out.

They could not bear the creature I had become.

Once I had moved out, the kids didn't want to see me and Robert had to look after them most of the time. I imagine he would have surmised that if I ever got better then there was always a chance of a relapse. Once I was better, it was impossible to persuade him it was the drugs rather than a mental illness that had caused my decline. After all, he'd witnessed me walking into the street unaware of traffic, forgetting to dress myself in the morning, dribbling, rocking backwards and forward whilst struggling to stay seated during meals, unable to clean myself. These are all not so well-known side effects of antipsychotic and antidepressant medication. A clue lies in the experiments carried out with healthy volunteers, who are given psychiatric medication. In 1993 expert David Healy took 60 volunteers from the medical staff and students at Bangor University and gave some of them an antipsychotic drug, droperidol, as part of a trial to test different drugs.

This is what happened to one of the volunteers, Gwen Jones-Edwards, a consultant psychiatrist. [3]

I was given my juice at 1.15 pm on 28 November 1997. Like all the participants I did not know whether I had been given droperidol, lorazepam or a placebo. I was in a buoyant mood, having had a fulfilling morning's work and a drive through brilliant November sunshine to the unit in Bangor. After drinking the juice I went on to do some clinical work. An hour later came the first lot of tests on a computer. I had done these previously and had no qualms about doing them. However, as soon as I sat at the computer I began to feel drugged – very drowsy. I had to concentrate very hard and felt as if I was looking down a tunnel… the next hour was very bad. I did not know what to do with myself. I brought papers to read but I could not be bothered to look at them. I thought of going home to find out how my 3-year-old daughter was – she had been unwell. I picked up the telephone, but could not be bothered to dial… I wandered aimlessly around the unit. I could hardly sit down.

The effects went on the next day. A colleague noticed she looked like 'a chronic schizophrenic':

They were fascinated by my incongruous personality, apparently my speech was normal and sensible but physically I was behaving very oddly indeed.

She was so unwell, she had to cancel the day's work and had to get her husband to pick her up, and she spent the next day in bed. Even the following day, she had to turn back while driving to see her favourite music guru. By now she had started to get parkinsonian symptoms:

I could hardly move, I had a coarse tremor, the muscles of my hand were going into spasm and I had a pain behind my right eye, which I attributed to spasm of the ocular muscle.

THE PILL THAT STEALS LIVES

This was now forty-eight hours since taking the droperidol and it took a further ninety-six hours before the akathisia (restlessness) subsided. Even five full days after she had taken the drug, she was in a terrible state and had to be sent home.

> My head kept telling me I would be better once the drug was metabolized, but my heart simply didn't believe it. I was completely demoralized. Actually I was suicidal – I made no plans but I did feel that death would be better than what I was going through.

She says the effects of that one dose of the antipsychotic droperidol lasted a total of three months.

Richard Bentall, a professor of psychology at Liverpool University, took droperidol as part of the same experiment. He describes something similar:[4]

> For the first hour, I didn't feel too bad. I thought maybe this is okay, I can get away with this. I felt a bit light-headed.

Then somebody asked him to fill in a form.

> I looked at this test and I couldn't have filled it in to save my life – it would have been easier to climb Mount Everest. It was accompanied by a feeling that I couldn't do anything, which is really distressing. I felt profoundly depressed. They tried to persuade me to do these cognitive tests on the computer and I just started crying.

He too developed restlessness (akathisia) and it took him a week after finishing the drug to feel normal.

So that's just on one dose... I was taking this medication for the best part of a year.

Antipsychotics are known to affect brain function. I was on two – one called olanzapine (marketed as Zyprexa) and another called quetiapine (Seroquel). In the trials, twelve people committed suicide on olanzapine and four people did the same in the Seroquel trials. These deaths were excluded when the trials were published in scientific magazines.[5] Despite this, and the fact it can cause diabetes, sales of olanzapine have now surpassed those of Prozac.[6]

If you're still in doubt about the excruciating chemical effect of these drugs, Gwen Olsen, an ex-pharma salesperson, points out in her book, *Confessions of an Rx Drug Pusher*, that the World Psychiatric Association condemned Russia's use of neuroleptics (antipsychotics) on Soviet dissidents in 1977, saying the practice amounted to nothing less than a combination of lobotomies and torture. The drug in question was haloperidol (marketed under the name Haldol). It was a drug Olsen sold and it is still prescribed.[7]

So there is some irony that one of London's most expensive private hospitals was charging £6,000 per week to administer me with the same class of drug that is used to torture prisoners of war. And that these drugs are regularly forced on some people who, if they weren't mentally ill to begin with, most certainly will be after they've taken them.

For the year that I was ill not a single psychiatrist, psychotherapist, CBT (Cognitive Behavioural Therapy) specialist, yoga teacher, counsellor, doctor or nurse spotted the fact that the reason I was wandering round like a dribbling lunatic was a side effect of the drugs so I can't blame Robert, whose speciality is intellectual property law, for not spotting it either, and for not believing it now.

Naturally our different views on what had happened in that last year took their toll on our relationship. We no longer talk and all communication is strictly by post.

The war that broke out on the therapist's couch two years previously continued and reached its climax at the Central Family Court on 30 April 2014 when the judge ordered that the house on Dundonald Road should be sold and the assets split. The loss of our family home and all it represented was the event that precipitated my year-long illness. Finally it happened – but this time I was going to have to face it drug-free.

It didn't take long before I realised we could no longer afford to live in Queen's Park, the area the kids had been brought up in. Every day I'd buy cups of coffee for the estate agents that lined the main high street, Chamberlayne Road, and see what had come onto the market. I came to the gradual realisation that no amount of cappuccino buying would alter the fact that the most we could afford would be a two-bedroom flat, if we wanted to stay in the area. The other factor in all of this was that during my 'illness', I was too unwell to manage my financial affairs. An unpaid gas bill almost completely blighted my chances of getting a reasonable mortgage, giving me a poor credit rating. I remember the desperation a year back on learning this, the feeling that I had let my children down so badly that I would never be able to provide them with a proper home.

I'd almost given up but then I saw a picture of a house in

a property magazine. The photo was of a kitchen with light flooding in from all sides and sliding doors out to a small, but beautiful garden. Without knowing where it was, I decided this was the house I wanted to buy. I'd never been to Harlesden and when I visited, even though it was just two miles from Queen's Park, it was like another country. Disaffected kids lined the streets, there were almost no recognisable shops on the high street, and there was also a feeling you might get mugged any minute. However, the house was more beautiful than its photo.

When we moved in, there were teething problems. On her first day, Lily ran home from school in floods of tears and told me we had to move house: spotting her lack of street savvy, a guy had followed her. In those days she wandered around in a skirt so short it scarcely covered her, and would think nothing of having her phone in her hand despite me nagging her daily. Her distress tore my heart apart and once again I had this terrible feeling I had let the children down but then Lloyd came into our lives.

Lloyd is a half-Jamaican fifty-something whose details were given to me by a friend. For him life started out in a supermarket plastic bag, having been dumped by his parents, and he was subsequently brought up in children's homes. His experience of being bullied made him into a self-defence expert. As an adult he devotes himself to running self-defence and street awareness classes for kids.

I put postings aimed at local parents on community internet sites and gathered together a group of kids and asked Lloyd to come over once a week to our house and teach them how to defend themselves. They looked on in awe as he taught them in the space of one hour how to concuss a potential assailant by using pressure points. A few sessions later, both Lily and Oscar and all the other kids were transformed. Now they wander the streets with an air of confidence and know exactly what to do, should anyone approach them.

Moving to Harlesden proved a shrewd move. Since our arrival, it has become a mecca for other middle-class families migrating westwards in search of more space. Gastro pubs, bijou cafés and delis have sprung up between the Poundland and mobile-phone shops. But even before that, my love affair that began with our grey terraced house had spilled out to embrace the multi-cultural, multi-lingual, multi-faceted, thriving, thronging, jostling, jiving streets of this up-and-coming north-west London suburb that I am proud to call my home. I suppose somewhere in my psyche championing the underdog is something that extends to places as well as people. As you're about to find out.

Immediately after my recovery, it took all my energy to get a job, buy a house and furnish it and get fit again. But I was inexorably drawn to the whole subject of antidepressants. Wherever I went, it seemed I came across stories of people whose lives had been blighted. There was a friend whose teenage daughter had tragically hung herself after taking Prozac, another whose sister had started off with a drug addiction, went to a private hospital, was told she was bipolar and after taking similar medication to what I was on, she committed suicide. Then a guy I went on a date with who had thrown himself under a train after changing his antidepressant dose (not after the date with me, I might add!).

Also, I started reading up on the subject and it didn't take me long to come across cases around the world of people who, like me, had become psychotic on the drugs. Unlike me, though, in many cases they had gone on to kill.

One of the first people I spoke to was Kim Crespi from North Carolina. Ten years earlier she'd been happily married to her husband, David, a very successful bank executive. When David was feeling stressed at work and unable to sleep his doctor prescribed Prozac. Immediately he started acting strangely and told his therapist he was worried he would harm someone. Kim noticed he couldn't sit still – akathisia.

A week after David was prescribed Prozac, Kim went to have her hair done and when she came home, she found the street had been cordoned off and there were police helicopters. When she asked if she could go to her house, she was told that David had killed their five-year-old twins by stabbing them in the back. It wasn't until two months later that Kim was allowed to visit her husband. Still on the drugs, he was coldly mellow and didn't seem to show any signs of grief.

During the police interview David seemed confused and out of it. Later he talked of being told to do it by the lawn sprinklers and was convinced that his wife could bring the twins back to life. As he admitted murder there was no trial and he was given two life sentences. It was only two years later when he came off the medication he was now being given in prison that he emerged from his drugged-up, zombie-like state and realised what he had done.

Kim visits David every week and they are trying to get his plea set aside so the District Attorney would have to rethink the homicide of their twins, Tess and Sam. David has been medication-free for seven years now and works as a chapel clerk and teaching assistant in prison. Ironically, Kim and her grown-up children were offered antidepressants to help them deal with the trauma.[8] Details of their story and their fight for justice can be found at www.crespifamilyhope.org.

Then there was David Hawkins in Australia. He is now ninety years old and I spoke to him over the phone about the awful day he killed the wife he adored after taking Zoloft in July 1999. David was prescribed it because he was grieving for his daughter, who had died of breast cancer. When he couldn't sleep, he took more than he should, and the next morning, when his wife, Margaret, passed him on the doorway to make a cup of tea, he strangled her.

When I asked him what it was like, he described an out-of-body experience that I remembered so well from when I went psychotic on the escitalopram (Lexapro). While I could see myself being stabbed in the stomach as if I was looking down, he describes how he saw his own face, all bloated as if from above and it was as though he was watching himself doing what he was doing.[9]

The judge said: 'I am satisfied that but for the Zoloft he had taken, he would not have strangled his wife.' And accepted a defence of automatism – meaning he wasn't responsible for his actions. In spite of this Pfizer, the drug manufacturer, insisted that it was Hawkins's depression that was responsible for his actions.

As I started to talk to some of these people, I became passionate about telling their stories. I was struck by how easily I could have been one of those people, that it was sheer luck that I didn't kill my kids the night I went psychotic on escitalopram (Lexapro).

At this point I should tell you a bit about my career and myself. I'm a documentary filmmaker and I cut my teeth at the BBC. Dame Esther Rantzen gave me my first job on the *That's*

Life programme when I graduated from Warwick University. She was my mentor and I owe an enormous amount to her. She demanded rigorous standards of journalism but had an extraordinary populist touch. It was thrilling to work on various campaigns in the eighties and to see the law being changed as a result. I will never forget her simple dictum, which she taught me as I grappled with whether a story worked, or it didn't – 'If it moves you, Tinks, it will move others.' And actually that simple piece of advice has guided me through my career, which soon took me to producing and directing documentaries.

It's always been ordinary people rather than celebrities I've been interested in and so, when I read up on cases of people like me who had killed because of these pills, it ignited a passion in me. Not just because of the injustice brought about on ordinary folk, but also, I suppose, because I understood in a way that few others would just how possible it would be to kill on the pills.

Usually, but not always, I work on films that have already been commissioned – that's to say a broadcaster has already told a production company they want to make the film, and the production company ask me to direct it. But sometimes I've come up with ideas that have then gone on to be commissioned. It's notoriously tough, though.

In the year following my recovery I put together a film proposal called *Getting Away with Murder* that featured some of these cases. There had been a few foreign films featuring these stories but oddly none in the UK so I'd used archive from these films and knocked together a pilot to see if I could get interest from a British broadcaster.

When I talked to people in the industry and bemoaned the fact I didn't have a British case, they said, 'Look, you're the

British case. You need to be in it.' I resisted this, saying, 'But I haven't killed anyone.' To which they replied, 'It doesn't matter, you nearly did.' I've never wanted to be on camera and dismissed what they said but recently I started thinking about it again. Maybe they were right. I realised the story wasn't going to work unless it was told by us as a family so I had to get Lily and Oscar on board. We had a talk. And when we talked, I realised how they had come to care passionately about this subject. Not just because of what happened to me, but because of what had happened to others and what could have happened to them.

To understand this, you need to understand the journey that we three began shortly after my recovery. I decided that I wanted to train for a half-marathon to get fit and to raise money for RxISK (http://rxisk.org), the charity that raises awareness of the dangers of prescription drugs. I got in touch with their media department and spoke to a man called David Carmichael in Canada. The reason he is now working for the charity is because it would be hard for him to get a job anywhere else: he killed his eleven-year-old son shortly after taking the antidepressant Paxil (Seroxat or paroxetine).

To begin with, he did well on antidepressants. He took Paxil for what he now calls a nervous breakdown in 2003 and it seemed to help him. A few months after he came off it in 2004, he was sleep deprived, relapsed and went back on it. He started becoming more anxious, couldn't sleep, had no energy and began having suicidal thoughts so he upped his dosage and, like me, became psychotic. His suicidal thoughts got worse and then he became severely delusional and convinced that he had to kill his son because it was the morally right thing to do.

David told me how he took Ian to the family holiday home on the lakes in Canada. He planned a suicide/murder by tying both of them to the anchor of their boat. But he forgot his bathing suit and in his deranged thinking he thought it was a message from God that he wasn't supposed to die, just Ian. A week later, he took Ian on a trip to a hotel in London, Canada, and strangled him at 3 a.m. After kissing him on the lips, he told him he loved him and that he was in a better place now. He didn't cry, he watched TV until the morning, then he calmly rang the police and told them he had killed his son.[10]

In every case of people I've come across who have killed on antidepressants it seems to follow the same pattern. They feel an inner restlessness and turmoil with a growing sense of dread. Often they can't sit still. They keep hearing voices telling them what to do; they have thoughts of both suicide and killing others. It ends with the person calmly ringing the police and confessing to the crime then showing no remorse until they come off the drug.

When I came off the phone from speaking with David for the first time, I was shaking with emotion. His psychosis had enough similarities to mine to make me realise it was luck that it didn't end with me killing the children, myself, or indeed anyone else who was around while I was psychotic.

I felt I had to get the story out there. Here was a man who was obviously not mentally ill; he would have had no motive for killing his son. Every time I've spoken to him, he has cried when recounting the terrible events of that night. Luckily, his wife and daughter have stood by him – they understand it wasn't him that killed Ian, but the medication.

I need to point out here that the manufacturers GSK have denied their drug caused David to kill and it wasn't used as part of his defence. However, he is now suing the drug company for $22 million.

I realised that there was no point in me running this half-marathon unless I told people what had happened to me, what happened to David Carmichael and what had happened to others. Even if most people disbelieved it, if just one person did, then it was worth it.

David sent some RxISK leaflets and Lily and Oscar agreed to hand them out at the race. They were designed to get people to report adverse drug reactions.

As I completed my first ever half-marathon on a rainy April day in 2014 in Hastings just a few months after I'd got better, Lily and Oscar were waiting at the finishing line. Unusually I didn't have to bribe them to wait the two and a quarter hours it was going to take me to complete the task. I'd simply reminded them that the reason we were doing this was because of people like Ian Carmichael, who was the same age as them when his dad killed him.

Crossing the finishing line on Hastings sea front and seeing Lily and Oscar's faces cheering me on are moments I will cherish for the rest of my life. They encapsulated so many things. Of course, there was the fact that there could be no surer proof that I was 100 per cent better; physically fitter than I'd ever been. And this was no small feat. Six months earlier I was smoking 70 cigarettes a day, was too ill to leave the house, and was 3 stone heavier and walking around in a dressing gown all day long, unable to wash or care for myself. By then the children had given up any hope of having their mother back again. There was also the fact that we had raised £2,500 in sponsorship money for RxISK.

But those were not the things that caused me to cry on

Hastings sea front that morning, nor was it the fact that my whole body was aching from the effort of running 21K and that for the last 5K, I honestly thought I couldn't carry on any further. As I hugged Lily and Oscar against my now sweaty RxISK T-shirt, as the race organisers handed out water and goody bags with cereal bars, the tears became sobs and Lily and Oscar looked on with a mixture of amusement and consternation. As the three of us headed off for fish and chips, hailstones came pelting down and I was suddenly freezing cold.

'Poor Rell,' Oscar said as he put his arms around me ('Rell' is his pet name for me – it came from 'Rule' because I had so many rules). 'Let's get you nice and warm.' But I was crying because I felt very lucky. Unlike David Carmichael, I had my kids to share this moment with me. I didn't kill them, or myself, and I know that both of those scenarios were once a possibility. The tears that were streaming down my face were for the death of David's eleven-year-old son, Ian. As promised, I texted David, telling him I'd completed the race in 2:15. I didn't send him the photo I'd asked a passer-by to take of all three of us at the finishing line – it seemed just too cruel to remind him of the different outcomes of our stories.

Despite the fact I'd run further than I'd ever run in my life, and my pink Garmin watch proudly announces that I've burned over 1,000 calories, I've no appetite for the fish-and-chip lunch I've promised the kids as we huddle in the warmth of a seafront restaurant.

'Why are you so sad, Rell?' asks Oscar.

I reply that I'm not really sad, just thinking. I'm thinking that although we've raised £2,500 today, and we've told family and friends how antidepressants took away a year of our lives, it's not enough. For me that rainy day in Hastings in April 2014 was just the beginning.

So when I broach the subject with the kids eighteen months later of whether they would consider being filmed about our story, their answer is a resounding 'yes'. Not just because of the unspoken promise of an iPhone, also because by now, they know a hell of a lot about the subject, and they truly care. So on a rainy day, in September 2015, the week before they go back to school, I get my friend and cameraman Steve to come round and we dip our toe in the water: I interview them, they interview me. Actually it's the first time we talk properly about how it affected each of us. And we all cry tears that perhaps have been waiting two years to be shed. And we all hug. And I realise that I'm not the only one who hasn't expressed the full horror of that year. And at the end, I think to myself, if nothing comes of the film, that day was worth its weight in gold for the therapy it provided for all of us.

Chapter 16

SUNDAY, 6 SEPTEMBER 2015

Today we have a family lunch party to celebrate the children's joint birthdays. Their birthdays were both in August so there is just a year and three weeks between them. They are very close and I'm grateful they had each other during the trauma of the last few years.

I take some tea up to Lily, who is now rubbing her eyes. Our black cat Rocco has jumped onto the bed and is licking her nose. Lily's quieter than usual and there is a look of sadness on her face. I snuggle up to her, relishing the smell of her skin and the feel of her hair against my cheek. Not so long ago this physical and emotional interaction between mother and daughter was something we simply didn't have. I'm reminded too of something Lily told me – when I was ill she used to sleep with me because when I was asleep, she could pretend I was normal.

I know what's wrong with Lily, but I ask anyway.

'It's brought it all back, hasn't it?' I say to her. She nods, her green eyes swelling with tears.

She's talking about the filming but also about the day the previous week when we were visited by a journalist called Caroline Scott, who had seen an article about my story and the half-marathon on the RxISK website and came to interview us for a piece to go in the *Daily Mail*.

I'm usually wary of tabloid journalists, but I trusted her because I had seen articles she'd written for the *Sunday Times*. She obviously has a genuine interest in mental health issues but I was still worried that she wouldn't really understand. Even when I explain to people, they still talk about my 'depression'. I feel like screaming at them that I wasn't depressed, I was poisoned. Would she get it? I wondered. Does she understand that these drugs can cause ordinary people to want to kill themselves?

When I saw her at Willesden Junction station, where I was picking her up, I knew I'd like her. In her forties, she has blonde hair scraped back in a ponytail, and looked just like the kind of person I'd get on with. She's a bit hassled and breathless when she gets into the car because she's late, and then she talks about the holiday she's just come back from with her kids. Whenever people talk about their kids, I tend to bond with them.

We came back to my house and over cups of coffee in the living room she interviewed me for three hours. It was the most I've ever talked about my experience. Her gentle, probing questions took me to a place I hadn't been to before because in two years no one has really talked to me about it.

If I'd been taken hostage for a year, or had cancer, or been in a coma, there would be a conversation – more than a conversation. There would probably be therapy, a fuss; people would say, 'Wow, what was the chemo like? Did you ever think you were going to get out alive? What was it like, waking up?'

But friends and family don't ever say, 'You went away for a year, can you describe that land so that we can understand?'; 'What was it like being in such a state that you wanted to end it all?'; 'You were prepared to jump under a train and never see your kids again?' 'Christ, that's something, can you explain what that was like?', Or even show polite interest: 'Tell me, what were the nurses in the mental hospital like?'; 'How was the food?'; 'Did your room have a view?'... And so the whole thing goes unexpressed.

I've bribed the children to stay upstairs, do their homework, practise the piano and get ready for the start of school. It's been partly successful and I've only had to break with the interview on a few occasions when they have got into a fight with each other.

Caroline wants a brief chat with them so we go upstairs. Oscar has abandoned his homework and has decided to embark on his own methods to de-flea our ginger cat, Choochee. I find him in the bathroom, with a very wet and bedraggled cat on his lap, and with him going through his fur with a flea comb.

She asks the children a few questions about what it was like for them to lose me for a year.

Did Lily have to grow up quickly?

Oscar tells her how during my illness he knew underneath he loved me but he grew to hate me. I'd heard this before but every time I hear it, I feel sick with sadness.

As we arrive back at the station, Caroline asks a question

that shows a percipience that had made me instantly trust her in our first conversations. She says, 'What's it like now, do you get flashbacks? It must be like having post-traumatic stress.' Her question reinforces my realisation that my memory has blocked so much out. As it has with the children too, I suspect. And perhaps the most important lesson I've learnt is that talking about upsetting things, and feeling sadness is no bad thing. In fact it's a rather good thing. And so I'm not at all worried about the tears in Lily's eyes, or the floods of emotions that have surfaced of late as we have revisited those terrible events of two years ago.

As Caroline leaves, I notice I feel different. Lighter. We all do. It's because for the first time someone has listened and believed us. Not only that, but she's going to put it out there in a national newspaper. And one thing that I've come to care very deeply about is that people understand the dangers of these drugs.

Chapter 17

A FAMILY LUNCH

In the next few hours I struggle to get lunch ready for our guests, who are arriving at midday. Thankfully it's a beautiful sunny day and we can eat out in our small, but pretty south-facing garden. I've tried to keep the menu simple – a poached salmon, a couscous salad, green beans and a chocolate cake Lily has made the day before. But somehow, as always happens, I run out of time and start yelling at the kids. As midday gets closer and the kitchen is still a mess, I start regretting my decision to host a party of eleven.

One of my realisations when my marriage ended was that in fact I hate cooking and that while I had managed to successfully host a number of impressive dinner parties, the cooking part made me miserable. I like ideas and big concepts rather than detail and that doesn't make for good cooking. For twelve years of marriage I bought cookery book after cookery book, hoping somehow that the right book would make it all different.

THE PILL THAT STEALS LIVES

It didn't, and now I try to keep things as simple as possible but even that dictum doesn't seem to work for me. Today I'm stressed and I have to stop my mind going into well-rehearsed mantra of self-pity about being a poor, struggling single mum with no one to support me. My kids often tease me and say, 'Aha, you're doing your "poor me" act! Isn't it time you stopped being a victim and got into the driving seat of your life rather than the passenger seat?' It always makes me smile when they regurgitate a version of something I have said to them.

I'd hoped people would be late, but at midday precisely the doorbell goes. It's my sister Amy and my twenty-six-year-old nephew Alex. When my parents named my sister, they must have had a prophetic insight into her character. Amy means 'loved one', and she is indeed one of the most loveable and loving people you could meet. She is absolutely the opposite of me in personality. I joke with her that we can't possibly share the same parents as she is so totally different.

While I'm creative, emotional and a bit of a risk taker, she's calm, logical, never takes risks and has great attention to detail. Eight years older than me, she is a successful partner in a law firm. While I have always been conscious of my looks and try to keep to a strict regime of fitness to retain my figure, she is more comfortable in her own skin and has a much more laissez-faire attitude towards her appearance. For a long time it mystified and rather annoyed me that despite this, she's the one who has never been single: she has stepped seamlessly from one life partner to another when her first marriage broke down after twenty years. It's only recently that I've understood that it's not a six-pack that gets you love, but being loving – and that's where my sister Amy wins hands down and why she will always find love.

A FAMILY LUNCH

Today I feel sadness when I see her because I know I won't share with her the news about the *Daily Mail* article or the film I want to make. Out of all my siblings, Amy was the most supportive at the time of my year-long illness; she took countless days off work to nurse me and spent hours visiting me when I was in hospital. But now there is a wedge between us and I don't know how to solve it. She seems not to believe that it was the antidepressant and antipsychotic drugs I was on that caused me to be ill. I wonder if it's because she feels she was somehow instrumental in getting me to take them and that she in some way feels responsible; she always said to trust the doctors. I know it's a conversation I need to have with her at some point.

My two brothers, David and Richard, also both older than me, are unable to attend the party. The next ring at the doorbell is my best friend Jim, his partner Maria and their two kids. Jim was unconventionally the best man at my wedding and he has known me for many years. He was with me for every stage of my illness. Next is my niece, Ellie, a theatrical agent, and her actor husband. Andrew.

People muck in as they see that I'm struggling to cope. Somehow the food gets served and we all sit outside on the decking in the September sun. The house is perfect for entertaining, with sliding doors that open out onto a south-facing deck and a seating area in the shade at the bottom. There is a point where I stop and contemplate the scene before me: the lime-green canopy and matching garden tables and chairs, the sunflowers at the bottom of the garden in bright blue giant flower pots we've painted, our family and friends assembled there as we all demolish the chocolate cake that Lily has made after we've sung 'Happy Birthday'. And the children running around, talking animatedly about the start of term, their faces still tanned from our camping trips and festivals over the summer. I've even remembered to polish their school shoes ready for the term ahead. And I think to myself, yes, it's done. The journey of the divorce and creating the best possible home that I can for them is now complete. Yes, it's well and truly over. What next, I wonder. But I already know the answer.

Everyone says the food is delicious and the best bit is Lily's chocolate cake. I'm thankful that everyone leaves by 3.30 because it gives the kids and me a chance to rush up to the Serpentine Lake in Hyde Park and have a swim. We gather up some towels and jump in my car. When I separated from my husband, I swapped the very sensible LPG black Citroën for an ancient electric-blue Audi convertible for the same price. I put down the electric roof, turn the radio on full blast and drive up to Hyde Park in the late afternoon sunshine. Oscar and I jump into the water that is significantly cooler than I remember it just a week ago – it really feels like the end of summer.

The beginning of autumn, the return of school, it's all bringing back that day in September, exactly three years ago. I can't go there now.

When we get home I start to become exhausted. Usually I cope with the terrible insomnia by having an afternoon nap but today I haven't had the chance. The kids need to pick up their sports bags from their dad, who now lives with his new girlfriend in Kensal Rise, just down the road. Whilst I've never regretted our marriage ending, I'd be lying if I didn't say that actually I'm annoyed that he has found someone else and I haven't. My mind has conjured up that they are living in a ménage to rival *The Waltons*, with her two children living there alongside Lily and Oscar when they are there. I find it hard enough to get men to commit to a second cappuccino let alone to sharing a house and a life. What magic quality is it, I wonder, that he's got, that I clearly haven't?

Coming back to the kids, I'm too tired to take them the two miles down the road so I ask them to order an Uber taxi.

I take a bath, and though it's only seven, I get into my pyjamas. On the way home, the thought of the Sunday evening ahead has made me anxious. Although the kids will be there, I know I'm going to feel lonely tonight. It's been nearly four years since I separated from Robert and since then I've not been in a proper relationship. I keep myself busy, but there seems to be a void I just can't fill. Sometimes I feel there must be something wrong with me. Why can't I be satisfied with what I've got – my gorgeous kids, a beautiful home, a wonderful family and a great network of friends? Not to mention the fact it was pure luck that I didn't lose my life because of the drugs, or become permanently disabled from them.

I try to read the newspapers but I'm so, so tired. Instead I pick up my phone and flick through my Tinder app in a desultory and not very purposeful manner. Two years of Internet dating has left me disillusioned and often heartbroken. I can hardly be bothered to chat to the people I've matched myself with.

Soon I fall asleep and half remember my kids coming in, taking off my shoes and then tucking me up in my bed.

Chapter 18

MONDAY, 14 SEPTEMBER 2015

I wake up at 6 a.m., which is good for me. I'm sleeping much better since I've started talking properly in detail about what I have now come to call 'The Year My Life Was Stolen'.

The kids are with their dad this week until Friday but I've agreed to take Oscar to the orthodontist in St John's Wood at lunchtime today.

After I've made myself some tea, my first job is to clear up the cat shit on the lawn. Somehow in the divorce split, my ex inherited the two pedigree Burmese cats, Rosie and Charlie, while I got Rocco, the sixteen-year-old black moggy that is now unable to make it to the raised flowerbeds and so shits on the lawn. I was quite happy with the two new kittens, Choochee and Precious, but one day Robert turned up on the doorstep and insisted that Rocco should reside with me. I wasn't sure why, but it became clear after I'd agreed and it transpired that Rocco was now incontinent.

Clearing up Rocco's shit first thing in the morning has become a metaphor for my life. If I put it off and it piles up, the job becomes untenable. So, along with paying parking fines, telling my Internet dates I don't want to see them again, and clearing out the fridge, my mantra is 'Do the worst first'.

As I contemplate stepping out into the September air in my grey towelling dressing gown, bending down with small black plastic bags scraping up cat shit, I muse on the fact that 'Doing the worst first', dealing with the shit that life throws at you, has a significance way beyond the Rocco's mess on the lawn.

How many times have I and others I know got into all sorts of problems because we haven't dealt with the shit life throws at you but have attempted to run away with drink, food, shopping, sex (if only!) or drugs – prescription or otherwise? And then the problem gets worse.

I know my case is extreme. Not everyone who takes antidepressants becomes a knife-wielding maniac and ends up nearly catatonic for a year. And I do know that some people are supposed to benefit from the emotional numbness that antidepressants offer. But even then, I wonder as I put on a pair of latex gloves, getting ready for the task ahead. Do they really help? Or do they just postpone the problem?

For example, let's take someone I know who told me he had been on an antidepressant for a number of years. His doctor put him on it when he was having sleepless nights and felt anxious. Why? Because he was having an affair behind his wife's back and his lover was pregnant and asking him for a large amount of money. How do you think the antidepressant helped? Well, it didn't. His marriage imploded, and he ended up dealing with that plus the fact he had become dependent on a pill, which he struggles to come off.

And that's because antidepressants can be extremely hard to come off. If you don't believe me, watch a film called *Numb*, which you can see on YouTube.[1] It's a documentary in which an American filmmaker tries to get off Paxil (Seroxat or paroxetine) after ten years. He took it for social anxiety phobia, which in my view seems to be a re-marketing of good old-fashioned shyness.

The forty-two-year-old filmmaker, Phil Lawrence, decides he wants to stop taking the drug. Why? Because it makes him feel flat – he doesn't feel anxious, but he doesn't feel anything else either. So he tries to get off it, but he experiences the well-known effects of withdrawal: ringing in his ears, he keeps losing his temper; he is unable to help his kids.

'Something in my head is messing with me and won't let go,' he says.

By the end, he is crying on camera because he can't get off the drug. So he goes back on – and will probably be on it for the rest of his life.

It reminds me of a Roger Cook report I saw, *Ada v Ativan*, which went out in 1988. A woman called Ada is addicted to Ativan (also known as lorazepam), which was a tranquilliser handed out for nerves and anxiety before antidepressants came along. Her attempts to withdraw, along with her resignation that she will be on it for the rest of her life, are a mirror image of the American filmmaker coming off Seroxat. Meanwhile, Cook confronts a big cheese from Wyeth pharmaceutical company on the golf course with the accusation that his company knew all about it. It makes me think, wow, history is repeating itself, only with antidepressants the number of casualties is far, far greater than with benzodiazepines.[2]

And this is reflected in the settlements. At the time of

writing GlaxoSmithKline plc (GSK) has paid out more than $2 billion to settle a variety of Seroxat (paroxetine) related suits, including claims it has caused suicide, attempted suicide and addiction problems. These claims included 3,000 people in the US.

Oh, and did I mention the $1 billion GSK paid out in further settlements to 800 women in the US, whose children suffered birth defects after they took Seroxat? The birth-defect settlements came about after a Philadelphia jury ordered GSK to pay $2.5 million in damages to the family of Lyam Kilker, a three-year-old boy born with a heart defect after his mother took Paxil while pregnant. During the trial the family made public internal GlaxoSmithKline (GSK) documents showing execs talked about burying negative studies about Paxil's links to birth defects and that its own scientists were alarmed by the rising number of children who had been affected by the drug in the womb.[3]

Meanwhile there are thousands of Seroxat sufferers in the UK who haven't been paid anything to compensate them for the damage caused to them, yet some have joined together in a group litigation action against the drug company. Suicides, addiction problems and violence are amongst some of the problems they allege were caused by the drug. The basis of their claim is that they were told that they would be able to stop taking Seroxat whenever they wanted as there would be no withdrawal effects. Instead they had more debilitating symptoms when they tried to come off it, including impulsive suicidal thoughts, aggressive behaviour and physical pain. The only way for them to avoid this was to go back on their daily dose.[4]

These cases include people who started out well on the

medication. Charles, a successful businessman from London, recalls how suddenly he was the life and soul of the party. Seroxat (paroxetine) disinhibited him, although he hadn't initially taken it for shyness but for stressful circumstances, including the death of his father. The emotional blunting meant not only did he not feel sadness, he didn't feel anything at all.

'Soon I didn't give a fuck about anything,' he explains.

Also, the drug made him want to drink and he became violent. From never having contemplated suicide before, he started planning his death and went to a DIY store to buy the necessary equipment. It took him 22 months to come off the drug and he had to get it in liquid form so he could reduce the dosage. In that time he kept a diary and says he was a tearful, confused wreck.[5]

Bob Fiddaman is another claimant. He believes Seroxat cost him his job, his life, marriage and his kid's childhood. Bob lived in a council flat in Birmingham and was prescribed Seroxat for work problems. At first it seemed to work, but then he no longer cared about anything. He told me: 'It was a chill pill, it made me feel flat. Not good, but as if I was in my own world. The bills mounted up because I didn't care when in reality I should have cared.'

Then he started having horrendous side effects – night sweats, confusion and blurred vision. Out of nowhere he became violent and tried to strangle his wife in his sleep. When he came off the medication, the pain was indescribable. It took him eighteen months to taper down from 40 mg of Seroxat per day to 22 mg daily. After eighteen months he decided to go cold turkey and in that time he had to tie ice cubes around his head to cope with the electric-shock sensations.[6]

Bob still has problems he attributes to the drugs, such as memory loss, and he feels it played a major part in causing his marriage to break up. He now pours his energy into campaigning for change and helping others withdraw from the drugs.

But it's not just Seroxat (paroxetine). Over the course of my research I have heard similar stories of people on each of the SSRI antidepressants. So my point is that presumably many of those people started out like me, thinking they could take a magic pill that would kind of take the edge off the shit life throws at you.

All this goes through my head as I head through the patio doors but as I open them the burglar alarm starts ringing loudly into the morning air. I rush to the hall to type in the code to turn it off. We have a young Taiwanese couple staying as Airbnb guests. Although I've rented out the whole house when we've been away, this is our first B&B booking of people staying while we are here. They have been staying in Lily's room. I told her we would split the money if we had them to stay and she could sleep in my bed. She was delighted as it brought her closer to buying an iPhone and it gives her the excuse to sleep with me, which she wants to do anyway.

Jason, a Taiwanese film student from the South Coast, and his girlfriend are visiting London for the first time. Their English is ropey and they haven't grasped the fact that the burglar alarm needs to go on when we are out, not when we are in the house. Consequently, I came home earlier in the week to find the house empty, the back patio doors open and the alarm off. Then another time, when they were in the house, the alarm was on and the front door double-locked.

But I like having Jason and his girlfriend around. He chose our house because it says on Airbnb that I make films. He's looked me up and wants to talk to me about the films I've made. I feel flattered and I also want to make sure they have a good time so I help them plan their days out in Windsor, shopping in Bicester Village and visiting Greenwich.

Also, having people in the house – anyone – feels good to me. My marriage was far from perfect, but one of the things I loved about living in Dundonald Road was that our big, Victorian house was always full of people. So my first experiment in renting out the children's rooms on Airbnb seems to work well as long as I can get people to understand that security is paramount, especially here in Harlesden. Our grey painted house sticks out like a sore thumb amongst the other terraced Victorian houses with net curtains and faded façades.

There are a few other yuppified houses in the area but ours may as well have a sign outside saying: 'We're middle class, come and rob us'. In fact that's just what happened shortly after we moved in. I bought the children two new bikes, parked them (locked up) in our small front garden and within a day they had been stolen. Then I got a builder to erect a gate and a fence around the front and now no one can come anywhere near our front garden. However, they are still trying to get into the back. Oscar had spotted hand marks on the kitchen skylights showing that someone had tried to break into the back bathroom window. When I called the local police, and asked them what the best crime prevention would be, to the children's delight they said my best bet would be to get a dog. Despite the fact we have three cats – Rocco and two other moggies – the children have since nagged me daily for a dog.

'But Mummy, the police said we *had* to get one.'

The dog and Lily's new iPhone are now daily topics of conversation and I'm tired of both.

Chapter 19

TUESDAY, 15 SEPTEMBER 2015

After the shit-clearing session and a few emails I settle down to the main task of the week: I've decided to do another day's filming. My editor Iain and I looked at the rushes of the kids and me, and it looks OK. It's hard for me to judge because I'm in it and of course, so are my kids, but Iain says it's good. And so does Steve, my friend and cameraman, who has also viewed the rushes.

I was taken by the kids' ability to express the pain of that year. Lily recalled about the time when I was too ill to look after them: 'I'd dream about what I'd say to you. I'd dream I'd show you a picture and you'd suddenly take an interest in me. Or we'd have a conversation. I'd talk about what I'd say to you and we'd laugh about it. I could take you out and we'd do stuff we used to do. You could help me with my homework and I used to miss the simplest things that we used to do because I didn't even know who you were anymore. I used to tell people it was like someone had taken you and replaced you with someone else, who I still loved but I just wanted my old mum back.'

Oscar remembers the appalling moment when, aged ten, he had resigned himself to the fact he no longer had a mother and that I would never ever get better. And he had an interesting way of describing how I'd become emotionally numb – 'You didn't laugh or cry for a whole year. If a unicorn came into the room, you wouldn't have reacted.'

I'm pleased enough with what we've got to think it's worth investing in another filming day. This will form part of the pilot that I will then pitch to broadcasters. I decide to use the money I've set aside to take the kids to Barcelona for half term. Added to that, there is the extra money from Airbnb.

I'm trying to get permission to film on Friday at a conference called 'More Harm Than Good'. It's a talk given by experts in critical psychiatry about the leading research that shows how antidepressants and antipsychotics are at worst dangerous, and at best ineffective.

I wouldn't usually choose to film at a conference but this is different. Conferences, experts, facts… in my experience none of these make for good TV. It's human stories that touch people, but this conference contains at least one human story that I want to tell.

Shortly after my recovery I got an email from a man called Luke, who told me he had had a bad experience with antidepressants and had set up a charity called The Council for Evidence-based Psychiatry (http://cepuk.org). It turned out he was Luke Montagu, son of the Earl of Sandwich.

We agreed to meet for lunch near his house in Clapham. Meeting Luke was a turning point for me – for a number of reasons.

When I walked into the Italian bistro in April 2014 my muscles were still aching from the Hastings half marathon I'd completed three days earlier. A man in his forties dressed in jeans and a blazer, with blond hair, stood up and greeted me. He looked pale and over lunch, he told me his sad story. Aged nineteen, Luke had had a sinus operation for which he had been given a general anaesthetic. He reacted badly and had severe headaches and was unable to leave the house for two weeks. His GP diagnosed him with 'a chemical imbalance' and prescribed Prozac then Seroxat. This began a lifetime of illness and drugs to combat the side effects of the initial medication. After withdrawing from the antidepressant in 2002 left him with crippling side effects, such as acute anxiety and feeling disconnected the doctors scratched their heads and put him on Effexor (venlafaxine), another antidepressant, as well as clonazepam (a sleeping pill) and two other drugs. Eventually he went into a private clinic to get off the sleeping pills; however the detox was so appalling, he thought his brain had been torn in two and suffered a host of horrific long-term withdrawal symptoms, which forced him to leave his job as CEO of a large film school. He's been off the drugs now for five years but still has agonising burning nerve pain throughout his body, tinnitus and a sense of extreme agitation.

Luke was the first of many people I met later on in my journey who suffer from the effects of antidepressants long after they have stopped taking them. But he is also one of the few people I've met who has managed to successfully sue his doctor (they settled out of court for £1.4 million in 2014).

It's notoriously difficult to do this in the UK because of something called the Bolam test. Mr Bolam was a voluntary patient who suffered injuries while being given electroshock therapy in the 1950s. But he wasn't given muscle relaxants and his body wasn't restrained, as is the norm. The judge ruled the hospital wasn't negligent as it was common medical practice to do neither. According to the judge a doctor is not guilty of negligence if 'he has acted in accordance with a practice accepted as proper by a responsible body of medical men skilled in that particular art'.

In other words, if it's common medical practice, it's not negligent. So the fact that lots of doctors prescribe drugs that have potentially lethal side effects means that if it happens to you, it will be hard to successfully sue your GP because it's common medical practice. To put it simply, the more doctors have fucked up before then the more difficult it is to take legal action when your own GP fucks up. Which is a bit of a fuck-up in itself, if you ask me.[1]

In the US individuals sometimes take on the drug companies. Andy Vickery from Texas is a top pharmaceutical litigation lawyer and does most of the US cases. He told me how difficult it is to take on drug companies. It can take years, and when he asks for a simple piece of information, the drug companies often provide box loads. The awards are much higher in the US than they would be in the UK as the jury can award damages for loss of love and affection. Also, US lawyers work on contingent fees. That's not the case here, so individuals don't tend to sue drug companies. In any case the drug companies now warn of the side effects, so if you go off and kill someone after taking medication that's tough because the instructions with the pills now warn of violence and hallucinations.

There have been some big cases in the US. One of Andy Vickery's big success stories was a tragic case involving a young man whose family was destroyed. I spoke to Tim Tobin from Montana, who was awarded $6.5 million by GlaxoSmithKline (GSK).[2] In February 1998, his life fell apart when his wife, Deb, and baby daughter, Alyssa, went to stay over the Wyoming border with Deb's parents, Don and Rita Schell.

Don Schell, an oilman, episodically had brief spells of anxiety and this time he had not been sleeping for a few nights. Unaware of previous poor reactions to an SSRI, a new GP diagnosed anxiety and prescribed Seroxat (paroxetine). Tim called to pick up Deb and Alyssa. On arrival, he got worried when no one answered the door. When he went inside, he discovered why: forty-eight hours after Don had been put on the drug, he put three bullets through the head of Rita, three through the head of Deb, and then three through the head of Alyssa before killing himself.

After the tragedy Tim was so devastated he couldn't think of anything for a while. Then he began to think rationally again and he and his family tried to work out what had happened. Their conclusion was that Don must have been affected by the medication he was on. Nothing else made sense.

He told me: 'The Don I knew just couldn't have done this. He had been depressed before but he didn't act odd. If anything, he became more loving when he was down.'

Tim was able to win a case against GSK and along the way he learnt that they knew all along their drug was linked with violence but had hidden the evidence. He told me: 'When I heard that I thought, wow, they actually knew. I lost my family, it ruined my life and for what? So someone could take a cruise to Hawaii for selling more drugs? This is about people caring for other fellow humans.'

THE PILL THAT STEALS LIVES

Ironically, Tim was offered antidepressants to cope with the grief of losing his family. I don't need to tell you what his response was.

These are tragic stories, and until I met Luke, I thought that these relatively few casualties were unfortunate but that the majority of people who took antidepressants benefited from them. But through Luke and the experts who are on the board of his charity, my view was about to change.

Over 57 million antidepressant prescriptions were issued in England in 2013 – a rise of over 500 per cent since 1992. Eleven per cent of women and 6 per cent of men are taking them yet research shows they are no more effective than a placebo.[3] When I first heard this, I thought it must be just one trial that had shown that and that there would be many revealing the opposite. Now I understand this isn't the case.

When drug companies test a drug, they only have to show two positive trials to get it licensed by the US Food and Drug Administration (FDA) and they can hide the rest. Not only that, but they can run as many trials as they want in order to get the two positive ones. This may surprise you, and you're not alone. It came as a complete surprise to one of the leading experts in the study of antidepressants.

Professor Irving Kirsch was a researcher at Harvard Medical School and a professor of psychology at the University of Hull. In 2008 he woke up to find that his research was headline news in all the leading national newspapers in the UK. This was followed up by countless TV appearances and the publication of his research in a book, *The Emperor's New Drugs: Exploding the Antidepressant Myth*.[4]

> Somehow, I had been transformed from a mild-mannered university professor into a media superhero

– or super villain, depending on whom you asked. What had my colleagues and I done to warrant this transformation?[5]

It all started in the mid-1990s when Professor Kirsch was approached by a bright young graduate student, Guy Sapirstein, with an idea to look at the extent to which antidepressants work because of their placebo effects. That's because when people take a pill, particularly if it is given by a doctor, then sometimes they get better regardless of whether it is a real drug or a sugar-coated tablet. Instead of doing a brand-new study, they decided to look at the old studies, a process known as a meta-analysis. Together, they analysed 38 clinical trials and were amazed to find that all of the groups got better whether they were receiving the drug, psychotherapy, the placebo or no treatment at all. They were sure they must have made a mistake, so re-analysed the statistics but they kept coming up with the same results and eventually published their findings that antidepressants, according to their data, appeared to be only moderately more effective than sugar pills.

Understandably there was a lot of controversy when the research came out. It was pointed out that their study didn't include unpublished trials by the drug industry. Kirsch and Sapirstein didn't even know at that time that the drug companies regularly withhold trials from publication. To their astonishment, they discovered that nearly 40 per cent of all the trials on antidepressants hadn't been published. To obtain copies, they had to use the Freedom of Information Act 2000 and once successful, they undertook a second meta-analysis, which included all the studies – published and unpublished.

This time around the results were staggering: they found antidepressants didn't work moderately better than placebo, they worked almost no better at all.

When they looked at all the trials, there was a tiny difference – 1.8 on the Hamilton Rating Scale (HAM-D), which measures depression. The National Institute for Health and Care Excellence (NICE), which drafts treatment guidelines for the NHS in the UK, has established there needs to be a 3-point difference between drug and placebo for it to be clinically significant. Even the small difference between drug and placebo can be explained by the fact that if you are taking the antidepressant, you will experience side effects – dry mouth, diarrhoea, and forgetfulness. And, as Kirsch states, if you get those side effects then you will think you have got the real drug and so will get better.

The results were better for people who were severely depressed, but even then they only rated 4 points better than the placebo on the Hamilton Depression Scale. The startling conclusion of Professor Kirsch's research was that 85–90 per cent of people aren't gaining any clinically meaningful benefit from the drug itself.

This was not the first time that hidden drug trials showed that antidepressants were ineffective. Four years earlier, in 2004, Professor Tim Kendall raised a storm when, as director of the National Collaborating Centre for Mental Health (NCCMH), he went public with the fact that he was handed previously confidential information.[6] It contained evidence Glaxo (GSK) had unpublished trials showing Seroxat was not effective in treating children for depression. Not only that but the unpublished trials showed a significant increase in self-harming behaviour (2.5 times that of placebo). The trials still haven't been published and as this book goes to press there is still no law that states drug companies must disclose their trials even to our regulators.

You might have thought that the media storm following the publication of both of these discoveries would have a major impact. But it didn't. In his book *Cracked*, James Davies tells how three months after Kirsch's discoveries a survey of doctors showed that only 50 per cent would change their prescribing habits.[7]

In their opinion, the antidepressants worked. Well, they were right – they do work, but in some cases for the wrong reason: the placebo effect. And what's wrong with that, you might ask. Well, rather a lot, I think to myself as I reflect on Luke Montagu's long-term side effects and Tim Tobin's $6.5 million settlement from Glaxo, which will do nothing to alleviate the pain of losing his entire family, or the 800 women whose children have birth defects as a result of their mothers taking Seroxat.

So on this Monday morning in September, I send another email to Luke to see if I can film at his conference, 'More Harm Than Good'. I want him to appear in my film. I'm also convinced there will be lots of people at the conference with similar or worse stories than mine and I want to get a flavour of that.

My phone rings and it's him. He sounds rushed and I can tell he's got a lot on his plate with organising the conference, which is for 300 people at the University of Roehampton and being live-streamed across the Internet too. He admits he's in two minds about the film – he's had lots of people asking him to appear in films, 'but on the other hand, you're the real deal,' he tells me. I'm pleased he thinks this because right now, I don't feel like I'm the real deal – or in fact, any deal at all. To finance the filming, I'm having to plunder the children's holiday budget; no one has commissioned the film and actually I'm still in two minds about whether I should be making it at all.

I try to put these negative thoughts behind me as I drive the five kilometres to St John's Wood. I'm excited to see my little boy in the middle of the day. We've arranged to meet by St John's Wood underground and as I draw up in the car, he runs towards me and jumps in, wearing his school uniform.

'Rell, Rell!' he shouts. After he'd named me 'Rell' (from my having so many rules), he then started to call me 'Rell de la Carotte' for no reason that I can understand. I've got the car roof down, and as he jumps in, he throws his arms round my neck and says: 'Rell, I love you so much. I love you, I love you!'

At this I joke that I'm going to kidnap him for the rest of the day and cuddle him to distraction before we go to park in a nearby multi-storey car park. I contemplate it nervously. Already our blue Audi that I only bought nine months ago is covered in scratches because unfortunately my impetuous and impatient nature extends to driving, and particularly parking.

As we head up the ramp to the car park, Oscar is already cringing and begging me to take care that I don't land yet another scratch on our already damaged car. I recall the euphoria of buying this car just before Christmas. I'd been banned from driving for a number of months because of my history with antidepressants. It took forever for the DVLA to give me my licence back and involved blood tests and reports from doctors even though I'd stopped taking any medicines more than a year before. When my licence finally came back, just two weeks before the holidays, a few days later Oscar and I went out to view a second-hand Audi in East London.

It was a Saturday and the woman selling the car also worked in film and took a liking to me. She let me test-drive the car and I'll never forget the joy of driving that car with its leather seats and the roof down that morning in December, just nine months earlier. I remember tasting the freedom of driving that I'd taken for granted for some thirty years until that privilege was suddenly taken away. In fact, I was so euphoric that despite the fact we hadn't had an RAC test on it, I agreed to buy it there and then. Oscar was with me on this, urging me to go ahead with it. He and I piled into the car and drove it back through London to Harlesden with the roof down and music blaring out at indecent decibels. It was the best Christmas present to ourselves we could have found.

Although our appointment at the orthodontist is supposed to be at noon, the woman behind the reception makes no apology for the fact that there are still two people in front of us. I decide not to make a fuss so as not to embarrass Oscar and as we sit in the waiting room, I pretend to be doing emails on my phone when really I'm on Tinder.

Oscar glances over at me suspiciously; he knows what's going on.

'Get off your phone!' he growls.

'Darling, you've no idea how much I've got on my plate – work, Ocado, deflea-ing the cats, organising the weekend…' I tell him.

But he's not fooled. He wanders over to look at my phone and I'm about to be rumbled when the receptionist announces: 'Oscar Newman!'

The kids know all about my dating. In fact they know all

about pretty much everything in my life. Since being single I decided that there would be complete and total honesty and transparency between us. That decision came about because I realised that in my early attempts to protect them from the truth of our marital break-up, I'd caused them more heartache. When their dad and I had decided to separate just before Christmas 2011, I couldn't stop crying and he moved into the spare room.

I couldn't bring myself to tell the children, then aged nine and ten, what was going on so I told them I was crying because I was stressed about Christmas. They looked at me in utter disbelief. The idea that their mum, who flitted between directing film shoots in Peruvian prisons to attending school speech days and organised with military precision the routines of our household – the thought that I would be remotely fazed by any aspect of Christmas preparations – held no truck with them. They pleaded with me to tell them what was going on, but I stuck determinedly to my story. Was it going to be the Nigella stuffing recipe, or the Jamie Oliver one? Silver ribbons on the presents, or red ones? All of these choices were giving me sleepless nights and making me feel, well, yes, very weepy indeed.

By January, the game was up as Robert and I decided that in everybody's interests, he should move out. I revealed to the children that in fact our marital breakdown was the reasons for my tearfulness, not the turkey stuffing. Their reaction left me dumbfounded: they said they were relieved.

'Relieved?' I asked. 'How come?'

They explained that my obvious lie about the stresses of Christmas had left them to conclude that the real reason for my tears must be that in fact I was ill, most probably dying of a terminal and incurable illness. They simply couldn't think of another plausible reason. On hearing this, I learnt a big life lesson: that in our efforts to protect and shield children, we make them weak and when we don't tell them the truth, we create fear and uncertainty. From then on, I made a decision: give them the facts and let them make up their own minds.

In my mind this principle should be applied to us, the public, when it comes to drugs. I see the problem is that the drug companies don't give us the facts so we can make up our own minds. In fact, they deliberately conceal them and the Food and Drug Administration (FDA) in the US and the Medicines and Healthcare Products Regulatory Agency (MHRA) in the UK allows them to do so. Adverse effects are hidden, as are the trials that are concealed when they're not positive.

Coming back to my decision with the kids, it meant that in January 2012, when all three of us huddled up together, sleeping in my old marital bedroom and desperately trying to adapt to the fact we were now three instead of four, I announced the new rule: no secrets. Sex, drugs and rock and roll had previously been taboo in our household (and probably still were amongst our well-heeled neighbours in Queen's Park and almost certainly amongst the investment banker parents at their school in Chiswick), but at number 28 Dundonald Road, now in this new climate of glasnost and perestroika, those subjects flowed freely between us.

So, at the ages of ten and eleven, Lily and Oscar knew I had experimented with recreational drugs, they knew the minutiae of why their parents' marriage had broken down, and they knew that their mum was on a single-minded mission to find a new partner. That freezing-cold January of 2012, I was determined to replace the emotional and physical void that engulfed us. All of us rattled around our five-bedroom house, trying to disguise from each other the pain we were feeling at the cruel and sudden disintegration of our little nuclear family.

The following month, when I took my first steps into the unfamiliar world of Internet dating by joining Guardian Soulmates and Match.com, they helped to choose the photos I'd hired a professional photographer to take and watched on amusedly as their mum, who hadn't been on a single date in thirteen years, launched herself timorously into a world she was ill-equipped to take part in.

Two years later, I had become an aficionado, a member of various different dating sites and one of the first to join the new wave of dating apps. When Tinder came along, the kids delighted in picking up my iPad and matching me with the most unattractive guys they could find and would then begin chatting with them as if they were me. Once, when Lily was particularly annoyed with me, she went into my Guardian Soulmates account and changed my user name from Fitandfunny to Iamhorrible. She then listed my hobbies as 'beating my children and making their lives miserable'. When I found out my technical incompetence prevented me from changing it back, I had to beg her to do so for me.

To Oscar's delight, the orthodontist announces that he needs a brace. I don't, and still can't, understand why the fact of having to wear a piece of steel in your mouth would be appealing to a thirteen-year-old (or indeed anyone else).

Who am I to argue, and thank God it's on the NHS, I think as we stride off and grab a quick sandwich at Pret A Manger in St John's Terrace before I drop him at the tube again so he can make his own way back to school.

Chapter 20

WEDNESDAY, 16 SEPTEMBER 2015

At last I get an email this morning from Luke Montagu saying we can film at the 'More Harm Than Good' conference.

Steve and Tom are my favourite film crew to work with. We've done some of my most exciting projects together. The most notable example was when we made a film called *A Murder in the Family* for ITV in 2006. Shot in the Philippines, it was about a woman called Margaret, whose son Steven had been murdered by his Filipino wife, Evelyn.

We all share a slightly quirky sense of humour and every day I'd make a variation of the same joke as we ate breakfast at the Shangri La Manila Hotel: 'The buffet is complimentary, it's just told me what a great director I am!'

Tom is available and when I speak to him, I rattle through my story (which I can now condense into around seven minutes if I talk very fast indeed). I'm now used to the gasps of astonishment, the 'Oh my God, I'm so sorry,' and then finally, for around half of the people I tell, they come back with: 'Exactly the same thing happened to my friend/uncle/ aunt/business partner, etc.' Tom is no exception as he reveals that his uncle committed suicide and his aunt is convinced that it was because of antidepressants.

But I still don't have a date from the *Daily Mail* when the article is going in. Worries that they'll drop it start to crowd my head. What if their lawyers tell them they can't publish it? Maybe they'll contact the doctors at the private hospital, and I'll get a call saying they can't run it because they say I'm a dangerous lunatic, a fantasist; that I made it all up, I'm really a paranoid schizophrenic and I'm always attacking myself and possibly other people with a knife.

That afternoon I get an unexpected visit from Lily and her friend Molly. Lily wants to pick up some things and also wants me to drive her to her piano lesson. Having the two of them in my kitchen is a welcome break from the doubts that have been whirring round in my head that morning. I love Lily's auburn-haired friend, Molly, who is a rebel. Although I pretend to disapprove when she leads Lily astray, actually I applaud her independent thinking. Recently I got a call from Lily on a Monday afternoon, saying that she and Molly wanted to go to a pop-up concert somewhere in the East End that evening and Molly's mum had said it was perfectly OK. Not wanting to be a killjoy, I said Lily could go, only to find out half an hour later that of course Molly's mum hadn't said anything of the kind. By then it was too late as the two of them were halfway to the pop-up concert even though it was a school night and they had homework to do. They got back safely but I had to pretend to be extremely cross

Molly makes me laugh a lot and I know I make her laugh too. I have a special act that I reserve for Lily and Molly, which is guaranteed to have them falling on the floor with laughter. When Lily calls me 'Mother', I look her straight in the eye and with mock seriousness, I say, 'Lily, please call me by my full name. It's Motherfucker! Or, if you can't manage that, it's Mrs Newman…' If that hasn't reduced the pair of them to helplessness, I continue.

'Lily, you and I need to have a very serious talk. You're fourteen years old now, and things aren't going to plan. I want to hear by the end of the week that you've snogged a boy and that you've started smoking and drinking, and by the end of the month, I'll be extremely angry if you haven't at least experimented with drugs – and I don't mean Prozac. And if that hasn't happened, then I'm taking away all your screen time. Understood?'

I haven't heard anymore from Laurent, a guy I've been on a few dates with, so I decide to be more proactive on the dating front. I log onto Guardian Soulmates because just being online gets you more visits. I'm no longer 'Fitandfunny' because this yielded men in Lycra, or guys who boasted they'd done Ironman triathlons. On one occasion, a potential suitor sent me his Garmin chart just to show how fit he was.

So I dispensed with 'Fitandfunny' and now I'm 'Elegantandeloquent'. The photo of me completing a half marathon is now replaced by one of me reclining on a sofa in a black, clingy dress. By now, I'd refined and polished my profile to reflect exactly the kind of person I want to be and precisely the person I want in my life. It began: 'I've got a great new life post marriage and I'm here to find someone to share it…'

Independent, but vulnerable.

I'm careful to underplay the fitness: 'I'm active but for me it's about fun rather than fitness…' There's a gentle hint of humour too: 'I've never fantasised about snuggling up with a bottle of wine and a DVD, but I'll give it a go…' and open-mindedness. Then there's a recent addition that I've put in just two days ago, which I'm very pleased with: 'I can come across as cool and confident but really I'm just a pussy cat wanting a lap to curl up on'.

I'm delighted with that – soft and vulnerable.

There's a section about the sort of person you are looking for and it contains my very best line, 'If you're a mix of alpha and alfalfa, strong but sensitive, you're the one for me'. Careful not to sound materialistic, there's a line that goes: 'I don't really care about money, but it would be helpful if you've got enough on your Oyster card to get to the first date'.

Ha, Ha! I'm now so pleased with myself, I'm wondering why I didn't have a career in comedy. And then in the final sentence, there is a line which sums up the kind of man I'm looking for: 'We don't need to share the same interests but shared values of truth, integrity, a desire to stand up for what is right rather than what is convenient – all those are important to me'.

As I drive Lily to her piano teacher's home in a Victorian house in Kensal Rise, I reflect that perhaps it has taken me a very long time, not just my two years of Guardian Soulmates' membership, to arrive at that conclusion. As the car pulls up outside the house, where the sound of a child trying to play 'Für Elise' comes drifting onto the street, I ask myself, why has it taken me so long to arrive at this place, and why is it that this person has so far eluded me?

Chapter 21

THURSDAY, 17 SEPTEMBER 2015

It's a bright and beautiful day as I drive down to Golborne Road to have my hair cut. Golborne Road feels like my spiritual home. I moved there from my two-bedroom flat in Acton when I was thirty and so began a love affair that still continues.

I remember my best friend Jim, saying to me, 'Don't expect your life to change, just because you're moving to Notting Hill.' But he was wrong: my life did change. I'd lived in Acton because I'd started my career working at the BBC in Shepherd's Bush and it was convenient. Aged thirty, just after I'd broken up with the guy who had broken my heart and whom I cried over for six weeks, I looked at my finances and realised I could afford a tiny flat in the more bohemian part of Notting Hill.

Golborne Road is known as 'little Portugal' because of the plethora of Portuguese and Spanish delis lining the street.

THE PILL THAT STEALS LIVES

Other than food shops, there are antique shops selling a vast array of usually overpriced furniture that you could get for a fraction of the price anywhere else in the country. Except on Fridays and Saturdays, when the early-morning market spills out onto the road and you can find genuine bargains.

The moment I saw the one-bedroom flat above the mirror shop bang in the middle of Golborne Road, I knew I wanted to live there more than anywhere else in the entire world. It was unique, because although tiny, large full-length French windows looked out onto a Spanish-style walled courtyard.

It was at that flat that Robert and I began our courtship in the spring and summer of 1999. Ironically, I was series producing and directing a series called *Looking for Love*, which was about singles in search of romance. He was doing well at the law firm where he still works, and had recently become a partner, aged just thirty-two. We shared a number of mutual friends, and our life together that summer of 1999 was like a Richard Curtis movie. Every weekend people would pile back to my little flat above the mirror shop, and the parties would go on all night.

We complemented each other very well. He was the slightly straighter, practical one; I was the creative, artistic one. We got engaged very quickly – just six weeks after meeting. I was the one who pushed things forward, not just because I was thirty-five and wanted kids, but also because there was an underlying anxiety that without the wild parties, the summer heat, that if we allowed reality in, then maybe there wouldn't be the 'happy ever after' ending that I'd already written in my head. Maybe he'd remember that actually he preferred taller, skinnier women. Maybe we'd discover that while he liked programmes like *Coast*, I preferred human-interest documentaries. Maybe we'd discover that he wanted a wife who stayed at home and looked after the kids, while I wanted a career. And that was why it was essential that we set a wedding date very soon and that whatever happened we kept throwing those all-night parties in my flat above the mirror shop on Golborne Road.

All this goes through my head as I park my car outside the Lisboa coffee shop and am greeted by my hairdresser Justin at his salon, 53AM.

Chapter 22

FRIDAY, 18 SEPTEMBER 2015

When I wake at 6 a.m. it's still dark outside. As I go downstairs and switch on the bright orange kettle, my stomach is churning with excitement. Today is the day we're filming Luke Montagu at the 'More Harm Than Good' conference.

I take my cup of tea upstairs, stepping over Rocco, who has eschewed the designer cat basket the kids have insisted I bought for sleeping on the stairs. After I log onto my Sonos App from my mobile phone, BBC Radio 4 plays throughout the house. Every time this happens I congratulate myself, because in the past, it was Robert who took care of every technical aspect of our lives. Organising Sonos players round the house was just one of the myriad of things that I couldn't imagine myself being able to do, yet it was another victory along the path towards self-sufficiency after we split.

Justin has cut my hair as usual in a short bob and coloured

it to cover up the grey roots. I grab a black strapless dress and a red velvet jacket. Recently I bought three identical figure-hugging dresses from American Apparel: a blue one for the *Mail* shoot, then a black and a red one. They were £40 each, and although I felt guilty at the time, Lily and I now share each other's clothes so I feel better about it. Sharing my wardrobe with my daughter is good on many levels, not least because she's interested in fashion and I'm not. The downside is that the words 'mutton' and 'lamb' may easily find themselves sharing a sentence to describe me as I squeeze into the short skirts, bomber jackets and crop tops that Lily has chosen for us both.

I've ordered an Ocado delivery for the 6 a.m. to 7 a.m. slot, and though I know I have to be out the door by 7, I'm sure as it's the first slot in the day that they will come at 6, leaving me time to unpack. As I force down a banana and a cup of coffee, I look at my watch: 6.30, and no sign of them. The kids are coming back from spending some time at their dad's this weekend and I've ordered £100 of groceries. I'm pleased with myself because yesterday I cooked a Greek lamb stew for tonight.

I'd spent the night putting together a rough call sheet, sending it out to Tom and Steve. I'm feeling hassled, unused to having to deal with the minutiae of logistics when filming. Usually there is an army of production assistants and runners to organise the details of a film shoot.

Today, I've enlisted the help of my friend and neighbour, Simon. I met him at Christmas through another single girlfriend, and we had formed a posse of single parents in Harlesden, having dinner at each other's houses and helping each other out. The other day I spoke to him about the film shoot, told him I needed an extra pair of hands, and because he works as a freelance videographer he said he would come along if he could talk to Tom, the sound recordist, and learn a bit about sound.

I'm getting nervous now because it's 7 a.m. and we need to leave. The doorbell goes and I open the door to find both the Ocado man and Simon standing there. I throw the perishables in the fridge, and leave the rest on the floor.

The Google map on my iPhone tells me we have arrived in the right place as we pull into a car park just off Roehampton Lane. A cursory recce of the area tells us there is no sign of the 'More Harm Than Good' conference. I ring Steve – where is he? He replies that the conference is in fact in a quite different part of Roehampton University: it's ten minutes down the road. The postcode takes you to the wrong place, he explains – he'd spent yesterday evening checking the map and working that out. As we drive down the road, still not really knowing where we are going, I'm feeling flustered, annoyed I'm having to do this all by myself. I smile as I say those words to myself, as I hear Oscar's voice in my head with his familiar chant: 'Ah, all by yourself, Rell. Poor Rell!' Yes, there were all sorts of things that I've had to do all by myself recently. Not just the Sonos and the various other multitudes of unfamiliar tasks I've now taken on as a single parent. This film, this story, I've had enough of doing this all by myself: I want to share the burden of it, I want to be part of a team working together, collaborating to get this story out. When we pull up into the car park on the other campus at Roehampton University, I'm so very relieved when I see Steve and Tom standing there waiting for me.

Simon runs off to get coffee for us all. I haven't seen Tom for a while but we have a familiarity born of shared experiences. We have, on our many filming trips, lived in close proximity and worked on a number of emotionally harrowing stories. Out of that comes an intimacy, a shared understanding. It doesn't take long for us to get into our familiar banter as he puts a radio mike on me and I pretend to flirt with him and tell him it's the most action I've had in a long time.

We've arrived early at the conference so we can plug into the live feed as Luke has already hired a crew, who are broadcasting the conference live across the Web. When I see Luke in the empty conference hall I'm once again struck by how tired and pale he looks. And once again, I feel so very grateful that my brush with psychiatric drugs lasted just a year and didn't leave me with long-term effects, unlike him.

I'd been in two minds about filming this conference but seeing Luke reminded me of the damage that psychiatric drugs can do. It confirms to me it was the right decision – right for lots of reasons. Not just because there will be lots of people here, like Luke, who have suffered at the hands of psychiatric drugs but because all the leading luminaries against psychiatric drugs are here today, and I want them to see us here as a proper film crew, actually filming, actually here making a documentary about the epidemic of psychiatric drugs and actually taking it seriously. And it's also right because if Luke can set up a charity and a conference despite his ongoing suffering, then surely the very least I can do is make a film.

So I sit in the audience and get talking to the man next to me. He's an old Etonian whose life was messed up by psychiatric drugs when he went into a private hospital and he now runs a support group. The room fills up with around

300 people, a mixture of people working in mental health, journalists, and many people who have suffered harm from psychiatric drugs.

I'm seated in the audience and I agree with Luke that in the second round of questions, I will ask a question. It's the first time I've shared in public my story. Christ, I'm about to stand up and tell everyone not just here but to the audience it's being live streamed to that I went a bit crazy and attacked myself with a knife! What if they don't believe it was because of the drug? What if they think I'm just a nutter?

A well-dressed woman in her sixties introduces herself as the wife of Brian – I know exactly who she is. Her husband runs a website called AntiDepAware (http://antidepaware.co.uk) and was one of the first people I spoke to as I recovered. Their story is tragic: their son, a family man with a successful career and no history of depression or mental illness, was prescribed an antidepressant because he was stressed at work. Six days later, he took his life. Brian was convinced it was because of the citalopram he was prescribed. The coroner agreed, rejecting a suicide verdict, and actually naming citalopram as a 'possible cause' in the narrative.[1]

On the AntiDepAware website, Brian identifies, documents and recounts reports of inquests in the British media where antidepressants are linked to suicide or homicide. At the latest count dating back to 2003, he had a list of over 3,500. He says that his motivation is to raise awareness of the dangers of the drugs, and to expose the prescribers and coroners who ignore these dangers.

In 2015 he wrote an article called 'The Lost Children', featuring some of the children who had taken their lives during the previous year. He was subsequently asked by a

Human Rights group if they could submit this article as part of a presentation to the United Nations on the Rights of the Child, which he did.

Brian's wife explains that he isn't here today because they have just come back from a conference in Copenhagen. She tells me the highlight was when five women, whose loved ones had taken their lives while on antidepressants, stood up and each gave a speech. I wish I'd been there. After our talk I don't feel quite so daunted about the prospect of standing up and talking about my experience.

The author and academic Dr James Davies is the first speaker. I'd met him through Luke Montagu at a lunch he'd arranged a few months ago and discovered he had written a book called *Cracked: Why Psychiatry is Doing More Harm Than Good*.[2] His talk is about the *DSM*, the psychiatrist's handbook that is used by psychiatrists in the US, which classifies disorders. Its full name is the *Diagnostic and Statistical Manual of Mental Disorders* and it was first created in 1952.This large tome, now on its fifth version, imaginatively named *DSM-5*, is edited and published by the American Psychiatric Association and is the bible by which psychiatrists in the US make their diagnosis. Unlike the Bible, however, the publication of this work, with its tightly guarded copyright, generates huge amounts of money – $100 million in total has gone into the coffers of the American Psychiatric Association.

It isn't used widely in the UK – our psychiatrists mainly use the World Health Organisation system of diagnosing mental health conditions – but the latest version of its handbook, *ICD-10*, is being updated and the *DSM-5* will undoubtedly have an influence on the mental health section in the new version. As the NHS website points out, the *DSM* has a major influence on how mental health is thought about and treated in the UK and guides research into psychiatric disorders taking place there.

When it started out, there were around 100 disorders. Now, however, there are over 300, ranging from all sorts of extremely interesting interpretations of what cynics may alternatively explain as variations of human behaviour and character. Early on, homosexuality was listed. Now that's off (how very enlightened!) but there are some interesting disorders that have appeared out of nowhere in the last sixty years. 'Social Anxiety Phobia', as I've mentioned (I think the good old-fashioned term was simply 'shyness'), General Anxiety Disorder (once called 'worried about everyday things'), Minor Neurocognitive Disorder (for normal forgetfulness in old age) and Caffeine Withdrawal Disorder (no explanation needed). If you have been suffering from grief for longer than two weeks after the death of a loved one, you have Major Depressive Disorder! And my favourite of them all: Oppositional Defiant Disorder. Looking back, I'm surprised that the doctors didn't give me this diagnosis, along with psychotic depression.

A group of mental health professionals have become so enraged at this medicalisation of normal human experience that 14,000 of them have signed a petition to get this topic into the public debate. They insist that with 34 per cent of Americans taking psychiatric medication, and 20 per cent in the UK, we are creating illnesses which purely serves the interests of big pharmaceutical companies.

The latest version of the psychiatric bible, *DSM-5*, lists endless new illnesses, almost none of which have any actual biological origin. That's to say, with a few exceptions, there is no physical test, no blood tests or biological markers for them.

James Davies talks about how he interviewed one of the members of the *DSM* taskforce, who tells him how they agree on a disorder. He says that in many meetings there are simply twelve psychiatrists who 'thrash it out' for three hours and then vote. A critical psychologist, Renee Garfinkel, who participated on the committees said: 'It more resembled a group of friends deciding where they want to go for dinner. One person decides: "I feel like Chinese food", and another says, "No, I'm really more in the mood for Indian food," and finally after some discussion and collaborative give and take they all decide to go and have Italian.'

The same psychologist, Garfinkel, describes how once there was a discussion about whether a particular behaviour should be included as a symptom of a disorder. One taskforce member piped up, 'Oh no, we can't include that behaviour as a symptom because I do that!' So it was decided that behaviour shouldn't be included.

The way in which criteria for being diagnosed for conditions is created seems equally arbitrary. For example, it was decided a patient should have five symptoms for two weeks in order to get a diagnosis of depression. When the chair of the *DSM* was interviewed as to why it wasn't four or six, he replied, 'Because four seemed like not enough and six seemed like too much.'[3]

Davies talks about the theory that psychiatry's claim that 1 in 4 people have a mental disorder is a way to sell drugs that they've just renamed 'painful life experiences' to create an illusion of an illness that only they can cure. It seems he's got a good point.

He has described in his book *Cracked* how the makers of Prozac created a new pill called Sarafem for a condition labelled

THE PILL THAT STEALS LIVES

Premenstrual Dysphoric Disorder (PMDD). According to the makers, Eli Lilly, a woman must experience at least 5 of the 11 symptoms for a diagnosis to be made: mood swings, irritability, tension, depressed mood, decreased interest in usual activities, difficulty concentrating, lack of energy, marked change in appetite, insomnia/hypersomnia, feeling overwhelmed, bloating and breast tenderness. In fact, Sarafem was just Prozac, but it looked a little different – a pink pill instead of a green one. The drug company marketed both pills at the same time – one pill for depression, one for PMDD – so it was the same chemical but rebranded. A lot of women would have had no idea they were actually taking Prozac.

Davies writes about how the same thing happened with a drug called Wellbutrin, which was well-known as an antidepressant. When GlaxoSmithKline plc wanted to sell it as a smoking cessation pill, they marketed the same chemical under the new name of Zyban but didn't tell consumers it was the same drug.[4]

If you look up some of these disorders in the *DSM-5*, they seem to be describing many people at some stage of their lives. For example, Avoidant Personality Disorder: feelings of inadequacy and inferiority, extreme sensitivity to negative evaluation, and avoidance of social interaction despite a strong desire to be close to others.

Apparently, 21 out of 29 people who were on the panel that voted on the existence of a disorder in *DSM-5* have financial ties to the drug industry.[5]

Depression is one of the disorders in the *DSM* and of course was the illness I was supposed to have that precipitated my year-long descent into drug-induced hell. Although I wouldn't have been diagnosed using the *DSM*, whatever psychiatrists and doctors here in the UK are using, I know only too well just how easy it is to get the label.

I reflect on the many people in the last two years I've spoken to who, like me, have been told by their GP that they are depressed. Almost every other divorcee I've met has been offered an antidepressant. I think back to how normal it is to react to a life event like a divorce by having sleepless nights, anxiety and a loss of appetite; how these days all those symptoms are proof that you need a pill.

I've had to deal with far worse situations than the event that precipitated my initial visit to that psychiatrist – the selling of our family home in Dundonald Road – yet I've managed to get through those sleepless nights, the stomach-churning anxieties, the fears about moving to Harlesden, the worry that the children will get mugged and afterwards decide to live with their dad, the icy-cold fear that descends when Tinder announces 'There is no one new around you'... Then there's the myriad of everyday anxieties and responsibilities as a single parent that now crowd every crevice of my brain – mowing the lawn, visiting the vet, organising the PEPs, the pets, the ISA, the life, car and home insurance, the broken Nespresso machine, the Sonos, the children's speech days, the dentist, the orthodontist... Yes, all of that I manage without a single pill. As Oscar would say: 'Ah, all by yourself, Rell.'

It's true that many GPs hand these pills out like sweets, but actually, my GP didn't. I'd visited the small practice in Queen's Park, tearful and sleepless, and they'd told me there wasn't much they could do: they were right.

This may sound a bit tough but in my view, if you go to your GP like I did and say, 'Doctor, I'm crying all the time, my marriage has broken down,' or 'I've just been sacked,' the answer should be, 'Good, that's exactly what you should be doing. That's what tears are for. Now if you think you've got problems, I've got worse. And there's a queue of people in my waiting room who are actually ill so would you mind leaving so I can get on with making people better'.

My doctor didn't exactly say that, but actually we put enormous pressure on our GPs to come up with solutions to problems they simply cannot solve. Sometime later, I told the head of the practice about my year of drug-induced hell, and he told me their policy is to try never to prescribe antidepressants. They know how dangerous they can be, and not just that: they also know that many of the articles written in respected magazines are not to be trusted, that often they are written by drug companies, who pay psychiatrists to put their names to them. The drug companies manipulate information to make it look like their trials show the drugs to be more effective than they are.

But this happens across the board and not just with antidepressants. One shocking example was with HRT (hormone replacement therapy). Lawyers representing 8,400 women who were suing the pharmaceutical company Wyeth for harm that resulted from the company's hormone drugs produced 26 papers in support of HRT. The articles had appeared in eighteen medical journals between 1998 and 2005, detailing the benefits while minimising the risks. Listed as sole author on one of the papers was Dr Barbara Sherwin, a psychology professor at McGill University in Montreal, Quebec. Yet she actually wrote only portions of the article. The rest was prepared by Design-Write, a ghostwriting firm hired by Wyeth.[6]

And this happens a lot with antidepressants, the process

whereby misinformation gets into respected journals being particularly interesting. David Healy explains this process in his book, *Let Them Eat Prozac*.[7] The ghostwritten article arrives with a covering letter, authorising him to alter the piece. One example was an article about the SSRI Effexor, again made by Wyeth. Here, the message was that compared to other SSRIs, which might get your patient well, Effexor got the patient fully better. Healy agreed to have his name on the article if he could make two important additions: one is a note that SSRIs can make some people suicidal (important to note because getting people better rather than just well isn't much help if you've killed yourself). The second addition showed data from trials with one of Effexor's competitors, Remeron, which didn't substantiate these claims. But the final article, published in the *Journal of Psychiatry & Neuroscience*, didn't contain either addition. It's estimated that 50–100 per cent of articles on drugs that appear in journals are ghostwritten, which is why my own GP reads few medical journals, prefers to make up his own mind and has wisely, in my view, decided not to dish out antidepressants unless his patients insist.

If you think this is bad, a recent *Panorama* programme, *Who's Paying Your Doctor* (14 April 2014), exposed the fact that two of Britain's top psychiatrists, Guy Goodwin and David Nutt, were paid by the makers of Nalmefene, a drug used to treat heavy drinkers, and Agomelatine, a new antidepressant. They gave a series of lectures that appeared to be talking generally about addiction and depression, but promoted these drugs as the cure. Later, it was revealed they were paid thousands by the drug company producing those drugs.

Professor Tim Kendall of NCCMH appeared on the

programme and even confronted Guy Goodwin when he refused to appear on camera. He told me the evidence about how good the drugs are was extremely slim. It makes me wonder how anyone, including our GPs, can be expected to know the truth when those in high-up positions are being paid thousands to promote drugs that others don't really rate.

Next up is a talk by Peter Gøtzsche, co-founder of The Cochrane Collaboration, a global, independent group of researchers and professionals, a not-for-profit organisation that gathers data and information. Their reviews advise NICE (The National Institute for Health and Care Excellence).

Peter kicks off by talking about how easy it is to get a diagnosis of depression. In America, 10 per cent of people are supposed to be depressed at any one time. It's easy to come away with a pill. You just have to say that 8 out of 14 days you have less interest in things, and then you add one extra symptom to that – overeating (easy in America!), not eating, not sleeping... and bang, there you have it.

In one of his books,[8] he tells how he and 7 other successful, perfectly normal people tried the tests for depression – ADHD and mania – and none of them survived all three tests. Two had depression, four had definite, likely or possible ADHD. Seven suffered mania and one needed immediate treatment. He concludes: 'It's not the least surprising that when therapists have been asked to use DSM criteria, a quarter of healthy people also get a psychiatric diagnosis.'[9]

He makes the point that bipolar in children has risen 35-fold in the US, and it's not just the loose criteria that are the problem. Remember, there was a point in my illness when I was diagnosed as bipolar (and Rebekah Beddoe too, see page 113), and many others. Well, that's because SSRI drugs cause bipolar-like symptoms such as disinhibition, mania and mood swings, as do ADHD drugs.

Peter Gøtzsche's position on drugs is unequivocal: they are dangerous, the trials are done by the drug industry and are biased, both by design and analysis. Even if the drugs seem to work, you've no idea what would have happened if you'd done nothing. Most depressed people get better after some weeks anyway, he says.

My favourite quote from this smart-looking Dane is that when asked the alternative to antidepressants, his reply is 'No antidepressants.' I like that very much and I think back to the many times when people have said to me, 'Well, what's the alternative?'

I've arranged with Luke Montagu that I'm going to ask the first question once Peter Gøtzsche's talk finishes, and in the meantime I try to focus on the talk rather than the worry of standing up. I'm comforted by the fact that I know I'm a good public speaker. I first discovered this skill at my wedding in October 1999. It was just four months after we'd met and once I'd finished the series I was directing on singles in search of romance, I devoted all my creative energy into producing my new show, which was to be The Robert and Katinka Wedding. And I'd decided it was going to be a wedding to outwed all others.

Our chosen location was Polhawn Fort in Cornwall, a medieval castle perched on a cliff-top, with its own private beach. We hired it for the weekend, and on the Saturday afternoon, we would have the ceremony there and afterwards the party that would undoubtedly go on all night, then a wedding breakfast the following Sunday.

At the candlelit ceremony in the vaulted arches, friends and family read handpicked speeches, sang songs and played instruments. After the Lebanese feast we'd transported in vans from London, much to the understandable annoyance of the in-house Cornish caterers, I delivered a speech after Robert's that surprised me as much as the audience. In my cream antique lace 1930s dress that I'd bought from a vintage shop in Holland Park, I stood up and talked for ten minutes.

I began timidly, saying that to begin with I hadn't been interested in Robert because he was too nice – in fact, he was the nicest person I'd ever met and I was only interested in men who treated me badly, who were cold and uncaring. The audience liked it. They were chuckling. Encouraged, I described how he tried to woo me: 'I was deluged with niceness. Every time I came home there was a nice message on my answerphone, or a nice email from Robert, or a nice bunch of flowers. Once he offered to come round and cook a nice meal. Our conversations were constrained by the necessity to be nice to each other – the weather was our main topic of conversation.'

The audience was really with me. More laughter.

'Then fate stepped in and I happened to meet Robert when he was with his younger brother. Not only was Robert not being nice, he was being thoroughly unpleasant. This was something I could at least relate to. A whole new Robert emerged – opinionated, bullying, unreasonable, even violent and abusive – all the qualities I had been looking for were there.'

Now I'd got them. The audience was roaring with laughter – I had them in my thrall as I delivered the rest of it. I continued with a confidence I'd never had before. I was unstoppable, pausing only for dramatic effect and delivering the jokes with perfect timing. Just when they were aching with laughter,

I quickly did a gear change. I slowed down my pace and changed the tone of my voice to reflect that the jokes were over. I paused, waiting for their laughter to subside, holding the guests in my gaze before continuing. The room became unusually quiet considering the amount of people there. Now for my grand finale.

'This last summer – the time I have spent with Robert – has been the happiest time of my life. The sun has shone, not only literally, but also metaphorically on our lives.

'Many of you, friends and family, have been fantastic. You're all great but to be honest, I wouldn't want to spend the rest of my life with any of you. There is only one person here I want to do that with, and that is Robert, undoubtedly my better half.'

And at that point I turned to him, seated behind me at the wedding table in his new blue Ozwald Boateng suit, flanked on both sides by his parents, and I said to him, in front of the 120 friends and family drinking champagne and now eating Lebanese baklava at Polhawn Fort on 16 October 1999, 'Robs, when I fell in love with you, it was the happiest day of my life, then when you proposed, that was the happiest day. Today, you have topped it all by marrying me and this is the happiest day of my life. Thank you.'

As the audience applauded, there is an image of Robert that I will remember for the rest of my life. Tears were streaming down his face and I saw a look that I don't remember ever seeing again in our entire thirteen years of marriage. It was a look of admiration and pride. And I thought then, as I may have thought later, that I may not be the tallest, skinniest girlfriend he has ever had, but I'll make sure I'm the funniest. Peter Gøtzsche's speech has finished, it's time for questions and I see Luke Montagu coming towards me with the microphone. Deep breaths as I stand up.

'I come here in two capacities, both as a filmmaker but more importantly as someone whose life was blighted by psychiatric drugs for a year. I know some of you here will be thinking only a year, and believe me there is not a day that goes by when I'm not grateful that it was indeed only a year.'

And so I go on, at breakneck speed, to tell my story. I want to get it all out: the psychotic incident, attacking myself with a knife, the cocktail of drugs, losing empathy and not being able to love my kids, and finally walking to St Charles Hospital a year later and asking to be admitted, racing to the finishing line, and concluding with my question: 'How can we get this message across, that the drugs don't work, they're no more effective than a placebo and they're dangerous?'

Even Peter Gøtzsche with his years of experience is impressed with how my story illustrates so perfectly everything that is harmful about psychiatric drugs. His answer acknowledges all of this, but doesn't actually give me an answer. And it's an answer I still haven't got by the end of the conference and actually I wonder if I will ever get it.

However, a man in the audience pipes up with something that people who have been around the subject for many years know better than me. He corrects me. 'The drugs *do* work,' he says. 'They're just not fit for purpose.' And this is an argument I will hear over and over again. That the emotional blunting they provide helps some people to temporarily get on with their lives. The counterargument is that this emotional blunting isn't actually helping people to deal with their problems any more than taking cocaine or drinking alcohol does. And in a large number of cases, the side effects of these drugs can be devastating. Peter Gøtzsche cites a study that shows 60 per cent of people taking antidepressants suffer sexual side effects. And he also mentions three recent cases of teenage boys who attempted suicide when they couldn't get an erection. And do antidepressants really help people get back to work?

Another speaker, Robert Whitaker, also an award-winning writer (*Anatomy of an Epidemic* 2011, *Mad in America*, 2010), cites a study showing that people claiming mental disability benefits have increased substantially since the introduction of antidepressants. The argument, therefore, of these experts gathered here is that they are ineffective in helping people with getting back to work, and helping with their relationships.

As the lunch break is announced, various people descend on me who have suffered similarly. The lunch is free, which gives us a great opportunity to indulge our favourite routine.

Tom says: 'Did you know the buffet is complimentary?'

'Yes,' I reply. 'It's just told me it likes my jacket.'

But I'm not really interested in the sandwiches in the conference room at Roehampton University, I'm nervous because I want to nab Luke Montagu in the lunch hour because we're heading off at two. Also, I'm conscious of being surrounded by people who have extraordinary stories to tell, and I want to make the most of the experience. I get into a chat with a woman called Sandra Breakspeare, who is involved with a charity concerned with the treatment of the mentally ill (chy-sawel-project.co.uk/). She tells me how her son took LSD more than twenty years ago and was admitted to hospital because he became psychotic. They gave him antipsychotic drugs – probably the same ones I was on. Of course these drugs make you go crazy, which has happened to him. That was twenty years ago, and he's been under section ever since – forced to take the drugs and subjected to ECT. Despite her efforts, she can't get him released from the secure unit where he's being held. My God, it reminds me of some of the people I met at the end of my six-week stint at St Charles, who had been there long term. No doubt they too had been fed a cocktail of drugs, which I now know may well be the cause rather than the cure of their madness.

Luke comes over. He looks hassled, but says he has ten minutes to knock off an interview. Great. We go out into the courtyard, and I ask him a bit about the impact drugs has had on his life, then the purpose of the conference. He gives me two excellent sound bites, one about himself, then another about how psychiatric drugs are more dangerous than illicit drugs. Fantastic.

Much as I'd like to stay, I cannot justify spending the rest of the day filming at the conference. Iain, the editor, has asked me to get some shots of me running and with the kids so we head to the river at Chiswick Mall, where I've arranged to meet the kids after school. I'd mentioned it to them the night before and told them we would meet and have an early supper at the Black Lion pub on Chiswick Mall.

As I get into my car and drive off, I log onto my emails and see that Caroline Scott has written a whole load of questions for me to answer. I decide to answer them over the phone and put it on loud speaker as we navigate through the traffic that is already gathering for the weekend exodus. The questions are pretty straightforward until, talking about my first visit to the psychiatrist when I was upset about selling the family home, she asks: 'So what would have helped instead of an antidepressant?'

I pause – the *Mail* isn't going to want to hear that there is no answer. They don't want to hear what Peter Gøtzsche has just said in his seminar that the alternative to antidepressants is no antidepressants. I'm not sure what to say.

'Nothing,' I say.

'What do you mean, nothing?' she says. She sounds a bit frustrated. 'What about a therapist, talking therapy, a chat with a friend?'

I had lots of friends; I was even seeing a therapist. I'm grappling around for something I can give her.

'A visit to an estate agent.'

She's not laughing and actually it's only a half joke: a visit to an estate agent would actually have been far more helpful than a pill in helping me to deal with the inexorable fact of selling Dundonald Road. It really would. It would have taken me into the world of reality and certainty, and far away from fear and uncertainty.

But Caroline isn't having any of it, and as we cross over Barnes Bridge, as I see the late afternoon sun hit the Thames, as I look at the blueness of the sky and contemplate the beauty of London as the seasons change into autumn, as I think of the scent of my children as I hug them in a few hours' time, I say something to her which I hope very much indeed she will put in her article.

'There's no magic pill,' I tell her. 'You have to face up to your problems.'

And as we hit Hammersmith, I pray that whatever else the article contains, she will include that quote.

Chapter 23

FALLING OUT WITH THE KIDS

As we unload the gear in the Black Lion pub car park, the recent rain showers stop and Chiswick Mall and the River Thames are bathed in warm, afternoon light. I try to remember not to drop the radio mike down the toilet at the Black Lion as I change out of my black dress and into my jogging gear. Again, doubts crowd in: what the hell am I doing? I've hired a crew to film me running. Have I gone completely mad?

Then I remember the words of the interview I'd done on film. Lily is asking me what it's like, coming off the drugs.

'I will never forget going for a run and looking around the river and looking at the beauty of nature and being moved by that, and I will never, ever forget looking in my children's eyes and being able to love them again.'

And standing there with Steve and Tom on that Friday afternoon in the warm afternoon light, with just an hour before I meet Lily and Oscar, I can remember very well what it was like two years ago when I came off those drugs. And soon I forget all about feeling ridiculous.

My Apple watch vibrates to tell me a text has come through. It's Oscar: he doesn't want to do the filming. OK, keep calm. I call him.

'Darling, don't worry, just come down to the river, it's just a few shots. Please don't make a fuss.'

But he's not having any of it.

'I don't want to do it, Rell. I'm too tired, I want to go home.'

Rising panic now; I've planned the day around the fact that we can get these shots with them here by the river. Then a text comes through from Lily: she doesn't want to do it either. Their friends from their school, which is just along the river, may see them.

Damn, why didn't they say this before?

They did, apparently.

What, did they?

'Yes,' Oscar says. 'They said it yesterday.'

OK, keep calm.

Oscar is dragging his feet as he arrives in front of the Black Lion. He grunts a 'hi' at Tom and Steve and sits down at one of the outside tables with his phone. Lily arrives shortly afterwards with an attitude and expression identical to Oscar's as she joins him at the pub table and adamantly refuses to be filmed.

'Come on, guys,' I say. 'Please, it's just a few shots, and then we can have a lovely dinner here and go home. It's our *journey*, remember: the three of us.'

'Mummy, I'm sorry, I'm tired,' says Lily. 'It's the end of the week.'

'Oscar, come on, just the two of us,' I say.

He shakes his head, saying, 'No, I refuse. My fuse is reed.'

Now I'm desperate. I'll do anything but I know that no amount of bribery, iPhones or any mechanical device will be able to wipe off the look of end-of-week exhaustion and annoyance from their faces.

It's my fault, they say. I didn't ask them if they'd be filmed, I just told them.

I don't often give up but the look on Lily and Oscar's face tells me that this is a lost cause. Tom and Steve shrug their shoulders sympathetically, and we decide to pack up and go, hopefully avoiding the traffic from the Rugby World Cup.

As we head off to the Hogarth Roundabout, Oscar breaks his silence to tell me he hates me. For once, the two of them are in agreement.

'You're the worst mother in the world,' Lily adds.

I'm so tired from the day's filming, I can't even gather the energy to come back with my usual riposte of: 'What about Rose West?' And anyway, they wouldn't find it funny, and actually right now I'm not finding *anything* funny. I've only got one more filming day, and I've no idea how I can fit another sequence of the kids and me into that. And I'm very, very tired right now, because I've been up since six, and all I can think of is that at least I won't have to do any cooking because of the Greek lamb stew that's in the fridge.

As we walk in the front door, I'm sure I can smell something… surely not?

Rocco has decided that that out of the 1,500 square metres that make up our house he will relieve himself on the designer cream sheepskin rug in the living room. As I'm wondering how the hell I'm going to extricate the excrement from the fibres of the single, most expensive purchase of the house, Lily's voice comes from the kitchen.

'Oh no, not stew!' she says.

I try to keep calm and focus on my task of removing the cat shit from the rug fibres with a disinfected cloth 'Fine, no problem,' I tell her.

Deep breaths. Christ, the smell is unbearable. I'm wondering if maybe the best thing might be to throw the rug away. But it cost an absolute fortune. The cat shit is just not shifting.

'What shall I have?' she replies.

More deep breaths. I'm wondering now if it would perhaps be kinder to put Rocco down. After all he is sixteen years old.

'I don't know, darling, anything you want,' I say through gritted teeth. 'Just help yourself.'

She opens the fridge.

'There's nothing at all in the fridge,' she says.

I tell myself to just count to three before answering. Stay calm.

'Lily, there *is*. I've spent over £100 on groceries!' I tell her.

'I don't like any of it…'

I'm now like a pressure cooker that explodes without warning. That's it.

I hurl the disinfected cloth, now stained with Rocco's cat shit, and the stainless steel bowl onto the floor.

'What do you mean there's no fucking food? The fucking fridge is full of fucking food! What the fuck do you think you're fucking talking about, tell the fucking refugees there's no fucking food in your fucking fridge when we've just had a fucking delivery from fucking Ocado costing a hundred fucking pounds!'

'I fucking hate you,' she replies. 'I'm not going to be in your fucking film and I'm fucking going to live with Daddy.'

'Great,' I reply. 'I'm going to order you a fucking Uber [taxi]. Right fucking now. You spoilt, ungrateful miserable fucking cow!'

'Well, you're a fucking terrible fucking mother too!'

I look at her, she looks at me, and we both start to giggle, first a bit, then a lot, and then uncontrollable laughter. We throw our arms around each other, and collapse onto the sofa, hugging each other, wiping tears of laughter and tiredness from each other's cheeks.

'I love you, Lily Newman.'

'I love you, Motherfucker.'

'Shall we order a fucking takeaway?'

'You fucking bet!'

Chapter 24

SATURDAY, 19 SEPTEMBER 2015

After the kids have done their homework, I've promised to take them to the newly refurbished Kensington Leisure Centre in North Kensington.

Their seven-year-old cousin is coming over. My friendship with his mum was one of the casualties of the break-up of my marriage, so I'm very happy when I get a call from her.

Lily and Oscar are delighted to have their blonde-haired cousin for the day. As we drive down Ladbroke Grove with their swimming kit in the back, I turn right at Lancaster Road then down St Marks Road in order to make a detour so I don't have to go down Cornwall Crescent.

Number 7 Cornwall Crescent is the basement flat where I moved to in April 2013, six months into my illness. I was there on my own, barely leaving the house and mainly only to buy cigarettes to fuel my 70-per-day habit. At night, I'd scuttle out to buy vodka from one of the all-night shops on Ladbroke

Grove, hurrying back and downing it with sleeping tablets to try and escape the inexorable and awful numbness that had invaded my mind and body. The children would rarely visit me. And when they did, they'd cry and want to leave.

'Rell, you're going the wrong way,' chimes Oscar, as I take a sharp right turn down Blenheim Crescent.

'No, this is the right way, darling. We can get there this way,' I say.

Oscar's in a good mood and seems to have forgiven me for yesterday. He's wheeling out all the other pet names he has for me: 'Metawi', 'La Souta', 'Screlex'… all of these inventions from I don't know where punctuate his conversation.

I feel guilty because even though I've got the kids, I've agreed to see Laurent tonight. He's a guy I met through OK Cupid, or OK Stupid as my friend calls it. He's a very good looking and charming Frenchman. We've had a few dates and decided we are just going to be friends but actually I'm secretly hoping for more.

A text came through on Thursday asking if I wanted to do something on the Saturday. Even though I'd read somewhere that you shouldn't accept a date for a Saturday night after Wednesday, I rationalised that Laurent isn't actually a date, he's a friend – isn't he?

I haven't had time to change out of the short denim skirt I've been wearing all day, and the tight top that Lily and I share. I'm careful not to spill any of the meatballs and spaghetti that I'm dishing up for the kids before I hurry out the door. I make them promise to tidy and clean the kitchen after I've gone.

'How are you going to leave it?' I ask.

'Immaculate,' they say.

Exactly.

We've arranged to meet at an Afghan restaurant in Kilburn. Laurent doesn't have any suggestions so I step in with an art-house documentary at the Tricycle and this local restaurant. I've decided I really must pay for him this time because he always insists on paying. And although this place is cheap, the food is fantastic.

Unusually he's late, so I decide to order some starters as his text comes through: 'Central London traffic was bad. Losing precious hugging time. '

Mmm, I think, as I contemplate the array of unfamiliar Afghan dishes. The idea of precious hugging time with Laurent fills me with a frisson of excitement. I've no idea what any of these starters are, so I ask the waiter to choose for me.

I remember I didn't have time to put on any make-up so I reach for a mirror from my handbag.

Damn, I probably look an absolutely sight, I think, as I spot that I have spilt some of the meatball sauce on my skirt. But before I get my mirror out, a plate of dumplings arrives on the table at the same time as Laurent.

As usual, he is impeccably dressed and after he's pecked me on the cheek, in a rare show of assertiveness he asks the waiter if we can move tables away from the air conditioning. I note that I like it very much when he takes the lead.

Very much indeed.

We've only forty-five minutes to eat dinner, and despite my protestations, once again he absolutely insists on paying. Laurent exudes affluence, always arriving and departing in an Uber, describing a world of private schools, nannies and foreign holidays. He lives in South Kensington and unusually his two small boys live with him. He's modest about his work but I know it involves computers and coding – he once told me he invented his first programme when he was fifteen.

The film at the Tricycle Cinema is called *Looking for Love* and it's a low-budget documentary about black people talking about sex, dating and the secrets of a long-term relationship. I'd chosen it as a last resort, because Laurent wasn't coming up with anything, and as I had the kids, I wanted something local. But as we settle into our seat in the half-empty cinema, I congratulate myself on my choice: a film about love, dating and relationships, sitting next to the guy who is right now my best romantic bet, now seems an inspired choice.

As the film starts, to my delight he timidly takes my hand in his. This is a definite and unequivocal progression in our two-month friendship. Never has this happened before. And it gets better. As the film unfolds, containing interviews and poetry, both moving and funny, from people all talking about love, Laurent starts first to stroke my hand, then my arm, and then he has his arm around me, caressing my hair. I'm transported by this rare and utterly delicious experience of male physical contact.

When did a man last hold me? Yes, I remember it was on the August Bank Holiday weekend. I'd migrated to West Hampstead, avoiding the carnival, and I'd been invited to a party by a girl I hardly knew from the Serpentine Swimming Club.

The discovery of this community of people swimming between 6 a.m. and 9.30 a.m. every day of the year in Hyde Park Lido was an important milestone in my post-divorce recovery. It meant that whenever I woke up and the emptiness of the house was too much to bear, I knew I could drive to the Lido in just twenty minutes. I knew that if the cold water of the lake didn't offer a panacea to my loneliness, the crowd of friendly faces, all taking their kit off in the communal changing room, making each other cups of tea, would. One of the new friends that I'd made sitting out in the early morning sunshine, having a post-swim breakfast in the Lido café was the girl who was having a party at Hampstead Mansions on a Saturday night.

I was determined to get there at 8 p.m. because I didn't want a late night. It was the first time I'd worn the red version of the triumvirate of strapless, figure-hugging American Apparel dresses that I'd bought. The voice on my phone told me I'd arrived at my destination, but after I'd parked my car, I couldn't see any sign of Hampstead Mansions. I was annoyed now because I was wearing high platform sandals in cherry red to match my dress and I knew I couldn't walk far.

As I walked up Hampstead High Street, I caught sight of a man in his mid-forties, coming out of a smart-looking house. When I asked him if he knew where Hampstead Mansions was, he replied in an Italian accent that he'd help me find it, but first he had to deliver pizzas to his ex-wife and children. We never found the party at Hampstead Mansions but we ended up in the pub on Holly Vale, exchanging stories of our failed marriages, of exes, of children, of love, life, disillusion and disappointment.

It came as a surprise at the end of the evening when he put his arms around me and pulled me towards him in that red dress. But then it always comes as a surprise to me if men find me attractive. As I've mentioned earlier, I was chubby as a child and it's as if my brain has a default factory setting to which it reverts, telling me I'm invisible to men. In the past I've spent hundreds, probably thousands of pounds, on therapists telling me the absolutely obvious, which was that this is no doubt a result of being brought up by a depressed father who didn't seem to notice me. Despite the fact these observations cost me on average £60 per hour, there hasn't been a single therapist able to offer a solution to my lack of confidence around men. And so, I was very surprised indeed when Antonio kissed me on the lips standing outside the Holly Bush pub in my red dress and cherry platform heels on that late summer Saturday night of the August Bank Holiday.

And very pleased too.

After that we spent a few evenings together. He cooked delicious Italian food for me, we went to a jazz concert in Highgate and we kissed on the Heath on a balmy summer evening. But it didn't go any further. I didn't feel he was the one for me, and that was a barrier to any further intimacy.

With Laurent I felt differently. And so as he caresses my forearm, and I caress his, and as his hands twirl my hair as he draws my head towards his shoulder, my mind goes on a flight of fancy, to a world where our caresses don't stop there in the middle row of the Tricycle Cinema. And my imagination is now leaping ahead at a pace I can't control, as we've now gone beyond the physical and we're in a world where our separate lives start to merge, where he comes to my house in Harlesden first as a visitor, then more frequently, and now I'm thinking how my friends and family would approve of this kind, gentle man with his good looks and charming manner, and most importantly of all, Lily and Oscar. Yes, at first they'd joke about his French accent, but they would undoubtedly like him, and now I'm wondering about his kids. What are his two small boys like? Do they too speak with French accents? Would they like me, and would they get on with Lily and Oscar?

Christ, what am I thinking, I tell myself that I really must focus on this film.

There are scenes from the carnival, poetry readings and general musings about love: what it is, and what it isn't, what it takes to make a good relationship. One moment I'm laughing, the next I'm moved, and often the subject of this film makes me reflect on my own life and as my mind drifts back to Polhawn Fort, I wonder if love was truly present on that day in October 1999.

The readings in the film remind me of the many readings I'd chosen for my family to read at the ceremony presided over by a registrar. One reading particularly stands out. My mother, then aged seventy-five, delivered a reading, which ends, 'Love is not about finding the right person, it's about being the right person.' I wonder now if that's the key, that somehow in all my efforts to gain love – by being thinner, cleverer, and funnier – that my focus was on being loved rather than on being loving. So maybe that was it. And I thought of a quote in a French film, and I can't remember the title, but I remember it had Gérard Depardieu in it, and I remember the soundtrack was a Schubert 'Impromptu' that is one of my favourite pieces to play on the piano. He leaves his wife for an ugly, frumpy woman, and when the stunning wife confronts the plain mistress and asks how on earth she could have got her husband, she replies quite simply: 'A loving woman will always find love.'

So, is that it, then? Is that all I have to do? Be more loving? And what will that look like, I think, as I make a conscious effort now to match almost exactly in tenderness the caresses that Laurent is landing on my arm.

The lights come up at the Tricycle. Laurent disentangles his arm from mine, and we walk to the car. There's no hint of the intimacy of the cinema as we walk in near silence, talking only occasionally about the film. Instead there's a polite distance as he says goodnight and pecks me on the cheek. His parting words and only reference to what had happened between us that night were: '*La chaleur humaine.*'

As I drive back through Kilburn, and hit Queen's Park at the road flanking our old house on Dundonald Road, my heart is heavy with disappointment. That was all it was to him – '*La chaleur humaine*', human warmth – a brief moment of platonic tenderness, two people coming close together for just an evening.

As I turn off Park Parade, into our street, Harlesden Mews, where Lily and Oscar will now be sleeping, I reflect.

La chaleur humaine. Maybe that's enough… for now.

Chapter 25

SUNDAY, 20 SEPTEMBER 2015

As my eyes open, I know I'm cross but I can't remember why.

Ah, yes, that's it – Laurent, I think, as I pick up my iPad to check the time. I'm cross because he didn't deliver what I secretly hoped for; because at the end of last night he didn't promise anything beyond a fleeting tenderness. After his abrupt goodnight on the pavement, I wanted to be sure so before I went to sleep, I sent him a text: 'Thanks for a lovely evening and lovely to be held in your arms.xx'. It's a clear invitation; my words are resonating with warmth, beckoning him to take us further. He replies: 'Sleep well xx.' And that's it, nothing else. I conclude he's deliberately put an invisible full stop there, a barrier to prevent us deepening our friendship into something more meaningful.

I'm disappointed and still cross as I put on my grey sheepskin slippers and head to the bathroom. And just as cross when I go upstairs to wake up Oscar at 7.30 a.m. and ask him if he wants to come swimming at the Serpentine. His sleepy eyes tell me before he does that he's going to stay in his snug warm bed, under the pale blue lambswool blanket and Egyptian goose down duvet I bought to replace the cheap IKEA acrylic ones we'd had at Dundonald Road. Lily, too, tells me apologetically that actually, she'd rather not.

And I'm still cross by the time I come down and make myself some coffee and grab a banana from the giant orange designer fruit bowl perched on the marbled kitchen surface. As I peel back the skin, I reflect that my anger is perhaps with myself: how come I have written this particular script with Laurent as the protagonist and me the helpless victim, waiting to be chosen by him? Would I choose him is surely the more pertinent question, I think as I bite into the banana, discarding it as the slightly tart taste tells me it's not ripe enough.

And actually, I'm not entirely sure I would, I think, tossing the half-eaten banana into the lime green and white food waste caddy sitting on the counter. Because for all Laurent's Gallic charm, for all his intelligence, good looks, manners, and general savoir-faire, for all of that, there is one thing he lacks, I think, as I tie up the overfull food compost bag: he doesn't really make me laugh. And it may well be that in his native tongue he's a comic genius. For all I know he may have his French friends eating out of his Gallic hand with his witty repartee and sparkling wit. But in English – which, is after all, the language he and I converse in – Laurent is not actually very funny, actually not funny at all. I wonder, as I take the caddy outside into the September air, whether indeed this is something I can live without. And I rather suspect, as I empty the plastic food bag into the compost bin and shut the lid, it's not.

This morning I've arranged to meet my friend Maria at the Serpentine at 8.30 a.m. I'm looking forward to meeting up with her. She is an old school friend and I'm hoping to bump into some new friends I have made recently by joining a group of swimmers from the Serpentine Swimming Club who go once a month on an evening swim up the River Thames. Sixty people accompanied by boats descend the steps just outside the Black Lion pub and swim the 1.5K up to Chiswick Island and back again. Then we all have supper together on the wooden pub tables flanking the Mall, the exact same place where we'd been filming the other day.

The first time I'd done this, I'd forgotten that I suffer from extremely bad circulation, so I'd gone into hypothermic shock once out of the water and was unable to stop shivering despite everyone offering me layers of clothing and hot drinks.

'It's because you're so thin,' they say.

'Not at all,' I tell them, 'I've been fat too and I still get cold.'

So this time I'd stretched the family budget to buy a short wetsuit, congratulating myself on finding a child's size on the Internet for £20 cheaper, which I just about managed to squeeze myself into.

As I turn off Bayswater Road and drive into the park, the thought of a girlie gossip with my friend over a cappuccino and slice of spelt cake at the Lido café is a welcome antidote to Laurent's indifference. Maria' s marriage has recently broken up and our friendship has got stronger recently as now I am able to help her along the same path I'd travelled, three years earlier. Taking in the view of other swimmers bobbing about, the joggers, the mums with their strollers, couples holding hands, people reading papers, others eating breakfast, the young, the old, the happy, the sad, the general medley of people who are out in Hyde Park that Sunday morning, I reflect on Laurent's parting words. And I think to myself that Laurent is not the only source of *la chaleur humaine*. Because it's right here, right now in glorious Technicolor.

After our swim, we sit with our breakfast on the terrace overlooking the lake, huddled in puffer jackets and wearing woolly hats to stem the further escape of body heat that began as earlier we plunged into the cold water. We begin the conversation with Maria's more pressing life drama, as she talks about the meetings with divorce lawyers, her teenage son's reaction, and whether they will have to sell the family home in Highgate. When she talks about her ex I cut her some slack as she launches into the usual rant that I've heard so many times when people are at the very beginning of their break-up. Their usual explanation for their divorce is their partner can't feel empathy, they explain, as if it's a rare medical condition. In Maria's case, her therapist has confirmed it. I nod, twiddling my hair, and remembering how I'd regaled friends with my discovery that Robert had a condition called Narcissistic Personality Disorder.

Maria is one of the few people who have told me she benefits from taking an antidepressant. She's been on venlafaxine (Effexor) for many years. I know about this drug because I was on it towards the end of my illness. And I remember very clearly that it was only when I came off the last remaining pill that I got back my sex drive, its disappearance being one of the many horrendous side effects of the drugs.

My mind goes back to the dark days of my illness, seeing the fountain pen of one of the doctors write the words 'female anorgasmia' on my notes, as if this was something that had come out of nowhere rather than a direct consequence of his poisons.

I'm curious about whether Maria's experience is the same. I've not discussed this with her before, but I'm going to throw it out there, not knowing where it will land. I'm surprised by her candour when she confides in me that she hasn't had an orgasm in ten years. Christ, ten years! I muse, wondering how that must have impacted on her marriage and actually, not just that. How could this woman with beauty, brains and wealth elect to take a pill that interferes so cruelly with her biology, preventing her from having one of life's most life-affirming experiences?

I'm trying very hard to be even-handed, and impartial.

'So, just explain to me how you think it helps,' I say.

'Well, it helps to stop me feeling,' she tells me.

'And?'

'I'm frightened without it I'd be swamped with emotions.'

For the second time that day I notice the swimmers, the joggers, the people reading papers, eating breakfast; the young, the old, the happy, the sad, and the medley of people here in Hyde Park.

But it's not the second time I've noticed the glazed look in Maria's eyes.

'Isn't that a bit like having a gastric bypass operation in case you enjoy food?' I say.

She laughs, and I like it when she does this, because she looks very pretty in the morning sun and there is a light in her eyes that I don't often see.

At this point, like a salesman faced with the chink of an opening door, I decide to take my chance.

'You don't need it, Maria. You can deal with any feelings that are thrown at you, I promise you,' I tell her.

And at this point, I can't stop myself from grasping her hand.

207

Her eyes tell me she doesn't believe me.

'How do you know that?' Her voice is shaky, and I try to cast my mind back three years ago to re-experience the hell that she is going through right now.

How can I tell her that what I'm about to tell her is more valuable than anything the string of professionals she sees can tell her? And not because I'm more intelligent or wiser, but because I've experienced a year of the most expensive mental health care in the UK and a fair share of NHS care too.

And in my year of £6,000-per-week private healthcare, not a single one of the psychiatrists, psychotherapists, psychoanalysts, CBT specialists, nurses or doctors was able to help because they didn't tell me what I now know with 100 per cent certainty to be the truth: 'Because you're a human being, and that's what human beings can do.'

And as I grip her hand, and look into her beautiful eyes, I feel a mixture of sadness and joy. As we clear away our trays, I gaze back at the lake where the early-morning swimmers are now getting out. The sun is higher in the sky, and the cafe is now preparing for lunch. The park is filling up with more faces: the young, the old, the happy, and the sad. I focus on the day ahead, wondering if Lily and Oscar have left the kitchen immaculate, as instructed, and I think of the moments of laugher and no doubt tears that lie ahead as our unplanned Sunday together unravels. And as I drive away, I very much hope that one day Maria will stop taking the venlafaxine.

I hope that very much indeed.

Chapter 26

MONDAY, 21 SEPTEMBER 2015

At 7.46 p.m. I get an email from Caroline Scott that sends waves of anxiety through me: the *Mail* have decided to run the piece tomorrow instead of the following Tuesday, which was the date she'd previously given me.

So it's actually happening. Definitely. In less than twelve hours, it will be coming out. Their lawyers haven't vetoed it on the grounds I'm deluded and depressed and have nothing better to do than spread bad news about antidepressants. And the doctors at the private hospital haven't managed to prevent it by telling them I'm a dangerous, knife-wielding lunatic.

But there's one problem: I'm thinking, should I be filming the kids and me getting the *Mail*? Should I? I don't know; I can't judge it. Is us sharing our story part of the unfolding narrative of the film? I don't know. Who can I ask?

I know, Steve – my cameraman friend who has been shooting the rest of the pilot.

THE PILL THAT STEALS LIVES

So I ring Steve and I explain: 'Should we get it, do you think?'

'Maybe,' he answers, 'might be nice.'

'I think we should. If we don't get it, we can't redo it, can we?'

'True.'

'Great, so, er, are you kind of available tomorrow morning? Yes, it does have to be early. Well, yes, pretty early. Before they go to school – 6.45 a.m.?'

The second and far greater problem is the kids: they're at Robert's. First, I ring Oscar.

'Darling, there's a chance, a small chance – well, actually, quite a big chance – that the *Mail* article may well come out tomorrow. If that were to be the case, can Steve and I film a tiny sequence of the three of us reading it before you go to school? It'll only take a few minutes. Remember what we all agreed, that it's our journey, didn't we? You do remember that, darling, don't you?'

'No chance,' he says. It's too early and he wants to go to school on the train with Daddy. And anyway, it's not a problem because we can re-enact it another time.

I sigh. How many times have I heard this argument from various contributors over the course of my twenty-five years as a film director? And I reckon I'll have no more luck explaining to my thirteen-year-old son than I have to anyone else that you simply cannot substitute drama for real life. Even if he was Ralph Fiennes, it's just not going to be the same. But he's not going to be swayed.

'Come on, darling, it's our journey. Remember?'

But he won't do it; he refuses – his fuse is reed. Even though Oscar's fuse is reed, he's also clearly chuffed: 'Exciting, isn't it, Metawi? Clever Rell!'

Damn, his words confirm my feeling that maybe we really should be filming with him.

As I ring Lily, my anxiety levels are rising.

'Hello, Mummy,' she says.

'Sweetie, I know this is probably asking rather a lot, but the *Mail* article is almost definitely coming out tomorrow, and it would be really, really great if Steve could film us getting the paper and reading it together. Remember what we said about it being our journey?'

I hold my breath.

She giggles before saying, 'Yes, that's great. I'd love to.'

At this I offer up a prayer of gratitude. It's not ideal, just having Lily, but it's OK – and way better than neither of them.

'OK, honey, brilliant! I'll text you where to meet. It will be around 7 a.m., OK? And then we'll go for breakfast after. And I promise I'll drive you to school.'

She sounds excited.

I feel a bit guilty because I haven't told Robert about the *Mail* and about the filming. But my reasoning is that it would only cause him angst. Things have been so bad at various points since my recovery that he wouldn't put it past me to badmouth him to a national newspaper. The truth was that I'd told the *Mail* how supportive he'd been but I felt it best to let him discover this once the article is out.

Then I ring Steve.

'It's not great, but it's not awful: we've got Lily,' I tell him triumphantly, as if I'd bagged an exclusive interview with a politician or a superstar celebrity rather than my fourteen-year-old daughter.

'Where are we going to do it,' he wants to know, 'your house?'

'I can't,' I tell him, 'not enough time to get them here and get them to school. How about we get a shot of us going into a newsagent close to Robert's, we buy the paper and just read it outside?'

I can tell he's not keen.

'Have you looked at the forecast?' he says. 'It's pouring with rain tomorrow. And at 7 a.m. the light's rubbish, and I'm not going to be able to film you with rain pouring down onto the camera.'

He's right, I think, as I jump into my car and drive to Chamberlayne Road, to recce the newsagent on the corner of Wrentham Avenue.

As I walk purposefully into Runners, I'm betting the Indian guy behind the counter won't recognise me. I couldn't look more different than the person I was two and a half years ago, who used to come here every day like a drug addict looking for a fix. Back then I was three stone heavier, dressed in baggy, unwashed clothes, almost certainly dribbling, and I would buy packets of sugared popcorn, Liquorice Allsorts, chewing gum, Diet Coke, chocolate Reese bars, sweets, biscuits, cakes, ice cream... You name it, mountains of it, that I'd take home and gorge in one sitting, much to the children's utter astonishment.

I'm right, I think, as I wander in, his gaze taking in the short skirt and Lily's tight American Apparel top. He has no idea I'm the same person even though I came here every single day. I flash him a smile that would have Oscar cringing with embarrassment.

'Stop it, Rell!' I can hear him hissing, but happily he's not here to witness my shameless flirtation with the man behind the counter as I ask if please could we film, just for a very short time in his shop tomorrow morning, just a tiny sequence of me and my daughter buying a newspaper.

'No problem,' he says.

I drive back home and now I'm beginning to feel excited.

Chapter 27

TUESDAY, 22 SEPTEMBER 2015

My insomnia is a much-discussed topic of conversation. For the last two years, I regularly wake at three, four or five in the morning and never sleep beyond six. Oscar's theory is that it's the array of electronic devices that litter the floor charging overnight beside my bed – the iPhone, the iPad, the new laptop, the recent addition of the Apple watch, not to mention on the other side of the room the TV, the Internet router, the Freeview box – all emitting a blue glow into the bedroom air.

During one of Oscar's investigations, he ascertained that when I wake, I log onto my emails, and even worse, onto Tinder and occasionally Happen too.

'Right, that's it, Rell!' he announced one day. 'I'm confiscating all of your devices.'

But even after Oscar has determinedly moved everything to recharge downstairs, I still wake up and even without the obvious distress of discovering there are no further matches on Tinder or Happen, I still can't get back to sleep.

On that Tuesday morning, when I wake at 2 a.m. after just two hours' sleep, nothing can stop me reaching for the Apple laptop lying beside my bed. I've no idea when the *Mail* is published online, but I wonder.

After returning home from Runners newsagents, doubts have crowded into my head before I drifted off into the lightest of sleeps. What if it all comes out wrong? A story is about to go out to millions of people in a national newspaper about how I became a knife-wielding maniac, followed by a dribbling emotionless zombie for a year. How do I know that Caroline Scott will have made it clear this was caused by the antidepressants? So when I wake at 2 a.m., I can't resist the temptation to find out the truth.

My computer whirs into action as I type in my password, and then click on *Daily Mail*. The headline reads: 'How Depression Pills Turned a High-flying Film-maker Into a Zombie Needing 24-hour Care'.[1] It's a sweet picture of the three of us on our cream sofa, flanked by patterned cushions, I think, as I click onto it.

But there's more at stake, I think, as I see that there is an entire full page devoted to our story. I read through it and as I do so, I breathe a huge sigh of relief. Caroline Scott has told our story brilliantly, her skills as both a tabloid and broadsheet journalist melding together to make a story that is touching, inspiring and most importantly, 100 per cent true. And on top of that, there's quotes from leading expert David Healy about how common my experience is, quotes from the children about losing their mum and thinking they'd never see me again, and finally, the article, which now goes onto another page, ends with a paragraph that, had I known where Caroline Scott lived, I would have gone to her house in South London right now in the early hours of the morning and thrown my arms around her in a hug of gratitude.

It ends: 'Katinka has become a passionate campaigner against SSRIs. "We all want to believe in a magic pill. We want to think that if the going gets really tough there's something that will make us better," she says. "But there really isn't – I needed to face my problems and work them out. Having paid the price, I want to tell people, it isn't worth taking the risk."'

And as I lie on my bed at three in the morning, my eyes mist up with emotion. The story is out. And I think back to the letter I received from the main doctor in response to my complaint. How he claimed I'd got it all wrong, that it was nothing to do with his drugs; it was a coincidence I'd got better. I'd been ill, he insisted, with *psychotic* depression for a year and should be grateful it has just magically disappeared. I think also of the friends and maybe even members of my family who still don't know the full facts, and that my life was stolen for a year, not by a mysterious illness but by a cocktail of drugs so lethal, I would have arguably done better to have mainlined heroin for a year.

I don't mind that I know I won't get back to sleep. And oddly, I don't bother to log onto Tinder as I usually would. So the tears start streaming down my cheeks, because I feel so very, very grateful. Grateful not just to have my life back after a year, but to feel heard, to feel believed, not just by a few, but also by many. I know that tomorrow, there will be people out there reading my story, who may just pause for a moment before they take a pill so powerful it can devastate lives.

And though the house is empty, though it's just my black cat Rocco and me in the large superking double bed, and though it's three in the morning and there is no chance I will get back to sleep, somehow I don't feel lonely at all.

Chapter 28

STILL TUESDAY, 22 SEPTEMBER 2015

It's 5.45 a.m. when I jump into the shower and I've hardly slept a wink all night.

It's raining and my stomach is gnawing with anxiety about filming. I'm furious with myself for messing things up. Why didn't I predict the *Daily Mail* was running the story this week? I could have made sure the kids were staying with me. We could be filming a lovely breakfast scene of the kids and me reading the *Daily Mail* at the breakfast bar in my kitchen, perched on the multi-coloured swivelling designer kitchen stools, like a Ready Brek commercial, with me wandering around like Nigella, serving them homemade bread and granola. Bugger! It's a disaster. We're filming outside a newsagent on the Chamberlayne Road. Oscar won't be filmed at all, and I bet Lily will cancel because of the rain. And Steve will be worried his camera is getting wet.

As the windscreen wipers fight the rain off on my journey

down Park Parade I'm hit by a clarity of thought unusual for this time of the morning. I reflect that the art of documentary making is in some ways identical to the art of living. That if you dwell on what wasn't, you miss what is. That the more I think about the idyllic breakfast scene we could have had, the less likely I am to capture the reality of what is actually unravelling before me right now.

I accelerate through Harlesden and pass by the plusher houses in All Souls Avenue. My heart quickens with excitement as I begin to appreciate the preciousness of this moment, that right now the *Daily Mail* is hitting the newsagent shelves across the country, that there is a full-page article of our story on page 37, and that I have two young children who will be excited to see it. And even if I never use the sequence, that I only have a 45-minute window to capture that moment on camera before Lily goes to school.

At 6.45 a.m., I greet Steve outside Runners newsagents, and tell him I'm going to pick up Lily. If I offer to collect her in the car, I think, she's more likely to come. On the way, I have an idea. There's a café, Zest, on the Chamberlayne Road, and I've met the owners at my friend's wedding reception. Don't they open at seven? I park on the double yellow line outside, put the hazard warning lights on and leap out. Do they remember me – you know, Juliette's friend, her wedding? Anyway, I know it's short notice, but if I bring my kids here for breakfast in a minute, please, please can we film it? Yes, they say.

Phew!

I text Lily. I'm outside the house. It's all looking good. Damn, I think. I really want Oscar too. It's our bloody journey, the three of us. Doesn't he realise that? I've texted him again this morning, but no, he's adamant: he doesn't want to be late for school. Christ, why is he such a Goody Two-Shoes?

Lily comes out in her school uniform and we zoom up to the newsagent. OK, outside Runners. Radio mike on, all set. Breathe deeply. OK, Lily, this is it: be calm, just don't look at the camera. Otherwise just be yourself. So, in we go, mother and daughter, Lily and me.

We buy the *Mail* and go outside to read it. I pause as Lily takes it in. She reads it, she giggles and then she throws her arms around me. And I hug her. And she hugs me. And I hug her tighter still. And she hugs me tighter still. And I can sense that unless we stop hugging each other, we will both start crying on the pavement in the drizzling rain outside the newsagent on Chamberlayne Road. Because actually this is a very important moment: for her more than me. And that's because the full-page article on page 37 has a significance way beyond the novelty of seeing a photo of us three in a national newspaper. And I'm thinking what it must have been like for Lily during that year I was stolen from her. The whispers of her school friends about the dribbling wreck her mother had become. Her schoolteachers gently pulling her to one side – 'We know things are difficult at home, Lily. Is there anything we can do?' The doctors' insistence that I had a chemical imbalance. Would she then deduce that if I had it, surely so might she? I can now picture her face midway through my illness as we sat in the kitchen, or at least everyone else was sitting while I paced around from the medication like a caged animal. It's after yet another meeting with the hospital doctors. And she's asking my sister, 'Please tell me, Aunty Amy, please tell me, when will Mummy get better?' And my sister, desperately trying to offer words of reassurance;

desperately trying to hide the fact she really doesn't know when or even if I'll ever get better from this mysterious illness that the most expensive healthcare in the country can't seem to cure.

I understand very much why Lily is tearful at seeing our story in the *Daily Mail* today. Because despite the conversations we've had, despite my reassurances that I'll never, ever get ill again, despite the endless books and films we've devoured on the subject, despite all that I know that seeing our story in black and white in a national newspaper will prove to her beyond doubt something that is vitally important to her: that her mum wasn't nuts, but that the madness lies somewhere else.

Right now I don't give a stuff whether we ever use this sequence in the film or indeed if the film ever gets made. All I care about is that I have to get hold of Oscar to share this very special moment with him too. I ring him and suggest breakfast at Zest. We rush down there to meet him.

Two minutes later, Oscar arrives in his school uniform. And the three of us pore over the article in Zest, punctuated by Oscar's 'Ah, Rell!' Then he throws his arms around my neck and squeezes me very hard. And I squeeze him back. And he squeezes me harder. And I squeeze him harder still. And we pour out onto the street, and Oscar insists on going to school by train so he won't be late, and Lily and I speed off in the car to school in the drizzle on the Chamberlayne Road.

After I've dropped Lily off at school, my head starts to become dizzy with tiredness. The fact I've only had about two hours' sleep is catching up on me. Having a story go out in the national press is a bit like Christmas, I think, as the emails come through, and the Facebook messages from people I haven't heard from in ages.

THE PILL THAT STEALS LIVES

The most important people, of course, are my family and I've not been quite sure how they will react to me splashing this story out there so publicly. So I'm relieved when I get emails from my two brothers saying they thought it was good.

By midday, I'm worried because I haven't heard from my sister, Amy. I know she never fully accepted that the drugs were the cause of my illness.

Brian from AntiDepAware gets in touch and I'm moved when he says: 'No one will listen to me. I'm just some guy whose son died, who nobody believes. But people will listen to you.' I reflect that it's only been since the journalist Caroline Scott visited us a couple of weeks ago that people have listened and believed me.

There is a quote in the article from a professor saying: 'There's nothing in the literature that suggests SSRIs can make you suicidal.'

Really? In the States, by law drug companies have to put on the drug packages that antidepressant drugs make children suicidal and so it's on there in a black box label. Or doesn't that count? And I'm wondering what literature Professor Allan Young MB, ChB, MPhil, PhD, FRCPsych, FRCPC, who is Chair of Mood Disorders at King's College, London, has read. I log onto his website and see he has a lot of links with the pharmaceutical industry. It says: 'Paid lectures and advisory boards for all major pharmaceutical companies with drugs used in affective and related disorders'. Even more puzzling then that he hasn't read a single piece of literature that SSRIs can make you suicidal, particularly as it's in the package inserts of the drugs he purports to be an expert on.[1]

Finally, mid-afternoon, comes the phone call I've been wishing for all day: it's my sister. Nervously, I answer her call.

She explains it's taken her so long to call because I sent the article to the wrong email. But what did she think of it? I pause, not knowing what to expect. She liked it, she says. She liked it a lot.

We talk more on this subject than we ever have. And I remember how my sister, with her full-on job as a partner in a law firm, with her own son, who was ill at the time, how she came to visit me every single night after work at the hospital. How she took weeks off work to nurse me at home, how she must have spent countless hours and sleepless nights worrying if her baby sister would ever get better.

'They were going to give you ECT, you know,' she tells me halfway through our conversation.

My blood chills at the thought of the doctors calmly expatiating on the benefits of electroconvulsive therapy to my attentive family, all desperate for a solution to jolt me out of the world I'd disappeared into.

There's a feeling that comes over me, that I thought I'd put away some time ago, but hearing my sister tonight, I note its presence mounting inside me and settling somewhere around my neck. An image of the doctor in charge of my treatment driving around in his aquamarine Jaguar flashes into my mind.

We wind down our conversation with a final thought that comes unexpectedly to me. 'Non would be very proud today, wouldn't she?' I say, referring to our mum, who we called 'Nonnie'. 'Imagine, an article in her favourite paper, the *Daily Mail*!'

My sister chuckles with a laugh that takes me all the way back to our childhood. For the second time in twenty-four hours, there are tears in my eyes.

My memory has cleverly hidden away in the furthest recesses of my mind the thought that I never got a chance to say goodbye to my mum. Her last memory of me would be of a dribbling wreck, someone almost unrecognisable as the daughter she had brought up and loved. We shared so much, Mum and me. Like me, she was a journalist and a single mum. A love of words and a sense of the ridiculous were the currency of our very special relationship. I wonder what it was like for her to see me rendered speechless and emotionless by these doctors' poisons. How she must have missed our laughs, our private brand of repartee, the banter that had danced through our lives, which suddenly and inexplicably stopped in her final year. I reflect that the night she died, aged eighty-nine, she knew the daughter she adored was incarcerated as a mental patient in St Charles Hospital.

As the day draws to a close, I think of my mum, Nonnie, who lost her daughter for her last year of life. I think of my siblings and all the time they took off work to nurse me. I think of Lily and Oscar, who thought they'd lost their mum. I think of Brian from AntiDepAware and David Carmichael, who lost their sons. I think of Luke Montagu with his tinnitus and ongoing side effects and his young family. I think of Maria and her glazed eyes. And I think of the doctor who treated me with his look of genuine concern and his smart fountain pen.

And I think to myself that for me this really isn't the end of a chapter, this is just the beginning of something much, much bigger.

Chapter 29

SATURDAY, 3 OCTOBER 2015

It's been nearly two weeks since the *Daily Mail* article came out.

There are posts that are published online in response to the article. There are people who say the article is irresponsible because their lives have been saved by antidepressants. Then there are others praising the article, who say their lives have been destroyed by antidepressants. They are in roughly equal numbers though slightly more horror stories than lives saved.

Here are some horror stories that emerged from the posts. A twenty-nine-year-old left with permanent brain damage from being on venlafaxine for a year after a grief-related breakdown. A woman whose son now needs a liver transplant from being wrongly prescribed SSRIs. Another woman whose mum became a zombie like me but could no longer take it and drove her car into a wall, killing herself earlier that year.

THE PILL THAT STEALS LIVES

Here are the lives saved. A woman from Cornwall who says antidepressants are a godsend to many, including herself. And a woman from Canada: 'SSRIs have turned my life around. Before them I was a mess of anxiety and life was almost too hard to live. When used properly, these drugs do save lives.'

Then someone else: 'My Antidepressant saved me TOGETHER WITH COUNSELLING – it's taken ONE YEAR but I am back with the human race + functioning again. I feel very sorry for this lady BUT as others have pointed out – IT IS A MISLEADING, NON-STORY.'

The best response, however, was from someone from Canterbury, who was referring to the fact there was an advert for sausages on the same page as the article. 'The Sainsbury's sausages sound like a good deal, but are they any good for the treatment of depression? I think they probably are, as you can't beat a good plate of bangers and mash to cheer you up, especially when it's cold and wet outside.'

So there you have it. Obviously this is not a clinical trial, but interesting to see the response. So do SSRIs do more harm than good, as Luke Montagu and the critical psychiatrists claim? Or do they do more good than harm, as the doctors at the private hospital I was at and most of our medical profession will say? Or might a good old-fashioned plate of sausages be as good a treatment for depression if prescribed by a proper doctor, as would be suggested by the placebo studies, which show that if patients are told by a medical professional that something will make them better then it works?

Whatever the truth, I feel that people should be given more information about these pills. What I will say is to quote a leading expert: there is plenty of evidence to suggest that antidepressants work in the short term for some people, but little to suggest they work in the long term. And I'd like people to know more before they sign up to take them.

A piece of paper inside a pill packet which says somewhere in small print that in 1 in 1,000 cases may suffer violence and hallucinations is insufficient. These are my suggestions, which I think should be in large print on the outside of the box.

> 'This pill has caused healthy people with no mental illness to be seized with an inexplicable desire to harm themselves.'
>
> 'Courts have ruled people have killed their own children, best friends and partners because of these pills.'

And then something to address the more common side effects:

> 'You may lose your sex drive on these pills. And it may never return.'

And this is the truth. Expert David Healy has patients whose 'ability to make love', I think was the way he delicately put it, has never returned.

And finally, because I don't want people to think I'm too one-sided, something balanced.

> 'While these pills may make you feel good in the short term, long-term use can cause irreversible brain damage. And you may not be able to come off them.'

I'm not the only person who thinks there should be clearer

warnings on these pills. Professor Tim Kendall of NCCMH told me he'd even go as far as to have a flashing blue warning light on them to warn people under thirty.

Since 2004, in the USA, the US Food and Drug Administration (FDA) has required the pharmaceutical industry to put a black box warning on all their antidepressants. This sounds more impressive than it is. It's actually a warning with a black box border on the package inserts, not even on the box. However, every SSRI in the US carries this black box warning that the pills may result in increased suicidal tendencies in children, adolescents and young adults aged eighteen to twenty-four. Clearly there must be absolutely no danger once you have reached your twenty-fifth birthday despite the fact there have been countless cases and settlements to suggest otherwise.

This warning came about after a group of parents of suicidal kids and mental health professionals lobbied the FDA. The hearing in 2004 was televised[1] and is possibly one of the most distressing things I have ever seen in my life. It begins with a man saying: 'I'd like to introduce you to my daughter, Caitlin Elizabeth McIntyre. It's actually only a two-dimensional image of her, but it's all I have. She died age twelve, eight weeks after being put on Paxil and Zoloft.'

Then there is a forty-one-year old woman, Pamela Wild, with a deformed face, who took an antidepressant because she was shy. She put a Smith & Wesson revolver to her head and blew half her face off. She says: 'In going through withdrawal from Paxil, I lost all ability to cope and reason and without realizing it, became suicidal. I suffered from sleeplessness, night sweats, light and sound sensitivity, irritability, and dizziness. I was in a constant state of terrible anxiety and felt as though the only thing holding me together was my skin. I couldn't understand why others weren't seeing things my way, as though I was speaking in another language. I was told by my therapist that I had drifted into a fantasyland.'

Then more and more similar cases… It is, quite frankly, staggering and even more staggering that it took a full thirteen years until the FDA put a black box warning on its pills.

And staggering too that our own Medicines and Healthcare Products Regulatory Agency (MHRA, the UK government's medicines and healthcare products regulatory authority, who license our pills) has not followed suit. Critics have pointed out that the MHRA (like the FDA) is funded not by the taxpayer, but by the pharmaceutical industry. Therefore it takes fees from those it regulates. The chairman of the MHRA is Dr Ian Hudson, former head of Global Safety for Glaxo (GSK). In 2000, he defended the company in the trial involving the death of Donald Schell, the guy who turned a gun on himself, his wife, daughter and granddaughter forty-eight hours after taking Seroxat (paroxetine), whose trials with kids showed that eleven became suicidal on the Seroxat and only one on the comparator. This is the outcome that Glaxo touted, sold as 'safe and effective'.

I've read the transcript of this trial and it seems Dr Hudson's department had a file about paroxetine called 'The Aggression Study'. The clue is in the name, but to confirm any doubts, it's an internal investigation, which uncovers how Seroxat (or Paxil) can make its users violent. Strangely, Dr Hudson kept this report to himself and his department at Glaxo. This fact was important in winning the surviving relative, Tim Tobin, a $6.5 million dollar settlement and Glaxo was subsequently fined for withholding information.

So yes, that's the very same Dr Ian Hudson who is now chairman of the MHRA, the UK agency that protects and informs the general public. Now it's possible when he joined the MHRA as director of licensing in 2001 he turned over a new leaf. Maybe he had a 'Road to Damascus' conversion, eschewing his company Mercedes for an Oyster card to get to his new job in Belgravia. From now on he's going to tear up invitations to pharma Christmas parties, forget the champagne in a Royal Opera House box, listening to *Cosi Fan Tutte*. He no longer cares about the corporate Centre Court Wimbledon tickets. From now on he's going to focus on defending truth and justice and making sure the public is properly informed about the drugs he once used to sell.

Sadly, the evidence doesn't seem to support this. After Dr Hudson joined the MHRA, there was a four-year investigation into why GSK had knowingly withheld safety data regarding children taking Seroxat. And the MHRA decided to let GSK off the hook. Yes, they did: they got off scot-free, with no criminal investigation. It was dropped. Glaxo didn't fare so well in the US, though. They received a fine of $3 billion in 2012 for withholding information on Seroxat, unlawfully promoting it for the under-eighteens and writing a misleading article about its benefits. But here, in the UK, Ian Hudson and his colleagues decided to let it go. The good news is that as this book goes to press a worldwide investigation is being launched.

Recently I rang the MHRA to get a list of all the suicides, homicides and adverse reactions. I knew the results would be disappointing, and they were: 30 homicides from all SSRIs. And suicides – citalopram: 67; escitalopram (the drug I was on): 18; Prozac: 106; fluvoxamine: 5; paroxetine (Seroxat): 65;

sertraline (Zoloft): 42. I also asked them about olanzapine, which is an antipsychotic I was on – 26.

But I don't believe these figures, and here's why.

Adverse drug reactions come to the MHRA via a yellow-card reporting system that doctors are supposed to get the patient to fill out. I know this doesn't happen. Most people won't have even heard of the yellow-card reporting system. When I was better, I contacted the psychiatrist who gave me the pill that made me go psychotic. He conceded reluctantly that as the symptoms went away, it must have been the pill. You might expect, at this point, that he might say, 'Please don't hang up before you give me your address so I can courier round right now a very important card. It's yellow. Please fill it in immediately and take it round to the MHRA. Ian Hudson or one of his colleagues will be waiting.'

Well, he didn't.

And when I finally confronted one of the doctors at the private hospital with a long letter of complaint, he steadfastly maintained his position. The last sentence of his letter of reply: 'You have been very ill for a year with *psychotic* depression' (my italics, not his).

Still no mention of a yellow card.

And when I left St Charles Hospital, after my mysterious symptoms disappeared, no one stopped me before I left. No, there wasn't a single person who said, 'Excuse me, Mrs Newman. You must be in a bit of a hurry to get the hell out of here, away from the lunatics, who have kept you awake at night with their screams, nicked your iPad and various other belongings. I'm sure you can't wait to see your kids who lost you for a year, but there is a very important card we would like you to fill out. And it's yellow. Would you mind?'

No, none of that happened. And over the course of the next two years I have heard countless other tales of minor and major drug reactions that will not be included in their press officer SarahRose Burke's emailed statistics to me. Both in the UK and in the US, research shows that only 1–10 per cent of cases are reported. For the most part, people simply do not realise that many suicides are drug-related.

An example is the sister of one of the most impressive people I've met. His name is Richard McCann; and Peter Sutcliffe, the Yorkshire Ripper, murdered his mum, a prostitute. He and his siblings woke up one morning in 1975 to find their mum hadn't come home. Her body was found shortly afterwards. Naturally, they were emotionally scarred beyond measure by this appalling event that terminated their childhoods; Richard was just five. However, after a brief period of trying to lose himself in drugs and crime, he got his act together and has written a number of bestsellers and now runs a successful motivational speaking company. But his sister, Sonia, turned to drink and antidepressants. She hanged herself at thirty-nine.

I got to know Richard through making a film about Peter Sutcliffe. When I mentioned what I knew about antidepressants he went very quiet. Then he told me how Sonia had been hallucinating before she killed herself. She'd texted her sister just before to say she thought there were crocodiles in the room. This was the first time Richard had realised his sister's death might be linked to the pills she was on.

Another example is that of fifteen-year-old-George Werb who 'calmly and deliberately' walked in front of a train at Seaton Junction, near Honiton, on 28 June 2013, a day after being released from The Priory Hospital, Southampton. The press reports focus the blame on the consultant who allowed George to go home, and on the fact that the hospital and Solent NHS Trust have now jointly admitted liability. Talking to George's mum Joanne convinces me the other culprit is the medication he was on, which is only given a tiny mention in press reports.

George suffered depression and believed he had various diseases from the age of thirteen. His parents became increasingly worried and despite going to various professionals, they weren't offered therapy for him. Eventually he saw a consultant who prescribed the anti-psychotic risperidone just a month before his death. As soon as this happened he started talking of suicide. He had such a bad reaction, he took himself off it after three tablets. But then, when he was taken to The Priory in Southampton in May 2013, he was put on the antipsychotic olanzapine and two days before his death, Prozac was added to that. During his last ward meeting with the consultant, George asked, as he had on many occasions, if the olanzapine could be reduced as it was affecting him. The doctor asked him if he would be happy starting an SSRI antidepressant and George tried to negotiate a reduction in olanzapine in return for starting Prozac. The same day George made a second case for olanzapine to be reduced but as the consultant wrote in his report to the coroner, 'I tried to persuade him that olanzapine was the answer to his problems not the cause'. It seemed that George knew the medication was poisoning him. He wrote about this in a three-page letter that was left under his bed before he took himself away that morning. His parents have shown extraordinary courage in allowing me to quote a couple of sentences from his last words because they feel so strongly about stopping this happening to others.

'I feel completely brain fried'; '20 mg was too much for me and someone should have protected me from myself'; 'By the way this is the only time in my life I ever strongly felt that suicide was the only option'. He went on to write: 'Thank you Mum and Dad for an awesome 15 years.'

There is more that convinces me that George Werb was suffering the deadly side effects of these pills when he chose to end his tragically young life. When I talk to Joanne about how George was when she picked him up from the hospital the day before he died, she describes wide, staring, expressionless eyes and he couldn't sit still. Yes, pacing up and down, the side effect that occurs in every single case I know of people who have killed themselves or others. Akathisia. As I contemplate my weekend with my kids around the same age as George would have been, my words of sympathy to Joanne Werb seem utterly futile and empty in the face of her appalling loss.

The strange thing in all of this is that I know too well from my experience and many other similar tales, that even psychiatrists and consultants who are at the top level of their profession, simply do not know how to spot what Lily and Oscar could spot a mile off. Wide staring eyes, akathisia, continuous violently suicidal thoughts – these are signs that people are in acute drug toxicity and suffering an adverse drug reaction.

All this goes through my head as I prepare to go for breakfast with a guy who has contacted me from the *Telegraph* dating website. He's an oncologist called Max and he lives in Notting Hill. Oscar has let me go, as long as I promise to be back at 11 a.m. He casts a disapproving look at me: my preoccupation with the film has meant I've let my appearance go. He's already pointed out grey roots and insisted on a visit to Justin. Now he's noticed the red shellac on my nails is coming off.

'Not good, Rell,' he says, shaking his head as I rush out, wishing I'd had time to put on more make-up.

It's the first time I've been out for ages, I think, as I drive down Ladbroke Grove towards Electric House, a members' club on Portobello Road. As soon as he arrives, I regret the fact I didn't make more of an effort. He's smart and sexy. On top of that, he's kind. Of course he would be. He's an oncologist, for God's sake – he saves people's lives from cancer. Why didn't I think of that? Damn, I think, as I clench my hands to hide my chipped nails, and wonder if I can get to the loo to put on some lipstick.

It doesn't take long for the subject to turn to my film. He's a medic, so he's interested. He deals with patients with cancer and prescribes antidepressants all the time. Does it help them? 'God, yes,' he says, 'especially Prozac.'

The waiter hovers with his pen poised. Are we ready?

'Eggs Benedict, please,' I murmur.

I pause; would that be the same Prozac that was refused a licence in 1984 by the German government because there wasn't enough evidence to say it worked? And the drug that Luke Montagu first took and has now left him with tinnitus and burning sensations? Oh yes, and the drug David Crespi took and then killed his twins?

Meanwhile Max is tossing up between the full English or the poached eggs and avocado. As I contemplate his tanned face and toned physique, my mind has wandered off through the doors of the Electric, onto Portobello Road, and now it's heading off right to Chepstow Crescent, where he has told me he has a house with a cinema in the basement. I'm being held in his arms, he's telling me how clever I am, and as he caresses my hair he's gently explaining to me the stuff I don't understand about the science of serotonin as he pours me a glass of chilled Sauvignon Blanc. He promises me that even if we don't see completely eye-to-eye on SSRIs, whatever happens he's going to stand by me in my fight against big pharma. And would I like to go away with him for a mini break to Babington House and if that goes well, then Christmas at the Four Seasons in Bali?

As I stir my cappuccino slowly, the pattern on top of the frothy milk now disappears. I can't stop the words coming out. What about the fact that Eli Lilly settled cases amounting to $50 million because of Prozac-related murders and suicides in 2000?[3] Those cases are the exception. Most benefit, he insists. So how do you know it's not the placebo effect? Doesn't he know about the hidden trials? What about the fact it has sexual side effects?

His patients would tell him if they couldn't get a hard on, he's sure.

'Really,' I say?

'Definitely.' They trust him so well, 'the guys even tell me if their wives complain their blow jobs taste different.'

'Really?'

This guy must have a hell of a rapport with his patients.

He tells me he's been on drug company trials. They wouldn't skew them, he would know. At this point in my head I've got up and left the cinema in Chepstow Crescent and Max and I are over: it's curtains.

I'm now thinking of Ben Goldacre's brilliant exposé in

his book, *Bad Science*.[4] Here are just a few tricks: Ignore the dropouts because they will make your drug look bad. Report anything that makes your drug look good and ignore anything that makes it look bad. If the difference between your drug and placebo becomes significant four and half months into a six-month trial, then stop the trial immediately and start writing up the results. Don't ask about annoying side effects. So, one 3,000-subject review on SSRIs didn't list sexual side effects on its 23-item side-effect table.

Do not ask about akathisia unless you see it in front of you.

One final, very sneaky one is to give a very high dose of the competing drug so patients report worse side effects. They did that with risperidone and olanzapine trials presented for licensing, the two drugs where nearly 1 per cent died in clinical trials after half the participants had dropped out. Where are we told of these dropouts and deaths? We're not.[5]

The waiter clears away the plates and brings the bill. Our body language tells a thousand tales as I sit cross-armed as Max politely pays, avoiding my gaze, and makes his excuses.

As I turn the key in the lock, Oscar rushes down the stairs and clocks my disappointed face. He raises his eyebrows in an 'I-told-you-so' kind of way (he still thinks it's the chipped nails). I suspect the more likely explanation is that clever medics don't like smart-arse women who think they're a medical expert just because they've read a few books and been in a couple of loony bins for a year.

Lily is at Westfield, shopping with her friends so Oscar and I decide to go for a bike ride. Without his sister, he's all affection. His new catchphrase, 'A hug is in urgent need of transferral', as he throws himself at me.

THE PILL THAT STEALS LIVES

We whizz along the Regent's Canal towpath, the wheels of our bikes kicking up autumn leaves.

'I don't just like you, Grout, I *love* you!' shouts Oscar.

And as we scoot up the ramp from the canal and I see Regent's Park, now bathed in a golden afternoon light, I don't mind at all that I'm not being held in Max's arms in his private cinema in Chepstow Crescent.

Chapter 30

SUNDAY, 4 OCTOBER 2015

Today, Iain has agreed to come round so we can get on with editing the rushes from the conference and the filming I've done with the kids. By the end of the day I feel disillusioned: it just looks like a middle-class whinge. Why would anyone care that my life was stolen for a year because I was foolish enough not to look at the side effects of a pill? It's not helped by the fact it was a private hospital, and our Harlesden house looks posh. Of course the shots of the designer-looking kitchen don't reveal that there are drug dealers outside and people trying to break in. I voice my concerns to Iain and joke that maybe I should rename it as 'The Year That Ocado Didn't Deliver'. He laughs it off politely but I can tell he agrees.

Iain goes off in the afternoon to watch the rugby and I'm beginning to question everything. Why did I start this in the first place?

It's Sunday night and I've no plans. My head has been

so full of the antidepressant stuff I haven't bothered with anything. Laurent has been in touch but only briefly and only suggesting lunch. I feel deflated by this obvious demotion. The Internet dating has dried up because I haven't bothered to log on. My Tinder account is untouched and the only new contact I've had is a man from Guardian Soulmates with the username Basilherb.

I'm thinking of heading down to the off-licence to buy a bottle of wine; I'm looking for numbness. I want to blot out this horrible sense of failure, wasted effort, feeling faintly ridiculous and aching loneliness. But I decide not to. Instead I remember the lesson I've learnt: listen to your feelings, your thoughts, your anxieties, and your doubts. Don't drown them, I think, although right now the idea is rather tempting. I resist.

Why did I ever think my story was important? Why? Think back. There is a film I've been meaning to watch, a documentary, about a twelve-year-old boy, Christopher Pittman, from South Carolina, who murdered his grandparents and set fire to their house.[1] The parents have always argued that it was Zoloft (sertraline, marketed as Lustral in the UK) that was the real killer.

I have a bath, get into bed and log onto my laptop. I'm mesmerised by this film, made ten years earlier, as the parents explain how much Christopher loved his grandparents.[2] They explain how he became anxious when his doctor prescribed Zoloft. As so often happens, the doctor didn't realise Christopher was reacting to the drug and he doubled the dose. They were at church – he couldn't sit still and was complaining that the drug made his skin feel like it was crawling. Of course this was akathisia, a sign of drug toxicity.

The parents explain how, after shot-gunning his grand-parents and setting fire to the house, Christopher is found in the woods, talking incoherently. The jury agrees the drug did all this to him but nevertheless end up having to find a twelve-year-old child guilty because South Carolina law doesn't recognise the role a drug can play in a homicide – and he is now spending thirty years behind bars.

Christopher Pittman doesn't come across that well. I can imagine that his monosyllabic style wouldn't have swayed the jury. But at the time of the trial he's about the same age as Lily. Christ, Lily's age, I think as I watch the film. The reporter asks him why he did it. He replies, looking her straight in the eye, no wavering: 'I thought it was a dream.'

As he says those words it sends shivers down my spine. I know he's telling the truth; he couldn't have made that up. And I know he's telling the truth in a way that others, including the jury, won't know – and that's because when I became psychotic I thought my life was a dream too.

Later I find that his testimony is used in the FDA hearings in 2004. His Dad read out a letter he had written from prison. It starts:

Dear FDA, My name is Chris Pittman. I am now 14 years old. I would like to tell you what happened to me, what the medication did to me and how it made me feel. When I was taking Zoloft, I took the lives of two people I loved more than anything, my grandparents. I went to the doctor and he gave me a sample pack of Zoloft. He told me to take 50 milligrams once in the morning and another 50 at night. I didn't notice a change in my behaviour until I was completely off the medication. It made me hate everyone. The smallest things made me blow up, and I started getting into fights....

He then goes on to describe the night he killed his grandparents.

When I was lying in my bed that night, I couldn't sleep because my voice in my head kept echoing through my mind telling me to kill them until I got up, got the gun, and I went upstairs and I pulled the trigger. Through the whole thing it was like watching your favorite TV show. You know what is going to happen, but you can't do anything to stop it. All you can do is just watch it in fright. Because of my own personal experience on the medication I would not want anyone to go through what I have then and now, losing the lives of my loved ones for the effects of homicide, or suicide or both, due to the medication. Thank you. Christopher Pittman.[3]

That night I can't get Christopher Pittman out of my head. He's innocent and he's been in prison for just ten years now out of the thirty he's been sentenced to. How many people out there are serving sentences for crimes they committed because they were off their heads on antidepressants, through absolutely no fault of their own?

Now I remember something that I'd read on the RxISK website about James Holmes, one of America's biggest mass killers, who gunned down and killed twelve people at a cinema showing a *Batman* film, *The Dark Knight Rises*, in Colorado. The article states that James was withdrawing from Zoloft.[4]

It's by Professor David Healy, who is one of the world's leading experts on antidepressants, and has been an expert witness in more trials involving antidepressants than anyone else. I email him and he sends me an unpublished paper. It looks really convincing: he's interviewed James Holmes as part of the defence team. In the end, the lawyers decided not to use the antidepressants as a defence (they didn't think the jury would buy it). Instead Holmes pleads insanity. But Professor Healy is convinced it was Zoloft that caused him to go crazy and become a mass murderer.

'How sure?' I email him.

'Ninety-five per cent,' he answers.

'Would he go on camera as saying that?'

'Yes.'

Blimey, I'm thinking, that's a hell of a claim. He's telling me he's sure that all these people would still be alive if that college kid hadn't taken Zoloft. And this isn't just anyone saying that: Professor Healy never, ever says anything he can't back up.

People have pointed out that 9 out of 10 of the high-school shooters were on antidepressants. Filmmaker Michael Moore raised the question that the two teenage killers in Columbine were both on Prozac.[5] He was unable to come up with any other plausible explanation as to why two healthy, balanced teenagers should suddenly turn a gun on their classmates and then on themselves. There is a chilling piece of interview where Moore says, 'Imagine if parents knew this, that this happened for no other reason than the fact that these kids were prescribed antidepressants.'

No one has really taken notice of claims that these mass killings are caused by antidepressants. I wonder if I can make people listen now through my experience.

THE PILL THAT STEALS LIVES

That night I'm so wired I can't get to sleep. I truly believe that I could have killed while on escitalopram (Lexapro). How can I persuade the world that what happened to me is happening to people across the globe: that a pill that 1 in 11 are taking here in the UK [6] has the capacity to turn ordinary people into mass killers? And that there are innocent people out there, some of them children, who are serving life sentences for crimes they really didn't commit?

Chapter 31

MONDAY, 5 OCTOBER 2015

Today, I have to vacate the house. I'm renting it out on Airbnb for the whole week so I can pay for the rest of the pilot. It's a big job, putting all the clothes in boxes in the loft, cleaning every inch and crevice, and finally putting out flowers, biscuits and a welcome note.

My friend Hannah has kindly agreed to put me up for the week and the kids are at their Dad's. She lives opposite our old house in Dundonald Road. It's odd to be revisiting the actual place that I'm revisiting in my mind as I cut the film. Iain and I had a stab at finishing the pilot, but by the end of the weekend we're a long way off. He has to go onto another job this week.

In my inbox is an email from Bob Fiddaman, one of a group of people suffering Seroxat withdrawal, who are taking a class action against Glaxo (GSK), the first of its kind in the UK (see also page 000). In the email is an article that chills me. It's about a coach crash in Switzerland in 2012 where 28 people are killed, 22 of whom are children. [1] It looks like the driver committed suicide (however, a possible suicide was never investigated by the Swiss authorities) and there is now a group of parents who are demanding a further investigation into the crash and into the fact that he was on Seroxat and with a view to coming off it had recently halved his dose. He could have been in agonising withdrawal.

In the course of my research I've talked to people who have undergone withdrawal from Seroxat, including Bob Fiddaman. The impulse towards violence and suicide is overwhelming.

Christ, I'm feeling sick now.

Soon Bob sends me a contact number for one of the parents – Olga Leclercq.

I know I can't wait until Iain finishes his job to complete my pilot so I email Allen Charlton, who cut my first proper documentary for Channel 4 (*Surrendered Wives*, 2000) – he'll do it. By lunchtime I've emailed to him the assembly of what we've done already. When I speak to Allen late afternoon he's already spent a few hours looking at the assembly and at articles on the Internet. He's totally got the story – not just mine, the whole thing. My psychotic knife-slashing incident, David Carmichael in Canada, the high-school shooters, and now the coach driver in Switzerland…

And as the hard drive containing the rushes travels in an Uber taxi from Queen's Park to Allen's house in Twickenham, I have total confidence that this story is in the right hands.

Wednesday, 7 October 2015. I'm staying in the small box room at the back of Hannah's house, diagonally opposite our old house in Dundonald Road. I'm annoyed because it turns out the Airbnb tenants in my house are a Chinese film crew, who have obviously been using the house as a film location (I went back to Harlesden Mews because I needed to pick something up). It reeks of cigarettes, and there are ill-concealed wraps of coke lying around on the glass shelves in my study. I know I can't chuck them out because I need the money for the pilot but I ring to complain to Airbnb and then go back to Hannah's house.

Hannah is bang in the middle of the same war I thought I'd already fought: she and her husband have split. They used to be regular friends of mine and Robert's. There was a pleasing symmetry as their two girls were best friends with Lily and Oscar. Between the shared suppers, the barbecues, the weekend camping trips to festivals in Oxfordshire, Hannah and I would huddle in our kitchens together and complain bitterly about our husbands.

Now there is a 'For Sale' sign outside her house. As I sit in her beautiful farmhouse kitchen, with sliding French doors opening to a long, thin, but picture-perfect wild garden, I see the worry etched on her face as she cuts me a slice of homemade banana bread that we share over a cup of morning coffee. She's at the beginning of the path I trod not so long ago: she is faced with the prospect of having to up sticks and move out of Queen's Park to somewhere like Harlesden, or Willesden.

I'll always feel gratitude to Hannah, but right now it doesn't feel the moment to express that. She is too caught up in the vortex that follows divorce and precedes the painful split of joint assets. And she's just at the start. I remember that Robert and I made a list of every single item in the house, down to the last IKEA bookcase and Jamie Oliver cookbook. The division of household spoils was the last round in our ferocious divorce battle. I remember the bemused look on the faces of our respective barristers as we instructed them to scuttle backwards and forwards from the two rooms in the Central Family Court like emissaries brokering a major treaty in a war tribunal. Only this time it was about Robert's tool kit, or the lime-green Weber barbecue.

At the time, it was of paramount importance to me that everything would be split 50/50 down the line. Each item was meticulously researched on the Internet to find its second-hand value. Afterwards, I spent hundreds of pounds storing my booty in a lock-up in East Croydon until I finally bought my house in Harlesden. But when I retrieved the spoils of our battle, I took one look at the Habitat faded fluffy cushions, the white flokati rug that had been cut in half because we couldn't settle who would have it, and the chipped Cath Kidston cups and decided I didn't want any of it.

No, not a single thing: *nada*.

And so, to Robert's immense fury, which the kids recounted animatedly, I put the whole lot, including a giant Liebherr fridge freezer, on the pavement outside the house we were renting in Kensal Rise, with a giant sign saying 'Help Yourself'. With the detritus of our failed marriage, I furnished the entire household of some astonished neighbouring Italian students. It was an interesting lesson in the simple pleasure you can derive from acts of philanthropy. And I also made a decision: that in our new house and new life, anything we don't like or that doesn't work is thrown away with immediate effect.

But right now that manifesto is on hold: because I don't like the Chinese Airbnb guests one little bit. However, I do need the money. So, as I watch Hannah clear away the breakfast plates and rinse the blue J-cloth, I resign myself to the fact that two miles down the road, the kitchen surfaces of my house in Harlesden, now occupied by the Chinese film crew, are no doubt being used for something quite different to bowls of homemade granola.

Hannah's face is etched with anxiety as she flicks through Zoopla, scribbling figures and rough calculations on pieces of envelope. I hope she's encouraged by the fact that I'm living proof there is life beyond the tree-lined streets of Queen's Park. And I think too of how grateful I am to her for the care she offered my kids when I couldn't be a mum to them.

I realise it's not the time to take either of us back to the dark time three years ago when her friend and confidante left the shores of sanity and became a virtual hermit in the house diagonally facing her. But sitting feet away from the Aga that warms her kitchen, with the taste of banana bread still on my lips and the smell of tonight's shepherd's pie drifting through the air, I remember that this kitchen was once a refuge for my children. It was here they fled, when their mum disappeared, first emotionally as the drugs that were supposed to cure me wrought their poison, and then quite literally when one day I upped and left them.

Yes, I left my children, I think, as I watch Hannah putting tortelloni in mini thermos flasks for her daughter's school lunch. And I wonder to myself what it was like for Lily and Oscar to come to this self-same kitchen three years ago, to see their friend's mother fretting and fussing over them, while their own mother had abandoned them in every possible way. I wonder how much consolation they could possibly have got from Hannah's homemade meals and assurances that of course, one day, your mum will get better, and of course she cares about you really, she's just gone away because she's very ill.

And I went away many times during that year. In total I was in hospital for fourteen weeks, the private hospital and then finally St Charles that saved me. And then the five months I lived apart from them in that ground and basement flat in Notting Hill. But it wasn't just the physical distance that was so painful.

I hear again the words of my children recorded in the documentary interviews. Oscar saying how he had just accepted the fact he would never have a mother again. And Lily's words, so poignant, striking me like daggers even though it's now two weeks since I first heard them: 'I'd dream about what I'd say to you. I'd dream I'd show you a picture and you'd suddenly take interest in me. Or we'd have a conversation…'

And as I hear those words in my head, my heart tells me it's time to leave Hannah's kitchen with the warm Aga and the smell of home cooking, and go upstairs to the small box room at the back, where my laptop is lying on a floral duvet cover on the antique French wrought-iron bed. I open it with renewed purpose and the first thing I notice is that there is an email from another mother like me.

Only Olga Leclercq is from Belgium. And her teenage daughter is dead.

The Sierre coach crash occurred on 13 March 2012 in Switzerland, when a coach crashed into a wall in the Sierre Tunnel. Of the 52 people on board, 28 were killed, including 22 children, and it was Switzerland's second worst-ever road crash. Most of the passengers were Belgian and the country declared a national day of mourning in memory of the 28 who died. Olga's daughter was one of them.

Olga speaks perfect English. Our conversation skirts carefully around the fact that her daughter died three and half years ago. Instead we talk about her conviction, along with the other parents, that this horrendous accident was caused by the fact that the coach driver was withdrawing from Seroxat (paroxetine, also known as Paxil). This is backed up by the official statement from the Swiss authorities (19 August 2013): 'The driver took this medication (Seroxat) for a duration of approx 2 years due to a nervous breakdown, the originally prescribed dosage has been halved by the beginning of 2012 with the intention of stopping totally.' Olga tells me how the bus driver's wife also told the media that on the day of the crash he didn't take his pill at all.

Seroxat has recently been in the press, with an exposé that Glaxo (GSK) failed to publish the findings of Study 329, a clinical trial on Seroxat conducted between 1994 and 1998, which tested its efficacy on depressed teenagers. Apparently they downplayed the negative findings and hired a PR firm to ghostwrite them.[2] Subsequently a group of researchers, including David Healy, who are part of a group called RIAT (Restoring Invisible and Abandoned Trials), conclude that Seroxat is no more effective than a placebo but caused a significant increase in suicidal ideation.

The RIAT study has just come out[3] but the news that Glaxo has hidden its data has been known for some time: as I've previously mentioned, in 2012 Glaxo were fined $3 billion by the Department of Justice for doing just that.[4] And early on in my research I met with Blair Hamrick, who worked for

Glaxo as a salesman and played a key part in this.[5] He was introduced to me by Bob Fiddaman, the Seroxat sufferer who has now become a campaigner.

Meeting Blair Hamrick was a fascinating insight into the workings of the drug industry. It was in the summer of 2014 and we met in a hotel in London with his girlfriend. He told me how he used to be a successful drugs salesman for Glaxo but one day he woke up and could no longer live with himself: he realised he was selling lies and risking lives.

Back in 1997, he joined GSK as a drug rep in the USA. It was great to begin with and he was taken in by company propaganda that they were helping patients and that they were all part of a big healthcare solution. When they played the music from their sales video, he got goosebumps. Added to that, he got an $80K basic salary plus a $40–$45K bonus depending on how many drugs he sold – plus of course a company car. He says they were under great pressure to sell drugs off label (that's selling a drug for something it's not licensed for). An example is Wellbutrin, an antidepressant. The reps were told to go out and sell it for weight loss and sexual dysfunction. They would tell doctors it was the 'happy, horny, skinny drug' and would often suggest it as an add-on to Prozac or antidepressants, which can cause people to gain weight and lose their sexual libido.

But there was a niggling doubt in the back of Blair's mind about all of this. He had a degree in marketing, not science yet here he was, telling GPs what to prescribe to patients. Then there was paying doctors $3K to give a talk they knew nothing about. That didn't matter because Blair would give them a script (written by GSK) and accompanying slides – and a few clinical trials (written by the marketing department of the drug company). This didn't just happen occasionally. Later in court it was found there were 40,000 (yes, 40,000!) doctors who were paid as speakers.

Blair had a personal epiphany in 2001. By then he had become a dad and his son was three. A child psychiatrist, Dr Paul H. Wender, MD from Boston, had written a book about ADHD and kids.[6] *ADHD: Attention-Deficit Hyperactivity Disorder in Children, Adolescents and Adults* mentioned favourably one of Glaxo's drugs – Wellbutrin. Even though the drug hadn't been licensed for children, Glaxo bought up thousands of copies of the book and started promoting Wellbutrin for kids with ADHD.

Blair knew that Wellbutrin is a form of speed and can cause seizures. In fact, this is stated quite clearly on the package inserts. He started to think: what if his own child was diagnosed with ADHD and was given Wellbutrin and died of a seizure? He could no longer live with himself while doing the job he was doing. He and three colleagues contacted the US Department of Justice. They carried out an investigation and some of this centres around how the company was promoting Seroxat for kids even though by now various studies in the 1990s and early 2000s had come out linking it to suicide and children.[7]

Blair no longer had a job with Glaxo and lost everything. He had to move back in with his mum and get a low-paid job as a supply teacher. But this story has a Hollywood ending. A few years ago the U.S. Department of Justice found GSK guilty, fined them $3 billion and in the US, under the False Claims Act, if you are a whistleblower you get rewarded. And when I say rewarded, I mean not just rewarded a bit, I mean rewarded, a lot.

THE PILL THAT STEALS LIVES

Blair's reward for being the White Knight of Truth and Justice was a cool $34 million. So sometimes the rewards go further than you think when you stand up for what is right rather than what is convenient.

Seroxat was also the subject of four BBC *Panorama* investigations (*The Secrets of Seroxat*), which went out between 2002 and 2007, and featured numerous tales of people becoming violent and suicidal on this drug. The programmes received an unprecedented public response with 1,400 emails and 5,000 phone calls after just one of the reports.[8]

All of this information that I have in the recesses of my mind comes back to me as Olga tells me that the Belgian coach driver, the man responsible for the death of her daughter and twenty-seven other people on 13 March 2012, was on this drug. His wife and doctor confirmed he was withdrawing from it.

Olga tells me how the parents commissioned the scientific expertise of Independent Forensic Services to recreate the crash, and they are convinced it was a suicide. It seems he drove the bus at 100 kph into a brick wall without applying the brakes. The report from the forensic experts concludes that the driver, Geert Michiels, must have been awake and conscious. I'm thinking back now to a conversation I had recently with a woman who contacted me after the *Daily Mail* article, who told me how her mother, on around the same amount of medication as me, had had enough and had chosen to take her life by driving into a brick wall. I think of all the other people who have gone into withdrawal on these drugs and felt suicidal, including me.

Could I have killed a whole coach-load of kids?

There were two occasions when the effects of these drugs were at their very apotheosis, once with the Lexapro. The second time was when I was withdrawing from all five drugs and was out of harm's way, under section at St Charles Hospital. So, could I myself have driven a whole coach-load of kids into a brick wall? Honestly? I was so deranged, on both occasions, in different ways. On the escitalopram (Lexapro), I wouldn't have known what I was doing. When withdrawing, I wouldn't have cared at the time.

I'm struggling to get a phone reception in the upstairs of Hannah's house, so the phone keeps cutting out. But not before I get a contact number for a woman who is helping Olga and the other parents with their investigation, a forensic medical investigator from Colorado called Selma Eikelenboom, who carried out the investigation for them and wrote the report.

Selma tells me about how she worked on the Sierre case and is convinced it was a suicide. In her opinion, nothing else could explain the fact that the coach driver drove at speed into a wall. She's frustrated that the Swiss authorities closed the official investigation.

As we end the conversation, I've now had to move to Hannah's bedroom at the front of her house so I can get a mobile reception. I can see our old house diagonally opposite, now with scaffolding on it for the renovations its new owners are having done. Despite the fact they've put in a new loft and side extension, they've kept the cheap wooden IKEA wooden slatted blinds in our old marital bedroom. Three years ago my view of those blinds was from the interior of the house. I remember how not long after my release from the private hospital in October 2012, I soon became nearly bedbound, and how my eyes would fix on those blinds as if they were the thing that was imprisoning me and stopping me from leaving the house.

THE PILL THAT STEALS LIVES

My mind wanders to territory I had completely forgotten. I'm now thinking of a morning that must have been about a month after I left the private hospital when I woke up so terrified, in such sheer utter panic, that I started screaming uncontrollably. Andrea, our nanny, alerted Hannah, who came running over from this self-same bedroom and held my hand, unable to extract from me what was making me scream. And I didn't know either. But I was still in sheer panic as they rang my sister, who rushed over, taking the day off work to look after me.

They also phoned one of the hospital doctors – what the hell was going on? He didn't seem to have a clue either but I remember someone handing me the phone and him saying something about the fact I must have missed a dose. The phone was handed over to Andrea, who rushed to get the pills and told me I must take another one right away. And now I'm thinking of Lily and Oscar's look of utter confusion and disbelief on seeing their mother gripped by an unnameable fear as Andrea desperately tried to calm everyone down and get them to school. And this was after missing just a single dose.

My sister had rushed over and then rang her office to tell them she wouldn't be in for the rest of the week. But my panic didn't go after I'd taken the pill, it just subsided, as I huddled up under a blanket on the sofa, shivering with fear. Every five minutes or so I would get to pace up and down, unable to sit still: it was akathisia, the condition that drives so many to suicide.

On that day, my sister tried to get me to go for a walk. I couldn't make it to Queen's Park, just a ten-minute walk away. It was to the small strip of greenery and playground known as 'Dog Poo Park' that we briefly ventured. My sister had no idea what was going on. She tried to get me to watch a TV programme but that was no good – I'd already lost the powers of concentration. Then she cheerfully announced another plan: that she and I should take a trip away together, to the seaside, perhaps, just the two of us. The sea would no doubt have a therapeutic effect – it was a well-known cure for depression, the disease I was supposed to be suffering from. This idea, that the two of us who were usually so busy with our own careers and family, should spend some quality time together would usually have me in paroxysms of joy. Back then, I couldn't contemplate leaving the house, or indeed my bed.

With my eyes fixed on those cheap IKEA wooden blinds.

And as I contemplate those wooden blinds from the other side of the street in Hannah's front bedroom, the only place where I can get a mobile reception, I make a promise to myself I know I will not break. Even if I have to plunder the children's holiday budget and we have to slum it in a tent next summer, and even if I have to let my house out to any number of foreign film crews who may or may not wish to snort cocaine off any of the surfaces of my interior-designed house in Harlesden, I promise myself that whatever happens, I will do everything in my power to make sure that I can tell the world about the story of the coach driver whose unexplained suicide killed twenty-two children, including the daughter of Olga Leclercq.

An email has just come in from her. Thanks for our chat. She's just read my article in the *Daily Mail* and seen the photo of us three on our sofa with the patterned cushions. Her daughter, Eline, she tells me, would have been the same age as Lily. It's the first time she's told me the name of her daughter:

THE PILL THAT STEALS LIVES

Eline. I feel slightly sick. Right now Lily is probably doing her homework just half a mile down the road at her Dad's. I remember I told her I'd call her today. The one thing my children know about me is that I never break my promises.

Friday, 9 October 2015. The car is all packed up for Brighton as I pull up outside Robert's new home to pick up the kids. I'm taking them to school on the way to Allen Charlton's house in Twickenham for my first day of editing with him.

The 'For Sale' sign is still up outside the semi-detached house just next to the bus station in Kensal Rise, despite the fact that they have been there for a month. It doesn't rival Dundonald in terms of size and location. And the kids say the buses flying past keep them awake at night.

I ring Lily's mobile to let her know I'm outside. Robert comes out and pretends not to see me as he heads to the station. As I see him dutifully walking off to work to support the increasing number of people who are financially reliant on him I can't help but feel a certain fondness for him. I guess that while some men are commitment phobes, he's the opposite: a sort of commitment addict, if there is such a thing. I reflect that while both of us are now equally vile to each other, this man is made of kindness.

I remember how kind he was to me in my marriage and even in the early days of my illness. He is a man born to please, I think, as I remember him mowing our lawn in straight lines at Dundonald and proudly announcing that he had now created a vegetable patch at the bottom of our garden. I recall how he would bring to the house his first crop of home-grown tomatoes and green beans in silver bowls from IKEA and deliver them to our pine farmhouse kitchen table. And the look of disappointment when he realised once again I'd forgotten we were now semi self-sufficient and had bought the same vegetables from Sainsbury's.

And how kind he was to the children, fussing around them on Sunday nights, polishing their shoes and preparing their school bags while my mind was on more important things – the detox I was starting that week, a new film, an important development in my career.

He looks greyer, I think, as I watch him in my wing mirror. I reflect on the enormous burden he's taken on: a new house, a new family. All this and the children's school fees.

The children tell me about the regime of thrift in the new ménage that has recently moved to Lynton Gardens. Everything is bought from the Sainsbury's basics range, they whisper in hushed tones, as if it's a confidence I absolutely mustn't tell anyone because of the ensuing shame it would bring on the family.

In my old life with Robert everyday economies would be juxtaposed with contradictory extravagances like holidays in the Maldives as if the weekly savings on the grocery bill could possibly have any real impact on these bigger purchases. There would always be an underlying atmosphere of scarcity, an unspoken rule that the bailiffs would be at the door if we dared to make purchases from the 'Taste the Difference' section. And then, suddenly, without explanation, like a binge eater breaking away from a fast, he'd announce a new car, or a holiday or a plan to extend the house. These memories make me smile as I see him head off with his battered briefcase towards Kensal Rise station, determined not to glance my way.

I can see he's noticed me out of the corner of his eye but he refuses to look this way.

THE PILL THAT STEALS LIVES

'Screlex!' shouts Oscar as he runs towards me with his bag packed for our trip to Brighton. Lily follows with another bag, but packed for her Duke of Edinburgh camping trip in the New Forest. Today is mufti day and without their uniforms, it feels as if the weekend has already begun.

I tease Lily about the camping trip.

'Is there a hotel near by, darling?' I begin, as her long legs clad in trendy torn black jeans stretch out in the passenger seat. Her long hair is unbrushed and I marvel again at the beauty of this girl, now on the cusp of womanhood, this girl that is Lily, not any Lily, but my Lily Newman. She raises her eyebrows because she knows where this conversation about hotels is heading.

One of my nicknames for her is 'Five-star'. It began when I took them on holiday to Vietnam at Easter last year. It was our first proper trip after my illness and divorce and I was determined to take them on an adventure. They had doggedly refused to take any interest in the two-week itinerary I'd put together that took us across the country, with various adventures along the way. When we arrived in the old district of Hanoi, just as I was downstairs talking to the receptionist and congratulating myself on finding one of the most charming hotels in this most exotic of places, Oscar came running downstairs to tell me there was an emergency.

'What is it?' I said.

'Lily's crying,' he told me. 'And she won't stop.'

I'm now thinking she must have somehow hurt herself. But no, it's far worse, says Oscar, breathlessly. It's because she thought we were going on a beach holiday and staying at a five-star hotel, like all her friends. And when I went upstairs, I found Lily crumpled in the bedroom of the three-star only boutique hotel, sobbing and telling me how all her friends were staying around the world in hotels like the Four Seasons. What the hell was she going to put on Instagram? she murmured between sobs.

And with my arms cradling my then thirteen-year-old daughter, I tried my best not to laugh or even smile. As we lay on the bed in that three-star hotel in Hanoi, I told her about the itinerary. Yes, there would be sightseeing, but also there were other plans afoot: a cruise on Halong Bay, an overnight train trip in a carriage all to ourselves, a speedboat trip up the Mekong Delta, and yes, finally, the icing on the cake was going to be in a hotel on the beach. At this her sobs subside.

'A five-star hotel?' she asks hopefully.

How am I going to break the news? I have to get it out.

'Four-star.'

There's a silence that tells a thousand words. And since that time, my nickname for her has been 'Five-star'.

As we head off to their school in Chiswick, she protests against my gentle teasing – she tells me that actually she has been camping before. And Oscar is all excited, because with our house occupied by the Chinese Airbnb guests, he and I are heading off to Brighton together. He doesn't mind the hotel is only four-star. It's got a pool, it's right by the pier, and his mind is already fixed on how he is going to persuade me to go on the scary rides.

As I pull away from their school and head off towards the Hogarth Roundabout, my mind can now turn to the film. Yesterday I'd filmed a Skype call with Professor David Healy, Professor of Psychiatry at Bangor University. This leading author and academic may not be a household name in every household but he is in ours. In the months following my illness, while other kids were reading Robert Louis Stevenson, I wouldn't mind betting Lily and Oscar were the youngest readership of his academic tomes, *Let Them Eat Prozac* and *The Antidepressant Era*.[9]

They provided a window to the mysterious illness that had stolen me for a year. Consequently, he has a pop-star status with my kids, who cannot contain their excitement when I tell them I'm speaking with him that afternoon on Skype.

'What, David Healy, Mummy? The *real* David Healy? You're actually talking to him in real, actual life?'

But it's not just his books that give him a pop-star status in our household. He's an expert witness in court cases around the world where people have killed or been killed by antidepressants. Christopher Pittman, the twelve-year-old boy who killed his grandparents on Zoloft; William Forsyth, whose son tried to sue because his dad stabbed himself and his wife; Tim Tobin, who successfully sued Glaxo (GSK) for $6.5 million after his father-in-law Donald Schell wiped out the family after taking Paxil. Not to mention the birth defect cases where parents on antidepressants are suing drug companies for the fact their babies are born with heart problems.

These facts alone would mean that if some clever marketing firm were to sell posters, T-shirts and key rings of their idol, Lily and Oscar would be queuing up to buy them. And there's more. Back in 2000 he was offered the job of clinical director of the Mood and Anxiety Program at the University of Toronto. Before taking up the post, he was invited to deliver a lecture in which he mentioned that antidepressant drugs can lead to suicide. Then he received an email withdrawing the job offer. Thinking this looked a bit suspect, he dug around to find that drug companies support 52 per cent of the budget for the university department. He suspects that the reason he was dropped is because senior figures are concerned that the drug companies might withdraw their funding. And it turns out he's right. He goes on to sue the university, arguing this violates the principle of academic freedom.

The case was settled out of court but the truth of what happened all came out. The university had been approached by Dr Charles Nemeroff, widely seen as the most powerful man in psychiatry at the time and the lead consultant for GSK, Eli Lilly and Company and Pfizer: they were told they had to get rid of David Healy.

Sometime later, in 2009, the extent of the amount Nemeroff was getting from Pharma was revealed in US Congressional Hearings on the Pharmaceutical Industry: it was in the millions. Despite this he has since been invited as a distinguished guest to lecture at our very own London Institute of Psychiatry. In fact he was invited by Allan Young, the professor quoted in the *Daily Mail* article about me, who said he'd never heard of SSRIs making you suicidal. Anyway, I digress because the point of this story is that David Healy fought this one out because he wanted a clear account of what had actually happened, and he got it.[10]

And this relentless fight for truth and justice is the reason why David Healy has become a hero not just to Oscar and Lily, but also to me.

And so as Steve arranges me on Hannah's kitchen table with my computer as we prepare to film the Skype interview, these thoughts are whirring through my head. What is it that drives this man to stand up for what is right, rather than what is convenient, I wonder. He could be writing out prescriptions in Harley Street with a smart fountain pen, not poring over

THE PILL THAT STEALS LIVES

Study 329 in a dimly lit office in Bangor University. He could be travelling the world in style, propping up the bar in five-star hotels paid for by drug companies. In return, all he would have to do would be to agree to promote their products: Prozac, Seroxat, sertraline, not to mention a whole host of other medication, antipsychotics and the like.

'Don't they have some rather nasty side effects? Kids, suicide? Sorry, what was that, can I have another Martini, please?'

Our call is due at 3.30 p.m. and at 3.25, I send him a text to see if he's ready. There's been some playful banter in emails, me asking for reassurance that he has a camera on his laptop, him refusing to pander to my 'neurosis'.

'You'll see,' he teases. 'Maybe we don't have such technology here in Wales.'

I come back with, 'We've discovered a new classification for the DSM, "Film Director Control Disorder".'

I joke that I'm going to go back on the pills and it will all be his fault. Despite this, he still hasn't told me definitively that he has sorted it out. As Steve is filming me interviewing him it's pretty crucial we can see as well as hear him.

As my computer dials his at 3.30, I'm anxious. The screen flickers and I breathe a sigh of relief as he appears from his office in Bangor University. He's ten years older now than he was in the *Panorama* investigation on Seroxat I've recently been viewing. I'm guessing he must be around sixty. I make some joke about the camera, but he doesn't come back with anything.

He's a busy man, I think. We need to cut to the chase.

I begin with general stuff. My stomach is in knots. He's answering in too much detail, I think. His lilting Irish voice is telling me about trial data too complicated to pack a punch; I need something pithy and direct.

I move on to James Holmes, one of America's biggest mass murderers – the student who gunned down and killed twelve people in a cinema in Aurora showing the *Batman* movie. OK, now he's warming up and he's improving. He tells me about how he sat with James Holmes for hours in his cell. He'd looked through his diary. James started having violent thoughts after he'd been put on Zoloft (sertraline). David is convinced it was because of the drug, but the lawyers made the decision that the jury wouldn't accept it. This is much punchier.

I know I've really got to nail this and I've only got a few minutes before Hannah's kids come back from school.

'So sum up how certain you are that James Holmes went on that gun spree because of the Zoloft,' I say.

And in Hannah's kitchen on 3.55 p.m., David Healy delivers me the sentence I'm after. He's sure, he says, in a sound bite that is about 15 seconds long.

And to emphasise the point I say, 'So, just to be clear, you're saying that that pill that 1 in 10 people take can cause people like James Holmes to go out and commit acts of mass murder?'

'Without the pill, he wouldn't have killed,' he says.

As his image disappears from my screen and the sound of the front door opening heralds the arrival of Hannah's kids, I look at Steve and ask him the question I already know the answer to.

'Am I missing the point or is this now quite a big story?'

Next up is Olga Leclercq. We knock off a quick interview with her in Hannah's living room. When I'm talking to her about the coach driver slamming into that wall in the Sierre tunnel, a chilling memory comes into my mind that I'd completely erased until now when it comes flashing back. It must have been the first night immediately after I'd taken the escitalopram (Lexapro) handed out by the private psychiatrist – my first dose of antidepressants. Andrea and the kids were sleeping. I was up all night as the drug first took hold of me, its effects ripping through my body, flooding my brain with serotonin and tipping my mind into psychosis.

I'm at my study desk in Dundonald Road in the early hours of the morning, gripped with an unnameable fear; I'm deranged. Like a caged animal, I've been pacing up and down, unable to understand what has taken over me. It's twenty-four hours before the proper hallucinations start but my mind has already started tipping over the edge. All I can think of is: there is no way out. There is a monster inside of me and out of nowhere I'm looking at the shed at the end of the garden, now bathed in early dawn light, and wondering if this affords an opportunity for me to end my life. And I grab sheets of A4 paper from my printer and start scribbling frenetically but I can hardly write because I'm so high on this drug.

Dear Lily and Oscar, I'm sorry, I have to leave you.

And then many versions of this, scribbled illegibly as the drug renders me incapable of holding a pen or a coherent thought.

As the Skype call ends, I sit frozen. Did that actually happen or was it a dream? I wonder, as Steve looks at me for direction.

As I turn off the Hogarth Roundabout and onto the A316 to Richmond, I think that maybe I need to recut the opening sequence to reflect the new journey of this film.

How did it start?

'This film is about a pill that 1 in 10 people take…'

No, that's rubbish! Who the hell wants to see a film about a pill? Some words are coming into my head: 'Three years ago something happened to me that set me on a journey to discover a horrifying truth. This isn't a story about us, it's a story about many. And it's a story of our time…'

I breathe deeply and pray that I can find a way to tell this story well. And as I turn into Riverview Road, where Allen Charlton lives, I reflect that although I've never been here before, I've arrived at exactly the right place.

Chapter 32

MONDAY, 12 OCTOBER 2015

I can't sleep.

It's been a hell of a day. When I came home this morning the house was a tip, thanks to the Airbnb guests. However, tonight it's not the Airbnb fiasco that's keeping me awake, it's a conversation I've had with Selma Eikelenboom, the forensic medical investigator from Colorado, who carried out the investigation into the Sierre bush crash.

Selma is interested in the role of pharmacogenetics in adverse drug reactions. She believes a lot of people who have bad reactions have something called a genetic polymorphism. Cytochrome P450 (CYP450) is the family of genes responsible for creating the enzymes essential to digest and break down antidepressants. Selma is of the view that when there are certain genetic mutations on any of the two alleles of one or several of these genes, the person is unable to produce the enzymes needed to digest the drug and the result is that the body becomes poisoned. Different forms of the same gene are called alleles, so for example the gene for eye colour has an allele for blue eye colour and an allele for brown eye colour.

She has a DNA test, and she has offered to test me. The other day, I carried out her instructions. Using Q-tips, I gathered swabs of mucus cells from my gums and sent them off to her laboratory. I know that it's early days for this test and the jury is still out as to whether it can really show the link between defective metabolising genes and people becoming violent or suicidal on these drugs but Selma has used it with a number of people who have killed on antidepressants, including James Holmes, the *Batman* killer who gunned down so many in the cinema in Aurora. He had four defective genes, and she says this meant not only could he not metabolise the Zoloft he was given, but also some sleeping tablets and other medication.

Selma believes it's not just antidepressants that cannot be metabolised when you have genetic polymorphisms. There are all sorts of other medications too, depending on the type of polymorphism you have. She says that often people who go into drug toxicity are on different drugs so it could start with taking a sleeping tablet or even a herbal tablet. Already your system is weakened. Then on top of that you take another medication you can't metabolise and bang, you go into acute toxicity.

All this is going through my mind as I toss and turn, trying not to wake up Lily, who is asleep next to me. How I wish it wasn't two weeks until that test comes back. I know it's not the definitive proof, I know it's just a stage prop, but I want that piece of paper so badly: I want to show it to my doctors at the private hospital.

'You see, I didn't have psychotic depression. I've got

polymorphism. You haven't heard of it? Really? All those years in psychiatric college and driving those expensive cars, and you haven't heard of polymorphism?'

'Is it important?'

'Well, yes, rather. Because you see there are some experts who think I was unable to metabolise the drugs you insisted I take. Do I know anyone else with it? Well, yes, I do, actually: James Holmes. You remember, the guy who gunned down twelve and injured seventy in one of America's worst mass murders. Yes, I know he wasn't one of your patients. And no, I haven't met him, but I know someone who has. But yes, he has got polymorphism, which may mean he reacted rather badly to the same drug that you are handing out liberally to your patients. Sertraline, marketed as Zoloft in the US. Wasn't that one of the drugs you prescribed to me?'

'Oh, yes, it was.'

I can't sleep, and I need to know more – now! I've got to contact Selma…

Colorado is seven hours behind us.

How certain is she that I'll test positive? Is it possible I could have had a toxic reaction and not be positive?

'Toxic reaction without polymorphism? Unlikely,' she replies, 'but it depends on the co-medication. But we'll see. Shouldn't you be asleep?'

I'm now thinking back to how I mixed the escitalopram (Lexapro) with zopiclone sleeping tablets that I had for jet lag. And wasn't there something else? Yes, I remember I was taking some herbal tablets too for the menopause.

Now something else comes to mind. As I sat in the private hospital in that pink floral dress, what was it one of the doctors said? Something about changing the medication because of my prolactin levels. Prolactin is a hormone and he seemed to be saying that a blood test revealed higher than usual levels, which is a sign your body is under stress. I wonder if it's a sign I'm reacting badly to the drug so I send Selma a quick email, telling her. She wants to see my medical reports from the private hospital. I send her the discharge summary and I quickly scan through it. Yes, there it is, on the third page: he changes the medication because of a rise in prolactin.

I send it off and head back to bed. It's now two in the morning and my mind is racing. There's no hope of sleep and while in the past I might have popped the odd sleeping pill, it's been two years since I promised I'd never take any medication ever again. That was even before I realised there might be genetic factors for me not being able to tolerate certain medication.

But it's not just the recent bout of poisoning that goes through my mind. As I toss and turn, I realise that talking to Selma and hearing about her DNA test allows me to open up a chapter that I'd hidden from my mind and from the world. At last, the thing that held me in fear, the thing I dare not talk about, is something I think I can now make sense of.

That episode three years ago was not my first brush with modern psychiatry. And it was not my first visit to that private hospital.

It all started in April 1996. I was working for Esther Rantzen's husband, Desmond Wilcox. I'd brought him a great documentary idea: it was about a group of British women who were going to Poland to have cheap plastic surgery. ITV commissioned it immediately. My prize was to produce and direct it, my first proper directing credit for a major network. I was green but I was going to do it all by myself. Did I want him to come along and report? No, Desmond, don't worry, spend Easter with Esther and the kids, I can do it. Did I want an assistant producer? No, not really. A producer? Definitely not! This was my baby and I wanted to do it all on my own. So off I went to Wroclaw with a Polish production assistant and a crew to film ten British women all being operated on by the same surgeon within the space of twenty-four hours.

As they leave the UK, we're filming constantly as we chart their fears and trepidation. We arrive and at midnight the surgeon began the first lot. As his scalpel prized off the face of the first victim, I started feeling sick. It wasn't just the blood, what if this went wrong? In my enthusiasm to make sure the slightly eccentric woman from Wales whose idea this trip was would have enough people, maybe I'd persuaded them to come along. Had I? I thought, as the polish surgeon stapled back the skin on Marilyn's face and wheeled another woman in.

I was so wired that night, I didn't sleep. And it got worse.

Then there were frantic calls with Desmond late at night. I'm close to tears as I explain to him that we missed the most interesting thing that day. Debbie's new breast implants. I fucked it up, I say, I was filming some stupid sequence that didn't go anywhere of Marilyn being stitched up. As my voice gets hysterical, he tries to calm me down from his Easter weekend in the New Forest. He tells me something which to him is obvious. But he's made over a hundred documentaries and this is my first. 'Tinks, calm down. You don't have to be there, the moment something happens. You can report back on it *after* the event. Get Debbie to tell you about her new fucking breasts tomorrow and now go and get some fucking sleep. The cameraman tells me you've been up for three nights and you won't let them stop filming. They need to get some rest too.' But I wouldn't listen. The cameraman had a monitor, and if I wasn't filming I was looking at rushes, thinking how I could have done it better.

And I still wasn't sleeping. And now I remember what happened: the Polish doctor, whom the girl with liposuction was dating, saw me getting more and more frazzled. He looked at me sympathetically; he had some blue pills that could calm me down.

'Yes, but I can't sleep,' I'd cry.

He had something for that too.

And I remember Selma's words: 'This is how it all starts with people who can't tolerate medication. Sleepless nights, sleeping pills, tranquillisers, more medication, and then bang, you are branded a psychiatric patient for the rest of your life.'

Two days before we were due to come back, I turned to Christina, the PA, and said I couldn't finish the film: I was a mess. I couldn't think clearly; I was convinced there was no film, that I would bankrupt Desmond, I'd never work again in TV. All of this I know I could have coped with but yes, by now there was a fog.

And now I know what had caused this.

I fly back home a day early and collapse in a crumpled heap in my flat above the mirror shop in Golborne Road. Later, I go to the doctor to get sleeping pills and complain of stress. She gives me more of the blue tablets the Polish doctor has given me and some sleeping pills. All of this makes me worse.

Eventually my mother came over from her flat in Chelsea,

where she'd lived since marrying my stepfather, and announced she knew someone who had a cure. That afternoon in April 1996, she bundled me into a waiting taxi and took me to the same private hospital, which had been recommended by her private doctor.

When we arrived at the hospital, I was seen by a doctor. Before he spoke, I burst into hysterical sobs.

'I've done the most terrible thing,' I cried.

He looked at me and he wasn't joking when he said, 'Have you killed anyone?'

'No, I've persuaded a whole load of women to have surgery they should never have had, and if it turns out wrong, it will all be my fault.'

They sedated me and gave me more blue pills. The doctor knew what I had: anxiety and depression. And he had a pill for it. It was Seroxat, one of the most lethal SSRIs, and the pill that Glaxo has paid out over a billion dollars in compensation claims to victims who have become violent and suicidal.

I can't remember how long it was after I'd been put on the pills that I went berserk. Akathisia at its worst, it was as if something had taken over my body and was causing my limbs to move involuntarily. One day when I was in a group therapy session I started trembling violently, then crying, and then screaming as the group looked on in shock. Nurses came rushing in, not knowing what was going on. I was like a deranged animal, writhing about on the floor. About four of them had to physically restrain me and carry me out, of the therapy session and into a private room where I was heavily sedated.

Not a single nurse or a doctor spotted what was going on: it was Seroxat. And I continued to take it. The doctors insisted.

Eventually it got too much for my family. I was talking

about suicide. Where did that come from? Out of nowhere. I started on about it. Why, people would say. But I didn't know why. Suddenly I just started feeling like killing myself – like all the other people that I've talked to, who have had the same reaction to the drug.

It ended quite by fluke. Somewhere down the line I saw the umpteenth therapist. I can't even remember who or where. When I started off on my usual rant about general feelings of despair, she wasn't having any of it.

'When did this start?' she asked.

So I told her about the film.

'Go and see it,' she said. 'Then go and get a job.'

'What? But I'm not well enough! I can't think straight, I get lost if I go out. I can't get a job…'

'Well, let's see. First, make a phone call to see that film and next week report back. When are you going to make that call?'

Four months after the Polish filming trip I went back into Desmond's office in Acton and sat in with the editor who had cut together the film.

It was fine – more than fine. It was mildly entertaining, occasionally insightful, apparently ITV loved it, and Desmond has been right all along. It didn't matter that I hadn't been there at the exact time that Debbie had got her new breast implants. And all of the women who had the surgery recovered too.

As I walked out of his office onto The Vale in Acton, I was so relieved that I chucked away the pills. Within a week I was back to my normal self. I always thought I'd got better because I'd faced up to the problem, which was partly true. My mother was victorious as she maintained I'd had a breakdown and it was the pills that had cured me. And so it went down in family folklore.

Chapter 33

TUESDAY, 13 OCTOBER 2015

I've only had a few hours' sleep but I know it doesn't matter. The hard work was done yesterday. The script is written and I can effectively sit on autopilot in the edit in Allen Charlton's basement flat as his Turkish wife Nilgun brings us cups of coffee and various home-baked treats.

Before I get the kids' breakfast ready, I still have time to log onto my emails. The first thing I used to do was log onto Tinder but I've now got used to the idea that right now my destiny is to remain single. I've long since resigned myself to the fact that my wish to snuggle up with someone who is a combination of alpha and alfalfa on a sofa with a DVD is not going to happen. Basilherb from Guardian Soulmates didn't follow through and Laurent has sent nothing more than a mysterious quote: '*Quand quelque chose manque à votre vie, c'est en général quelqu'un.*' (When something is missing in your life it's generally someone that is missing.)

No mention, though, of whether I'm the '*quelqu'un*' and I rather suspect I'm not.

I can't stop myself from opening up an email from Selma. She's seen the report from the private hospital; it mentions my father's suicide. Her email begins: 'Was your father on psychoactive medication? They would have started around 1965…'

I'm no longer listening to what's on the radio, and despite the fact the kids want breakfast, I'm glued to the screen.

'My father? I don't think so,' I reply. 'He was depressed because he had a stroke – then lost the feeling in his hand. I don't remember him being on pills.'

Driving the kids to school, I can't stop thinking about it. Already I've thought how others in my family have reported bad reactions to drugs. My niece, Sarah, confided in me that she was put on a pill for anxiety and reacted so badly she couldn't leave the house for two weeks. And I'm sure another family member said he'd had an adverse reaction to an antidepressant.

But my dad? Though I was twelve when he died, I felt I hardly knew him. He'd been depressed so long. But I felt genetically more linked to him than to my mum. This similarity meant I'd always been frightened that the disease that had taken his life would visit me. 'The Black Dog', I think I'd heard my mother describe it as.

One person who will know whether my dad was on meds is my older brother, David. He's on his boat in France, but he'll be picking up emails.

Another holiday, I muse.

He lives a simpler life than the rest of us, who struggle with bigger mortgages and private school fees in the metropolis. He's made a more intelligent choice.

THE PILL THAT STEALS LIVES

A hog pit roasting business just outside Chichester, boats and sports cars.

But he dropped everything when I was admitted as an emergency to St Charles Hospital after my year of being ill. Both he and my sister were granted Power of Attorney, but it was he who waded through the unpaid bills, found a home for my cats, and dealt with the divorce lawyers. Twelve years older than me, he'd taken the brunt of my father's illness: he'd been there when he'd killed himself at the hotel in Torquay. At first he'd tried to hide the facts from my sister and me – that he'd jumped from a balcony – but we found out later on because my mum told us. He always saw his role as to protect us.

So how am I going to broach the subject tactfully? My email header is an odd but very important question. In it I mention my suspicions that maybe reacting badly to drugs runs through the family. How I remember that my niece Sarah had a bad reaction to an anxiety pill. Maybe she has the same intolerance as me. And did he know whether father was on medication?

I send it from my iPhone once I've dropped the kids off in Chiswick.

David had done everything he could to make up for our dad's death, I think, as I head down King Street to the Hogarth Roundabout. I remember how he'd slog it from Torquay with his friends to my boarding school in Winchester for sports days. Other people had nuclear families, but I had my brother with his cool friends in open-top sports cars. And he had decorated a whole suite at the hotel for when I came home for the holidays.

What a strange existence that was, I think, as I head back

down towards Richmond again. Aged thirteen, while other kids were going home to farmhouse kitchens, I was going to a hotel in Torquay to spend it with a bunch of twenty-year-olds, with their fast cars and speedboats. But there were compensations. For one, I learnt to water ski. And his friends, seeing the void left by my father's death, lavished me with love and attention.

When I arrive at Riverview Road, there's already a response from David: he doesn't know if Father was on meds – and don't mention inherited genes to Lily and Oscar because it will make them anxious. On reading this, I'm cross. I've got my own manifesto – of giving my kids the facts and letting them make their own decisions. But then I stop myself as I remind myself of his extraordinary kindness and how he sees his role as protector.

But I do know there's going to be a tussle with him. I send another email. I've realised I've no clear memory of when my father was ill. His stroke, when did that happen? He replies that the first was when he was seventeen. The first? How many were there? Now he's getting cross: 'Three or four. But I can't remember. I'm stopping communication now. I'm on holiday. I'm back next week.'

And now I start to think; when there are things your brain can't make sense of, you just put them aside. And I had put aside things that never, ever made sense when it came to my father's illness and childhood. Those strokes, for example – Father was in his forties when he had them. And what were they? They were terrible chest pains, blackouts – all things that I had while on the drugs. I remember once calling an ambulance because I felt so faint. Then there were other things: a mysterious fire in his flat. We were told he had fallen asleep in bed with a cigarette. How likely is that when I know he never drank? So now I'm beginning to wonder. If the drugs acted the same on him as on me, was this perhaps another suicide attempt? And most importantly of all, I remember now my mum confiding in me that he was impotent, a well-known side effect of the drugs.

Allen has gone through my entire hard drive and chosen family photos and videos to put into the film, and he has cut together a horrifying sequence of when I go psychotic intercut with home videos of the kids to illustrate how close I was to killing them. We tell the story of Donald Schell, who turned a gun on his wife, daughter and granddaughter and then himself, twenty-four hours after taking the drug Seroxat. We use existing *Panorama* footage from their film, over ten years ago. There's an interview with the chairman of Glaxo, and I sit astonished as this man calmly says his drug doesn't kill. Yet his company has just been fined and a court has ruled they should hand over $6 million to the surviving relative, Tim Tobin.

How does this happen? I wonder.

I'd like to tell David Healy about my dad – I wonder if he'll have a view? So I email him. My dad killed himself and I'm wondering if it could have been the drugs. He comes back with: 'Do you know Sylvia Plath killed herself a week after taking an antidepressant, as did David Foster Wallace?'

Really? I Google it. Sure enough, there is an interview with Sylvia Plath's husband, the poet Ted Hughes. Sylvia was taking an antidepressant in the US and it made her suicidal. She knew she must never take it again but when she came back to England, she was given the same drug but under a different name. A week later, she gassed herself in the kitchen oven in February 1963. And there's more, because then I see their son, Nicholas Hughes, also committed suicide, hanging himself at his home in Alaska, in March 2009. I'm glued to the screen.

Could it be, that like his mother, Nicholas too was taking an antidepressant?

I need to take a break, I tell Allen, as I step outside into his garden. All these people, I think, who were supposed to kill themselves because of depression. And now it turns out it was a drug rather than a disease that killed them.

Am I missing the point, I ask myself again, or is this a very big story?

Chapter 34

WEDNESDAY, 14 OCTOBER 2015

I've given myself until Friday to finish the film. I'm interviewing Selma on Skype tonight.

I've arranged to meet Steve at my house at 7 p.m. I race home, but on the way, I phone my sister, Amy. She's just got back from a photography course and was with my brother on the boat in France. I try to be interested, but there's one question on my mind. After some pleasantries, I ask her straight out.

I'm approaching the roundabout at Old Oak Lane, heading towards Harlesden, in the early evening traffic when I ask Amy the question. I'm just five minutes away from home. As I pull up at some traffic lights, the windscreen wipers fighting away the specks of rain, her answer comes through the loud speaker on my phone.

'Yes, of course he was on meds,' she says. 'He was seeing a psychiatrist in Torquay.'

'Are you sure?' I say.

'Yes, of course I'm sure,' she says.

When I get out of the car outside my house I'm still shaking.

'What's wrong?' asks Steve.

'You'll find out,' I say, knowing we've only got fifteen minutes to get ready for the Skype call with Selma.

The moment Selma flicks up on my computer screen I like her and I know she's a gift to TV.

In my bedroom in Harlesden Mews, with my cat Choochee sleeping beside the computer perched on the grey throw, she is unpicking some of the world's worst killings.

With James Holmes, whom she interviewed, she describes a slow descent (like me) that began with sleeping tablets, and then escalated to other medication, ending with sertraline. A lot of people in antidepressant psychosis start thinking of doing things they would be remembered by, and he was no different.

This is good stuff. I tell her that I've found out my dad was taking meds. Could those drugs have caused him to kill himself, if he has the same adverse drug reaction that I have?

'Definitely,' she says. 'You inherit your DNA from your parents so half your DNA is his.'

The drugs that were around in those days, not just antidepressants but anti-smoking drugs or sleeping tablets, most definitely made people suicidal. I'm thinking of how my mum had a pill for everything.

What concoctions would she have had him on?

Chapter 35

THURSDAY, 15 OCTOBER 2015

I feel misty-eyed.
The children know.

'It's your dad, isn't it?' they say as they throw their arms around me and get out of the car to go to school. 'Poor Rell!'

Yes, it's my dad, I think, as I drive towards Richmond. And my eyes fill up with tears that were never shed. Yes, I hardly shed a tear for Dad, I think, as I remember the scene when my mum and my sister arrived unexpectedly at my friend's house in Eastbourne in July 1976. And as they walked towards the twelve-year-old me, I knew what was about to unfold.

'Daddy's done it,' my mum said.

But I didn't cry because I didn't feel anything – it was almost a relief. I'd often heard him talk about wanting to kill himself.

Today, we come to the section in the film where I'm at the

height of my illness, as my body fights with the poisons being poured into it, leaving me with an inability to focus, leave the house, wash or dress myself. I had lost interest in everything. And for the first time in my life I think I may have a window into the man who was my father.

On the way home, I ring my sister again. It's not just the fact that she's eight years older that separates us, it's the fact of our very different childhoods. I sometimes used to quiz her.

'What was he like to you?'

'He was a great dad,' she'd say.

'Did he ever hit you?'

'Never,' she told me.

And my mind would flash back to unexpected outbursts when I'd be cheeky and he'd hit me across the face. Then, remorseful, he'd come crying to me, begging my forgiveness. So that didn't happen to her then.

The uncovered trials of Glaxo come to mind.

The subject area is still tricky for us. She doesn't want to hear what I've been saying for quite some time now. I've told her before that the clinical trials show that antidepressants are no more effective than a placebo. And I've told her the idea of depression being caused by a chemical imbalance is a myth. But she insists doctors wouldn't say you were depressed if you weren't: they must know best. And I remember a time when I was seven years old, when she found me playing with card boxes in my Wendy house.

'They are for my fairies,' I told her.

For some reason, she told me then and there they don't exist.

Over forty years later, the tables are about to be turned.

As I tell her about the possibility our dad may have

been poisoned rather than depressed, she asks me why it's important.

Why is it important? I ask myself that night, first as I drive home to Harlesden, and then as I lie awake at night. Why indeed? How do I explain to her why it's important that it was a drug, not him that stopped him loving me?

How can I explain to my sister, who doesn't spend her life working out in gyms and obsessing over whether the Atkins Diet is better or worse than the South Beach Diet, who probably thinks a Brazilian is a type of takeaway, and who has only ever been out with two men in her life, both ending in marriage? How do I begin to explain to her what it was like to grow up unloved by the most important man in your life? To be invisible, occasionally noticed when his anger and frustration erupted into acts of unexplained physical violence. How do I explain that his absence led my childish twelve-year-old brain to conclude that I was unlovable, and that yes, there must be a reason for this.

Of course the reason was that I was fat. And so while my school friend marvelled at my willpower, as I restricted my food intake to two pieces of fruit a day, it was no mystery to me. I was on a single-minded mission to find love, somewhere, somehow, and if dieting until my hair fell out was my ticket then I was in. And so began a never ending quest to replace the love I never had.

It's midnight now, as I reflect my sister is six miles down the road in Wimbledon, in the arms of a man who loves her. But the scar of my dad's illness was not just about being unloved; it goes further than that. There's another thing that separates me from my sister: it's not her name that makes her more loving, or her DNA. The fact she was loved makes her able to love, in a way that I don't. The words of Gérard Depardieu come back to me: I'm not a loving woman.

And the single most frightening thing about my psychosis was that the drugs unleashed my subconscious mind to reveal a distortion of this fact. The game show televised to the world was an horrific exposé in which Robert was a more loving parent than me. And though I'm no psychologist, I suspect the reason for this is very simple: it's no coincidence that he fusses around the children on Sunday nights, polishing their shoes, while I think about myself. Our childhoods taught us very different lessons – him, how to love; me, survival.

Chapter 36

FRIDAY, 16 OCTOBER 2015

As I take the now familiar route from the children's school to Allen's house, I reflect that this journey is coming to a close. It's our last day of the edit. Is anyone going to listen, I wonder as I reflect that perhaps it's no coincidence there hasn't been a single TV programme on this subject since the last of *Panorama* reports in 2007. The fact there is no magic pill is not exactly a message people are going to want to hear.

And I remember reading about a vigil outside the courthouse during the 'Prozac trial' some twenty years ago when survivors of Joseph T. Wesbecker's gun spree were suing Eli Lilly. Scores of people who claimed they were suffering from depression turned up bearing lighted candles, one saying, 'We hope that this lawsuit doesn't take our drug away.'[1]

Recently I met up with Joanna Moncrieff. She is co-chairperson of the Critical Psychiatry Network, a group of psychiatrists from around the world who challenge the idea

288

that mental disorders are brain diseases and campaigns against the influence of big pharma. She sees many patients who have come to believe they are depressed and need antidepressants. Even when she suggests that what they are experiencing is an understandable reaction to life events or circumstances, that the pills are ineffective and have terrible side effects, they still want them. For various reasons they feel a need to have a medical label for their distress and they want to believe that a pill will make them feel better.

People have been encouraged in this view by advertising and professional educational campaigns. She goes on to tell me that some people who have been taking the pills for many years have got used to the side effects, the numbness and the lack of sexual functioning. On top of that, they have grown accustomed to the idea they are chronically sick and have to lead very restricted lives. For some people, being sick becomes what they are used to. We've become a culture that encourages people to view themselves as flawed and needing professional or technical help.

I wonder if the statistics bear this out. Officially, 1 in 4 people now suffer from a mental disorder. In 1950, it was 1 in 100 and at the beginning of the twentieth century only 1 in 1,000.[2]

Depression is set to be the second cause of disability by the year 2020.[3]

So are we becoming more miserable, are psychiatrists becoming better at diagnosing, or have we simply created more illnesses? If my own experience is anything to go by, I'd vote for the latter. I've been diagnosed with acute anxiety, depression, severe depressive disorder, psychotic depression, and someone once ventured bipolar. I don't believe I had any of those illnesses, and even if I did then the diagnoses were at best useless in helping me manage my life better and at worst positively dangerous in that they led to me taking drugs that made me extremely ill and for many people have serious side effects.

Recently I almost persuaded myself I had post-traumatic stress. A swift look at the NHS website tells me that I display many of the symptoms of post-traumatic syndrome – flashbacks, nightmares and physical sensations such as nausea or trembling. Also, avoiding going to places that remind you of the trauma. Yes, that's me, I think as I reflect how I still can't drive down Cornwall Crescent and in two years have avoided going anywhere near, where the private hospital is.

Whether I have PTS or whether I'm just a bit freaked out about what happened is a matter of opinion. If I went to a professional, it would depend on whom I consulted. A study in 2006 showed that two psychiatrists would give different diagnoses to the same patient for 32 to 42 per cent of the time.[4]

Post-traumatic stress disorder is treatable either by counselling or by the same drugs that made me ill for a year (paroxetine and sertraline). I can't afford the former, and I don't need to explain why I won't be using the latter. But that doesn't stop me using PTSD occasionally as a stage prop. If I'm invited to a dinner party, you can be sure that it will make its way into the conversation somewhere between the starter and the main course.

'Yes, my stolen year has left its scars,' I will say. 'I've tried to be strong, but however hard I try, I'm left with something rather debilitating.'

Pause here for a sip of Sauvignon Blanc, count to three for dramatic effect.

'Have you heard of PTSD?'

It may work with sympathetic strangers but not with Lily and Oscar. Recently I tried to use it with the kids to justify a trip away from them at Christmas.

'You haven't got post-traumatic stress disorder,' growled Oscar. 'More like Selfish Mother Syndrome.'

There has also been a huge growth in psychiatric disorders for kids. Now between 14 and 15 per cent of children are supposed to have diagnosable mental health disorders.[5] One of these is ADHD (attention deficit hyperactivity disorder), which has now rocketed to affect 5 per cent of kids.[6] Like other disorders, the diagnosis of this is down to opinion rather than a test. The symptoms are frequent fidgeting, difficulty playing quietly, restlessness, excessive talking and frequent daydreaming. I'm naturally sceptical about this, but my suspicions are confirmed by a Canadian study of 1 million schoolchildren in 2011.[7] The scientists were baffled that children seemed to be diagnosed in some months more than others. Then they realised that it was largely the kids born at the end of the year rather than at the beginning who were diagnosed. For the boys, 30 per cent were more likely to be diagnosed if they were born at the end of the year than at the start; for the girls, it was 70 per cent more likely. The younger kids were being diagnosed with ADHD when it was just immaturity, the fact some were eleven months younger than their classmates. And the same was found in other countries – the younger you are in your class, the more likely you will get a diagnosis.

In fact we are being bombarded by the idea that our kids are sick. Recently a report came out by a leading children's charity.[8] Three children in every classroom have a diagnosable mental health problem and half of those with lifetime mental health issues first experience symptoms by the age of fourteen. Depression and anxiety amongst teenagers have increased by 75 per cent in the past twenty-five years, and children are less likely to suffer from serious mental health difficulties if they receive support at an early stage.

But I don't need to look at reports to see that the idea our kids are sick has caught on. Some of Lily's friends have been put on antidepressants. I know, because their parents confide in me. And a recent study has shown that between 2005 and 2012 there has been a 54 per cent increase in kids in the UK taking antidepressants. [9] And it's not just the side effects that make this worrying. Joanna Moncrieff of the Critical Psychiatry Network sums this up when I interviewed her: 'What a terrible message it is, that when a teenager is going through the trauma of growing up, we tell them they are ill. And that they have to turn to something outside of themselves to get better.

'I was depressed as a teenager,' she adds. 'And like many people who are depressed, I thought I would be like that forever. But as I grew up, I learnt things, I became more confident, and it got better. And that, I suspect, is most people's experience of being an adolescent. It was certainly mine.'[10]

We're not the only country who thinks we are depressed. In every country around the world, in places where depression was never heard of, people are popping pills. In Japan, for example, sales of Seroxat went from $108 million in 2001 to $300 million in 2003. As well as ad campaigns there were 1,350 Seroxat medical reps visiting doctors. The ads were vague and gave the impression that anyone who was feeling low could be suffering from it.[11] Kathryn Schulz wrote in an article in 2004: 'The depression contagion was not spreading because more people were getting sick but because more and more people were being taught to redefine their existing suffering in these new disease-laden terms.' [12]

Every week I get emails from people with yet more horror stories. Recently it was the daughter of an eighty-four-year-old in Scotland, who has just been released after serving a sentence for killing the wife he adored after taking escitalopram. He remembers nothing about it and is now ostracised by the community who, I imagine, simply do not understand that it was the drug that killed his wife, not him.[13]

Then another case that sickened me. I spoke on Skype with a woman from Austria who has asked not to be named. It's the first time she's talked in details about the circumstances behind the tragic death of her four-year-old son. Four years ago, she was suffering panic attacks and was given Cymbalta. This is, in fact, the very same drug that caused the student Traci Johnson to hang herself while a volunteer on the drug trials (see page xviii). Within hours she suffered what I believe to be an adverse drug reaction. Her vision became blurred (a classic symptom), she couldn't keep still (yes, akathisia, once again), and from out of nowhere she wanted to kill herself. She took an overdose of sleeping pills and gave the same pills to her son. When she woke up from a coma in hospital, she read in the newspaper that her son had died. She has spent four years in a psychiatric institute and even now is forced to take medication or she will be readmitted. The doctors seem to recognise she cannot tolerate antidepressants, so she is now on a mood stabiliser, lamotrigine. Nowhere is it mentioned in the press reports that medication was a possible (and in my opinion very likely) cause of her son's death.[14]

Some of the worst cases are people who started out well but

293

are suffering long-term effects. These are very sad because there is simply nothing doctors can do. Take Carel, for example.[15] He took Prozac after moving to the UK from South Africa. Like many people, he felt better but as so often happens the effects wore off after six weeks. He suffered appalling 'brain zaps' when he tried to get off it so tapered – that is, gradually reduced – the dosage. Then, five months after stopping it, all hell broke loose: akathisia, indescribable anxiety, raw terror, insomnia. Unable to sleep, he was pacing up and down for up to sixteen hours per day. Eventually he had to stop work so in desperation went back on the medication. But then the symptoms came back.

He has contacted all the leading experts and there is simply nothing anyone can do. When I last spoke with him, he was walking round his house like a caged animal and has given up his work.

All of these side effects were apparent shortly after Prozac came on the market in 1988, yet somehow people don't seem to know about them. Dr Joseph Glenmullen from Harvard Medical School noticed in his patients tics, neurologically driven agitation, muscle spasms and drug induced Parkinsonism. When he dug around in medical journals he found thousands of similar cases dating back to 1991.[16] These included cases of people who have lost control at the wheel of their car, or fallen over furniture because of electric shock sensations, and visual hallucinations. Usually these stop once you stop the drug, but not always.

So how is it that we don't know about these side effects? According to Professor Healy, drug companies go to extraordinary lengths to make it difficult to report problems. If you manage to get through to them at all, they encourage you to report the problem to your doctor or the regulators because that way, your report will be dismissed as just an anecdote rather than a formal complaint.[17]

Allen Charlton wants to look back at the beginning of the film but I prefer not to.

'We're going to crack on until the end,' I say, thinking of my first half marathon in Hastings, my eyes set firmly on Lily and Oscar at the finishing line.

At 5.30 p.m., we're at the end. I write a hurried piece of voice-over that wraps it up:

> I began this film to explain to my kids that it was a drug that took me away from them for a year. Little did I know it could provide the key behind another theft, my father's life, and the theft of many lives around the world.

And then the title I've been searching for comes to me: *The Pill That Steals Lives*.

Allen's kids are back from school. He's going to send me the film by Vimeo, a website where you can upload videos and share them. It won't get there until the early hours of tomorrow morning.

The kids are at their dad's and I've no plans this weekend. It's my birthday on Monday; I'm fifty-one. My dad died when he was fifty-six.

I began this book six weeks ago and dedicated it to Lily and Oscar. I want to add to that a dedication to the man I never knew: my dad, Deryk Arnold Blackford.

Chapter 37

TUESDAY, 26 JANUARY 2016

I've recently asked for the private hospital's notes. Every patient can do this for a nominal charge.

When I declined to take yet more medication, this time lithium, the doctor writes: 'Once again, Katinka shows no insight into her illness.' And he references the fact I said 'elusions' instead of delusions. In fact it was a sign I was losing my speech because of his medicines rather than my mispronunciations.

At one point he actually says that I couldn't sit still for more than 15 seconds. He mentions my mouth is drooping and that I had 'dyskinetic buccolingual movements'. This is a medical term for the fact my mouth and tongue couldn't stop moving.

Lily and Oscar could now tell you that these are both signs of drug toxicity – tardive dyskinesia and akathisia. So how come a man who is kind, educated and wants to make people better didn't spot the fact he was slowly poisoning me and was instrumental in almost killing me? I guess he does what we all do: we choose the facts we want to believe and ignore the rest because it's convenient. I know I'm guilty of this too – I do it all the time. Whether it's believing in a magic pill and not bothering to read the side effects, or ignoring the cracks in my marriage.

Today, I may have a chance to change things. Because one of the doctors has agreed to meet me for a coffee.

I'm sitting in the atrium bar of a hotel in Central London and I've got there early. I didn't want to meet the doctor at the hospital because it remains one of the places I still can't drive past, along with Cornwall Crescent. He suggested Patisserie Valerie in Marylebone station but I said I'd rather come here, as it's quieter. His email responded 'very expensive' so I wrote back to say I would pay for the coffees.

As I listen to the somewhat annoying piano player and take in the other guests here, people having business meetings, a couple who look as though they are meeting on a blind date, I reflect on the irony of this. The fact that Robert's health insurance premiums went up so high after my year-long illness that none of us have been able to afford insurance since. In addition there were sessions with the doctors that weren't covered, for which we had to fork out hundreds.

But that's not all that is going through my mind today. I'm thinking that the last time he saw me was in September 2013 when I was a dribbling wreck, then on five different drugs including Lithium and three stone heavier. I had spent a night at the hospital to be told by him the insurance no longer covered me. And then when I was sectioned at St Charles, I'd rung him screaming, begging him to somehow find a way to get me back to the private hospital.

THE PILL THAT STEALS LIVES

He knows I'm dissatisfied because after I got better I wrote a long letter of complaint. His reply was an insistence that I was very ill with 'psychotic depression' but at the time he offered to meet up and now I've taken him up on his offer. I've decided not to tell him I'm writing a book, making a film, or that I've interviewed the world's experts on the subject.

Our meeting is at 3 p.m. and at 3.05 he arrives. I wasn't sure what to wear and eventually opted for one of Lily's American Apparel short black wraparound skirts, a bright blue crop top and a pair of black boots. I rise and greet him with a hug. It's probably the first time I've greeted him or any doctor with a hug, but somehow it seems the appropriate gesture. It's a tactical gesture on my part to disarm him, to give him a signal that while we may not see eye-to-eye on the details of my recovery, the important thing is now I am recovered and that's a jolly good thing, and by the way while I get the waiter's attention to order you the coffee I'm paying for, I just want to pick your brains if you don't mind about how the drugs you gave me took me away from my kids for a year and nearly killed me.

After we have got through some pleasantries about his work, about Robert, the divorce, the kids, etc., I take a deep breath and begin.

'You see, the curious thing is this: that whilst I was on the drugs I was very ill, then I went to St Charles and after coming off the drug, well, after three weeks, you see, I was just completely better. I'm wondering why you think that might be?'

I'm trying to appear nonchalant, kind of casually dropping these facts into the conversation as if they really don't matter, as if I'm talking about the weather, not the fact he and his colleagues nearly killed me.

He's stirring his coffee, his face is expressionless and he replies in a slow and measured way.

'I'm very pleased you got better,' he says. 'You have been very fortunate, you were very ill. It was the natural history of your illness you got better.'

I realise right then and there that I don't have a prayer of holding out on this politeness thing. Already I'm crossing the line.

'Come on, you honestly think that? You think it was a complete coincidence I came off all five drugs and got better?'

He pauses, and he has the demeanour of someone who is reading a press release or a witness in a courtroom.

'Well, I don't see why not,' he says carefully. 'The other option is that you were getting better and that when the drugs were removed, you were already better.'

Mmm… I'm kind of feeling we're going down a blind alley here so I change tack.

'OK, here is the other thing. You see, I don't think I was ever ill. This is what I think happened. You know the Lexapro…'

He stops me here: 'Sorry, I don't know what Lexapro is.'

I've used a trade name for escitalopram, which I really thought he might know (though in the UK the drug is often known by another trade name, Cipralex), but I tell him and continue.

'You see when I came initially to you and was talking about suicide pacts with God, I think that was caused by the drug, not at all what you said, which was that I had psychotic depression.'

He says he disagrees: it was his opinion I had psychotic depression. Why? Because of the pattern of my illness.

'Pattern, what pattern?' I say. 'You'd never met me before I turned up out of nowhere, talking about cameras filming me.

'Come on,' I add, 'it's just not normal, is it, for someone to come in talking about suicide pacts with God and film cameras in the ceiling just because they're stressed from getting a divorce?'

At which point he pauses and his next sentence sends chills through me. Despite the fact that it's two years down the line, despite the fact I know with 100 per cent certainty that it was the pills that made me ill, despite the books I've read, the experts I've talked to, the endless studies, the hidden drug trials, the pill package that actually states the side effects, the countless other people who have suffered similarly, despite the fact I know the only time I've ever in my life been mentally ill was as a result of those pills... Despite all this his next words spoken with utter conviction, and that look of concern, cause a sickness in my stomach.

'You're right,' he says, 'it's *not* normal,' all the while staring straight at me with a look of concern and sympathy that insinuates 'I know you better than you do and as an experienced psychiatrist, I can tell you with utter certainty you're an out-and-out fruitcake and I feel very, very sorry for you.'

I'm taken back to that time three and a half years ago when he gave me that same look and uttered very similar words. And it was that look and those words that caused me to be first physically and then mentally incarcerated for a year.

I want to leave there and then, I really do. Because there is an irrational thought that men in white coats are going to appear from behind the piano in the bar at the hotel, and on this doctor's instructions they will take me away right there and then to the hospital.

'She's still not normal, you see. She's very ill again, you see. Psychotic depression can reoccur, you know. It often does.'

But I stop myself from getting up and leaving. I remind myself that while geographically it's not that far from where I'm sitting and the hospital where he once incarcerated me, right now he has no power. None whatsoever. And it doesn't matter one jot what his opinion is about whether I am, or ever was, normal. Well, it doesn't matter in terms of whether I'm locked up or not. But it matters to me for another reason, I think, and I'm brought back to my purpose with a jolt by his next question.

'What exactly is it that you want from me, Katinka?'

Pleased he reminded me, I look him in the eye and tell him why I'm here: because I don't want this to happen to others, I really don't. Hallucinations are a known side effect of the drug – it says so on the packaging. I've never believed before I had a suicide pact with God or thought I was being filmed (unless of course I have been filmed, which, after all, is not unlikely given my profession), or lacerated my arm at any other point in my life except after taking that pill. I'm not a professional but in all my years I've never ever heard of anyone hallucinating because of stress, I really haven't. The words 'I've just been sacked from my job, and you'll never guess what, the next thing I knew I thought I'd killed my kids, and I was hearing voices from God' are not something I've heard before, or anything like it.

At last, the doctor concedes something. 'At the time I thought it was psychotic depression,' he says. 'One possibility is that it was the antidepressant.'

Hallelujah, praise the lord, I think. We're getting somewhere.

Now I move on to my thesis that the whole year's illness was caused by a series of bad drug reactions.

'Look,' I say, 'I know there are people who react badly to the drugs, lots of them, plus it says those are the side effects on the packaging. I've never been suicidal before or since. I don't want this to happen to others – I wasn't a mum to my kids for a year.'

'I understand that's your belief, and that's fine,' he replies.

'So it's possible?' I persist.

'Oh yes,' he admits, 'it's possible.'

'So you acknowledge those drugs can have severe side effects?' I say.

'Yes,' he replies.

'And why did you not think that was what was happening to me?'

'Well, I did. I was constantly changing your drugs because you were having adverse side effects.'

'Yes,' I reply, 'to different ones with side effects.'

I take a deep breath and go on: 'You see, I think I'm one of those people that just don't react well to drugs.'

'Well, you may be right,' he concedes, 'I'm not going to disagree with that.'

'Well, it's a bit unfortunate,' I say. 'Because it did take me out of action for a year, you see.'

'Well, yes,' he says, 'it was very unfortunate and I'm sorry that happened to you.'

'So you agree it's possible I couldn't metabolise the drugs?'

'That's possible,' he says.

At this point there is a huge gap between the doctor's words and the expression of boredom on his face: because he doesn't look at all sorry, not one jot. Which causes me to continue with: 'Look, I came to one of the most expensive hospitals in the country for you guys to get it wrong. And then I go to some NHS place and in four weeks of hell, I'm better.'

He seems unmoved.

I decide to move on and so I ask him why he'd told me, and more importantly Lily and Oscar, my illness was caused by a chemical imbalance. He agrees he may have said not quite that but something similar. 'So what's your basis for that?' I say. At this he fluffs around about the brain and chemical transmitters.

'Do you believe mental illness is caused by a chemical imbalance?' I ask him. But he's backtracking, saying there are neurons in the brain that are dependent on serotonin. That doesn't mean you've got a deficit of serotonin, it means the neurons might be modified by having more serotonin. There is a complex chain of events which includes a chain of neurons that are all connected to each other and you can affect this network in different ways, which means your mood can be improved. Medication or psychological therapy might help.

I'm not going to argue the toss with the doctor on this because although I know what he's saying is a long way from what he originally said, he's beginning to get suspicious of me now and he keeps asking me exactly what project I'm working on. We end with him saying maybe meeting me has modified his opinion but that it's not going to change his knowledge completely and that his views are based on the views of thousands of psychiatrists over 100 years about the nature of mental illness and psychosis. 'I'm not going to walk out today and say mental illness doesn't exist and I'm never going to prescribe another drug again, that would be bizarre,' he insists. 'But you agree it could have been in my case, that the drugs could have caused the psychosis?' I persist.

'We've already been through this, what did I say?' he says.

'You said yes?' I tell him.

'Exactly, so why are we repeating it? You're like a dog with a bone!'

He's right, I am: he's admitted to me that my illness may have been caused by the drugs, but it's a kind of Pyrrhic victory and it hasn't really got me anywhere.

Where the hell am I going with this, I wonder. I need to wrap this up.

'You acknowledge you may have got it wrong,' I say.

'Yes, I do,' he replies.

'That's great,' I say, 'because Lily and Oscar would love to hear that. They were nine and ten at the time, you see, when they lost me for a year. It was a bit of a shame for them, you see. Could you write them a letter, telling them that? You don't have to say you *did* get it wrong, just that you *might* have got it wrong.'

He hesitates – I notice his black coffee is untouched and now has a coat of film on it.

'I could probably do that,' he murmurs.

There is no eye contact.

'Do you promise?' I say.

'Yes, I should be able to,' he replies, looking at his watch.

But there is no warmth in his eyes. There has been no sign of his former bedside manner, his twinkling eyes or anything of what I remember about him when he thought he was making me better. I have no idea whether he believes he got it wrong, or whether he thinks I am barking mad. He has been looking at his Rolex watch rather a lot. And actually, I'm keen to wrap this up now. I tear a piece of paper from my notebook and scribble Lily and Oscar's names and our address on it and hand it to him.

'Thank you, it would mean a lot to them. And actually, it would mean a lot to me,' I say.

He gets up to leave.

Before he does, I get up and make sure I give him the warmest of embraces that I can muster.

EPILOGUE

Finally, as my mum used to say: don't let the facts get in the way of a good story. On this occasion, I hope I haven't let a good story get in the way of the facts, though. And that I've kept to my promise that I would give you the facts about antidepressants so that you could make up your own mind.

So here is a round-up of the facts. Contrary to what doctors tell you, adverse drug reactions can happen within hours. Around 1 in 5 people in trials experience 'activation' – that is agitation,– and approximately 1 in 100 become violent or suicidal.[1] If you experience akathisia, an inner restlessness and turmoil often accompanied by an inability to keep still, this is a sign you are being poisoned and you are in lethal danger of harming yourself or someone else. You should stop taking the drug immediately.[2]

And what about the rest, the ones who don't react badly?

That's not that many because 50 per cent of people who start out on antidepressants come off them within a month.[3] For the rest, various studies seem to indicate that only 30–40 per cent who are treated with antidepressants fully recover from their depression.[4] Sexual side effects occur in at least 59 per cent of cases and some people's libido doesn't return after stopping them.[5] The drugs are tested by the drug industry themselves, for only 6 to 8 weeks, and then they don't have to publish their results. People who have died on the trials don't turn up in the final data.

Some people are reporting long-term neurological damage even after they have come off the drugs. There have been billions of pounds of silent payouts to settle claims of birth defects, suicide, homicide and agonising withdrawal. Some people can't get off the drugs and will have to take them for the rest of their lives. It's hard to get an idea of how many casualties there are because there's no reliable system of reporting.

This is no small problem, it's actually a rather large one. As we go to press, over 100 million people worldwide are on antidepressants and on top of that there are many more millions taking other psychiatric medications which can have similar side effects – in fact, 15–20 per cent of populations in Europe and the USA. Along with China and Japan, it means a staggering 400 million worldwide are taking psychiatric medications. Even if it's a small percentage who react badly, the numbers are so enormous that surely this means a worrying number are walking around like a loaded gun.

Experts say if you try to come off these pills you need to do this slowly by tapering, i.e. you come off them gradually. Sometimes the best way to do this is by taking the drug in liquid form. I'd like to say you should do this with the help of a professional, but in this case, there are very few doctors who understand the complexities. There are details of support groups and charities at the back of this book (see pages 325–8).

One of the problems is that no one, not even our doctors and regulators, is given the full facts, not just on antidepressants but other drugs too. As Professor Tim Kendall says: 'Drug companies are all about making money, vast amounts of it, and have shown themselves to be completely dishonest in the past and there is no reason to suppose that will change while the profits to be made remain so large. The only way forward in all of this is to change the law so that they are forced by law to publish all their trials and data.'[6]

If you care about this issue, there is a campaign to change the law so drug trials are made public – it's called alltrials.net.

Whenever a report comes out in the paper, as has happened recently, about antidepressants causing suicides, there is an outcry from those who say what about all the lives that have been saved? To which I say, the facts borne out in trials show us that these people are in the minority, most would get better anyway, and we've no idea what the long-term effects are, even on those who start out well.

It is an uncomfortable fact that while there are some people who do well, they are in fact a small proportion of those who are prescribed antidepressants. In fact, half stop treatment within a month.[7] As Professor David Healy says: 'Of the remainder in any 100 taking part in clinical trials, very few people are actually helped by the pill. Some improve spontaneously, while others simply get better by seeing a doctor... Multiply this by all those who are put on medication and indeed many people have been helped but even more are harmed or don't benefit, and for the most part those people are voiceless.'[8]

In the last two years my own experience mirrors this as I've met many more people who have been harmed than people who have benefited from antidepressants. These are people I've met coincidentally through my everyday life, not as part of my research. Even with those who say they benefit, many confide the drugs have side effects, the most common being they can't have sex, put on a significant amount of weight and it's hard to come off them. A recent conversation with a close friend revealed to me that in addition to suffering both of those, she also kept on falling over from losing her balance. And this was someone who told me she benefited from taking Prozac! I haven't met anyone who has been warned of any of these side effects by their prescribing doctor.

Since I came to suspect my dad's suicide was linked to medication, I have come across a number of people who have told me how now they realise suicides in the family through generations may well be linked to adverse drug reactions rather than depression.

The results of my DNA test came back and showed I have three genetic polymorphisms. Selma Eikelenboom, the forensic expert who carried out the test, is sure these defective genes are responsible for causing my dramatic reaction to the drugs. Other experts argue that too little is known to conclude we have found defective genes that are responsible for causing adverse drug reactions.

So I've given you all the facts I know, but the truth is we never have all the facts, and even when we do, we choose the facts that support our beliefs and ignore the rest. And beliefs are only important in that they determine our actions.

THE PILL THAT STEALS LIVES

My decision now is to choose a set of beliefs that puts me in the driving seat of my life rather than a set that gives me a life dependent on badly tested drugs with terrible side effects, on professionals and big companies who are making money by convincing us we're ill.

I'm lucky because I don't have a real clinical mental illness, and in those instances, experts say these pills can really help. But I'm no different from most people around the world who are on antidepressants. A survey showed that as many as two-thirds of the antidepressants prescribed by GPs are for people much like me, even though the NHS guidelines say the drugs should only be used for those with severe depression.[9]

People say to me, so what's the alternative to antidepressants? The answer is that for most of us, it's probably what Peter Gøtzsche said: 'No antidepressants'.

Life can be shit, it's true, but is it any worse than it was for other generations who have coped without medication? Grief, despair, heartbreak, these are all perennial themes, not just inventions of us, the 'worried well.' My own experience tells me the mind and body have a unique ability to deal with life's ups and downs. If you try to short-circuit that process with any kind of medication – drink, drugs, prescribed or illegal – then you do so at your peril.

Everyone has their own individual solutions to problems, but the things that have helped me through are finding people with wisdom, confronting problems before they spiral out of control, and last, but most definitely not least, is the very thing that medication actually takes away by numbing us.

It's what I seek out now and nurture every single day. And it's what I try to gently suggest to my children as an alternative to Facebook, video games, or endless texting. It's what, if I were to win the Lottery or become prime minister, I would gladly pay Saatchi & Saatchi to promote with giant posters plastered everywhere. It's what makes us uniquely special, it's the very antidote to despair that is the essence of life, and in my very humble opinion is perhaps the altar we should be worshipping at. In the words of that good-looking Frenchman and at the risk of sounding terribly pretentious, it is *la chaleur humaine* – human warmth. And to take a pill that interferes with that, unless you absolutely have to, is, in my view, a very peculiar form of madness.

My final thought is for the people in this book who have suffered unimaginable loss and have chosen to deal with their pain without medication despite being offered it. They include Tim Tobin, whose wife, daughter, and parents-in-law were wiped out after his father-in-law took a gun and killed all of them after taking Seroxat (also known as Paxil) before turning a gun on himself. Olga Leclercq, whose daughter was one of many schoolchildren killed in the Sierre tunnel. She and all the grieving parents were offered antidepressants and she said no. And David Carmichael, who has to live every day with the agony of knowing he killed his son while psychotic after taking Seroxat. And those are just a few.

I'll never know for sure whether my dad was depressed or suicidal because of the drugs he was taking but I do know that my life is better now that I've stopped believing in a magic pill or that depression is hereditary.

So are Lily and Oscar's.

But that's just our story.

Postscript

On 13 March 2016, when I thought I'd concluded this book, the report investigating the Germanwings disaster came out.[1] A year before pilot Andreas Lubitz had locked himself into the cockpit of Flight 9525 and crashed the plane into the French Alps, killing 150 people on board. The investigators concluded he had done it on purpose and that he was psychotic, but they put this down to his depression. When I got to the section about his medical history a wave of sickness came over me. Ten days before the appalling tragedy, Andreas Lubitz had been prescribed 20 mg of the antidepressant escitalopram along with zopiclone sleeping tablets. He was also taking mirtazapine. This means that when he crashed that plane he was on exactly the same combination of antidepressant medication and sleeping tablets that caused me to become psychotic, attacking myself with a knife, thinking I'd killed my kids and that I was in a video game or a dream that I would wake from.

All the news reports have focused on Lubitz's apparent depressive illness. I already know from researching what happened to me that the chances of becoming psychotic because of depression are 1 in 20,000. The chances of becoming psychotic from antidepressant medication are 1 in 200.[2]

Gosh!

And that really is my final word.

SOURCES

Prologue

1. Professor David Healy, interview with author, October 2015
2. http://www.bbc.co.uk/news/world-europe-17362643
3. David Healy, *Let Them Eat Prozac: The Unhealthy Relationship between the Pharmaceutical Industry and Depression* (New York, 2006)
4. 'Student, 19, in Trial of New Antidepressant Commits Suicide', *New York Times*, 12 February 2004 (http://www.nytimes.com/2004/02/12/us/student-19-in-trial-of-new-antidepressant-commits-suicide.html?_r=0)
5. 'Antidepressants can raise the risk of suicide, biggest ever review finds', *Daily Telegraph*, 27 January 2016 (http://www.telegraph.co.uk/news/health/news/12126146/Antidepressants-can-raise-the-risk-of-suicide-biggest-ever-review-finds.html)
6. James Davies, *Cracked: Why Psychiatry is Doing More Harm Than Good* (London, 2013)
7. MailOnline, 15 May 2015 (http://www.dailymail.co.uk/sciencetech/article-3082987/Pets-Prozac-Dogs-separation-anxiety-feel-optimistic-taking-antidepressants.html)

8. David Healy, interview with author, October 2015

9. *Diagnostic and Statistical Manual of Mental Disorders*, Fifth Edition, DSM-5, American Psychiatric Association, 16 October 2014

10. Centre for Research on Globalization, 4 February 2014: http://www.globalresearch.ca/pill-nation-are-americans-over-medicated/5367349

11. Professor Dinesh Bhugra, interview with author, January 2016

12. *Daily Mail*, 22 September 2015, and David Healy, interview with author, October 2015

13. 'Antidepressants can raise the risk of suicide, biggest ever review finds', *Daily Telegraph*, 27 January 2016 (http://www.telegraph.co.uk/news/health/news/12126146/Antidepressants-can-raise-the-risk-of-suicide-biggest-ever-review-finds.html)

14. '"Staggering" rise in prescribing of anti-depressants', *Daily Telegraph*, 9 July 2014 (http://www.telegraph.co.uk/news/health/news/10957417/Staggering-rise-in-prescribing-of-antidepressants.html)

15. Professor Tim Kendall, interview with author, January 2016

16. http://davidhealy.org/prozac-and-ssris-twenty-fifth-anniversary/

17. http://www.alltrials.net

18. Dinesh Bhugra, interview with author, January 2016

19. 'How depression pills turned a high-flying film-maker into a zombie needing 24-hour care', *Daily Mail*, 22 September 2015

20. Joseph Glenmullen MD, *Prozac Backlash: Overcoming the Dangers of Prozac, Zoloft, Paxil, and Other Antidepressants with Safe, Effective Alternatives* (New York, 2001)

PART I: THE YEAR MY LIFE WAS STOLEN

Chapter 1: Saturday, 22 September 2012

1. Peter D. Kramer, *Listening to Prozac: A Psychiatrist Explores Antidepressant Drugs and the Remaking of the Self* (New York, 1997)

2. David Healy, *The Antidepressant Era* (Cambridge, Mass., 1999)

3. 'Depression is NOT caused by low serotonin . . .', *Daily Mail*, 25 December 2015 (http://www.dailymail.co.uk/health/article-3050380/Depression-NOT-caused-low-serotonin-levels-drugs-used-treat-based-myth-psychiatrist-claims.html)

4. Ronald W. M. Maris, 'Suicide and neuropsychiatric adverse effects of SSRI medications: methodological issues'; The Law Project for Psychiatric Rights (PsychRights) symposium (Philadelphia, 2002) (http://psychrights.org/Research/Legal/Evidence/MarisonSSRIsUnderDaubert.htm) See also http://ssristories.net/archive/show2ab0.html?item=2574

5. Akathisia: Wikipedia, March 2016 update (https://en.wikipedia.org/wiki/Akathisia)

6. M. H. Teicher, C. Glod, J. O. Cole, 'Emergence of Intense Suicidal Preoccupation During Fluoxetine Treatment', *The American Journal of Psychiatry* 147 (1990)

7. Richard DeGrandpre, 'The Lilly Suicides', *Adbusters: Journal of the Mental Environment* 41, 2002

8. http://missd.co

Chapter 2: Why I was Lucky to Survive

1. David Healy, http://davidhealy.org/prozac-and-ssris-twenty-fifth-anniversary/

2. John Cornwell, *The Power to Harm: Mind, Medicine, and Murder on Trial* (New York, 1996)

3. Ibid.

4. Joseph Glenmullen, MD. *Prozac Backlash: Overcoming the Dangers of Prozac, Zoloft, Paxil, and Other Antidepressants with Safe, Effective Alternatives* (New York, 2001)

5. John Cornwell, *The Power to Harm: Mind, Medicine, and Murder on Trial* (New York 1996)

6. Letter to the *BMJ*, 3 January 2005: Dr Breggin discusses the Eli Lilly Prozac documents.

7. Richard DeGrandpre, 'The Lilly Suicides', 2002, quoted in http://ssristories.org/deadliest-marketing-scandal-of-the-20th-century-the-lilly-suicides

8. Ibid.

9. 'Detailed Description of Antidepressant-Induced Homicidal Ideation After Only One Pill' (http://www.drugawareness.org/antidepressant-murdersuicide-airbus-co-pilot-deliberately-took-plane-down-echoes-egyptair-disaster)

10. http://www.drugawareness.org/why-i-took-a-gun-to-school-1/

11. Joseph Glenmullen MD, *Prozac Backlash: Overcoming the Dangers of Prozac, Zoloft, Paxil, and Other Antidepressants with Safe, Effective Alternatives* (New York, 2001)

12. 'Eternal Sunshine', *Guardian*, 13 May 2007 (http://www.theguardian.com/society/2007/may/13/socialcare.medicineandhealth)

13. David Healy, interview with author, October 2015

14. Ibid.

15. 'The Antidepressant Dilemma', *New York Times Magazine*, 21 November 2004 (http://www.nytimes.com/2004/11/21/magazine/the-antidepressant-dilemma.html)

16. David Healy, lecture: 'Hearts and Minds – Psychotropic Drugs and Violence', 29 May 2013

17. Ibid.

18. Gwen Olsen, *Confessions of an Rx Drug Pusher* (Bloomington Ind., 2009).

19. Yolande Lucire and Christopher Crotty, 'Antidepressant induced akathisia related homicides associated with diminishing mutations in metabolizing genes of the CYP450 family', *Journal of Pharmacogenomics and Personalized Medicine*, August, 2011

Chapter 6: Discovering I got off lightly

1. Interview with author, November 2015

2. Interview with author, November 2015

3. Interview with author, January 2016

Chapter 7: Sunday, 30 September 2012
1. Edward Shorter, *How Everyone Became Depressed: The Rise and Fall of the Nervous Breakdown* (New York, 2013)

Chapter 9: Final week at the private hospital, October 2012
1. David Healy, *Let Them Eat Prozac: The Unhealthy Relationship between the Pharmaceutical Industry and Depression* (New York, 2006)
2. Ibid.

Chapter 10: Friday, 12 October 2012
1. Joseph Glenmullen MD, *Prozac Backlash: Overcoming the Dangers of Prozac, Zoloft, Paxil, and Other Antidepressants with Safe, Effective Alternatives* (New York, 2001)
2. David Healy 'Shaping the Intimate: Influences on the Experience of Everyday Nerves', *Social Studies of Science* 34, 219–245 (2004)

Chapter 11: Why antidepressants make some people suicidal
1. Interview with author, November 2015

Chapter 12: The day my life was saved
1. David Healy, interview with author , October 2015

[section head]Part II: The Pill That Steals Lives

Chapter 15: Saturday, 5 September 2015
1. Rebekah Beddoe, *Dying for a Cure: A Memoir of Antidepressants, Misdiagnosis and Madness* (Sydney, 2007)
2. https://www.lawyersandsettlements.com/articles/zyprexa-suicide/zyprexa-fine-01864.htmlI
3. Gwen Jones-Edwards, 'An eye-opener', *Open Mind93*, September/

October 1998 (http://2spl8q29vbqd3lm23j2qv8ck.wpengine.netdna-cdn.com/wp-content/uploads/2012/08/Gwen-Eye-opener-Phil-Thomas.pdf)

4. Chris Barton, 'Unravelling Madness', *NZ Herald*, 4 April 2009 (http://www.nzherald.co.nz/news/print.cfm? objectid=10565099)

5. http://davidhealy.org/benefit-risk-madness-antipsychotics-and-suicide/

6. http://www.fiercepharma.com/special-reports/olanzapine-top-us-generic-blockbusters

7. Gwen Olsen, *Confessions of an Rx Drug Pusher* (Bloomington Ind., 2009)

8. Interviews with author, 2014

9. Interview with author, February 2015

10. Multiple interviews with author

Chapter 18: Monday, 14 September 2015

1. http://www.numbdocumentary.com/Numb_Documentary/Home.html

2. Conversation with David Healy, February 2016

3. Bloomberg Business (www.Bloomberg.com), 10 July 2010

4. Conversation with Darren Hanison from Fortitude Law, January 2016; see also: http://www.fortitudelaw.uk/product-liability/seroxat-group-action/

5. Interview with author, February 2016 (Charles is not his real name)

6. Interview with author, September 2014

Chapter 19: Tuesday 15 September 2015

1. Conversation with Darren Hanison from Fortitude Law, January 2016

2. Interview with author, June 2014

3. Council for Evidence-Based Psychiatry (CEPG) briefing note, 'The Harmful Effects of Overprescribing Benzodiazepines, Antidepressants and Other Psychiatric Medications', 29 June 2015

4. Irving Kirsch, *The Emperor's New Drugs: Exploding the Antidepressant Myth* (London, 2009)

5. Irving Kirsch, 'Antidepressants and the Placebo Effect', PMC (PubMedCentral) (http://www.ncbi.nlm.nih.gov/pmc/articles/PMC4172306)

6. Tim Kendall, interview with author, January 2016

7. James Davies, *Cracked: Why Psychiatry is Doing More Harm Than Good* (London, 2013)

Chapter 22: Friday, 18 September 2015

1. Interviews with author

2. James Davies, *Cracked: Why Psychiatry is Doing More Harm Than Good* (London, 2013)

3. James Davies, op. cit., interview with Dr Robert Spitzer

4. James Davies, op. cit.

5. Peter Gøtzsche, *Deadly Medicines and Organised Crime: How Big Pharma Has Corrupted Healthcare* (Abingdon, 2013)

6. *Toronto Star*: (http://www.thestar.com/life/health_wellness/2009/08/22/canadian_named_in_hrt_scandal.html)

7. David Healy, *Let Them Eat Prozac: The Unhealthy Relationship between the Pharmaceutical Industry and Depression* (New York, 2006)

8. Peter Gøtzsche, *Deadly Medicines and Organised Crime: How Big Pharma Has Corrupted Healthcare* (Abingdon, 2013)

9. Ibid.

Chapter 27 Tuesday, 22 September 2015

1. 'How Depression Pills Turned a High-flying Film-maker Into a Zombie Needing 24-hour Care', *Daily Mail*, 22 September 2015 (http://www.dailymail.co.uk/health/article-3243688/How-depression-pills-turned-zombie-high-flying-film-maker-ended-needing-24-hour-care-prescribed-medication-didn-t-need.html)

Chapter 28: Still Tuesday, 22 September 2015

THE PILL THAT STEALS LIVES

1. https://kclpure.kcl.ac.uk/portal/en/persons/allan-young(6bf03185-e533-4ac2-88ba-76349ba04ddf)/biography.html

Chapter 29: Saturday, 3 October 2015

1. Department of Health and Human Services, Food and Drug Administration, Center for Drug Evaluation and Research. Psychopharmacologic Drugs Advisory Committee With the Pediatric Subcommittee Of the Anti-Infective Drugs Advisory Committee. Bethesda, Maryland, Monday 2 February 2004. Transcript: http://www.fda.gov/ohrms/dockets/ac/04/transcripts/4006T1.htm
2. SFO investigating GSK: http://www.bbc.co.uk/news/business-27597312
3. http://www.nationalinjuryhelp.com/defective-drugs/prozac
4. Ben Goldacre, *Bad Science* (London, 2009)
5. David Healy, interview author, January 2016

Chapter 30: Sunday, 4 October 2015

1. Department of Health and Human Services, Food and Drug Administration, Center for Drug Evaluation and Research. Psychopharmacologic Drugs Advisory Committee With the Pediatric Subcommittee Of the Anti-Infective Drugs Advisory Committee. Bethesda, Maryland, Monday 2 February 2004. Transcript: http://www.fda.gov/ohrms/dockets/ac/04/transcripts/4006T1.htm
2. CBS News 48 Hours, *Prescription for Murder*, 13 April 2005 (http://www.cbsnews.com/news/prescription-for-murder-13-04-2005/)
3. Department of Health and Human Services, Food and Drug Administration, Center for Drug Evaluation and Research. Psychopharmacologic Drugs Advisory Committee With the Pediatric Subcommittee Of the Anti-Infective Drugs Advisory Committee. Monday 2 February 2004. Transcript: http://www.fda.gov/ohrms/dockets/ac/04/transcripts/4006T1.htm
4. The *Batman* killer: http://davidhealy.org/the-hidden-gorilla/

5. Columbine High School shootings: https://www.youtube.com/watch?v=DpinCRaAQOk

6.www.kcl.ac.uk/ioppn/news/records/2015/July/CulturalandeconomicfactorsaffectEuropeanantidepressantuse.aspx

Chapter 31: Monday, 5 October 2015

1. http://www.bbc.co.uk/news/world-europe-17362643

2. *BMJ* 'Restoring Study 329: efficacy and harms of paroxetine and imipramine in treatment of major depression in adolescence', 16 September 2015 (http://www.bmj.com/content/351/bmj.h4320). *BMJ* 2015;351:h4320)

3. http://study329.org

4. http://www.theguardian.com/business/2012/jul/03/glaxosmithkline-fined-bribing-doctors-pharmaceuticals

5. Interview with author, July 2014

6. Paul H. Wender, MD, *ADHD: Attention-Deficit Hyperactivity Disorder in Children, Adolescents and Adults* (New York, 2000)

7. David Healy, interview with author

8. http://ahrp.org/bbc-panorama-unprecedented-public-response-to-evidence-of-ssri-drug-harm/

9. Healy, David. *Let Them Eat Prozac: The Unhealthy Relationship between the Pharmaceutical Industry and Depression* (New York, 2006) and *The Antidepressant Era* (Cambridge Mass., 1999)

10. Interview with author

Chapter 36: Friday, 16 October 2015

1. John Cornwell, *The Power to Harm: Mind, Medicine, and Murder on Trial* (New York, 1996)

2. James Davies, *Cracked: Why Psychiatry is Doing More Harm Than Good* (London, 2013)

3. Mental Health, A Call for World Health Ministers (Ministerial Round Table 2001), World Health Organization

(http://www.who.int/mental_health/advocacy/en/Call_for_Action_MoH_Intro.pdf)

4. Daniel Carlat, *Unhinged: The Trouble with Psychiatry – a doctor's revelations about a profession in crisis* (New York, 2010)

5. Charlotte Waddell et. al., 'Child Psychiatric Epidemiology and Canadian Public Policy-Making: the state of the science and the art of the possible', *Canadian Journal of Psychiatry* 47(9), November 2002: 825–32

6. Guilherme Polanczyk et al., 'The worldwide prevalence of ADHD: a systematic review and metaregression analysis', *The American Journal of Psychiatry*, 164 (6):942–8, 2007

7. James Davies, *Cracked: Why Psychiatry is Doing More Harm Than Good* (London, 2013)

8. http://www.place2be.org.uk

9. http://www.bbc.co.uk/news/health-35756602

10. Interview with author, December 2015

11. http://www.nytimes.com/2004/08/22/magazine/did-antidepressants-depress-japan.html?_r=0

12. Ibid.

13. Sarah Rule, interview with author, January 2016

14. Interview with author, March 2016

15. Interview with author, December 2015

16. Joseph Glenmullen, MD, *Prozac Backlash: Overcoming the Dangers of Prozac, Zoloft, Paxil, and Other Antidepressants with Safe, Effective Alternatives* (New York, 2001)

17. David Healy, interview with author, October 2015

Epilogue

1. David Healy, interview with author, October 2015

2. Ibid.

3. David Healy and Graham Aldred, 'Antidepressant drug use and the risk of suicide', *International Review of Psychiatry* 17, 163–172 (2005)

4. 'A Deadly Emotional Disease', *Harvard Magazine*, July/August 2006; Aand 'Study of treatment-resistant depression' at the Clinical Neuoroscience Research Centre, published in *Biological Psychiatry*, 15 October 2003

5. A. L. Montejo et al., 'Incidence of sexual dysfunction associated with antidepressant agents: a prospective multicenter study of 1022 outpatients', Spanish working group for the study of psychotropic-related sexual dysfunction, *Journal Clinical Psychiatry*, 2001, taken from *Deadly Medicines and Organised Crime: How Big Pharma Has Corrupted Healthcare* by Peter C. Gøtzsche (Abingdon, 2013)

6. Tim Kendall, interview with author, January 2016

7. David Healy and Graham Aldred, 'Antidepressant drug use and the risk of suicide', *International Review of Psychiatry* 17, 163-172 (2005)

8. David Healy, interview with author January 2016

9. http://www.dailymail.co.uk/health/article-3024604/More-two-thirds-people-taking-antidepressants-NOT-actually-depression-Doctors-discover-not-meet-official-criteria.html (*Daily Mail*, 3 April 2015); and Rebekah Beddoe, *Dying for a Cure: A Memoir of Antidepressants, Misdiagnosis and Madness* (Sydney, 2007)

Postscript

1. Final Report, Accident on 24 March 2015 at Prads-Haute-Bléone to the Airbus A320-211 registered D-AIPX operated by Germanwings, BEA ,(Bureau D'Enquêtes et d'Analyses pour la sécurité de l'aviation civile), Ministère de L'Ecologie, du Développement durable et de l'Energie. (https://www.bea.aero/uploads/tx_elyextendttnews/BEA2015-0125.en-LR_04.pdf)

2. David Healy, interview with author, March 2016

HELPFUL INTERNET SITES

http://antidepaware.co.uk/
Promoting awareness of the dangers of antidepressants. Reports
on coroner inquests and possible links to antidepressant-induced
suicide.

http://ssristories.org/
SSRI Stories is a collection of over 6,000 stories that have appeared in
the media (newspapers, TV, scientific journals) in which prescription
drugs were mentioned and in which the drugs may be linked to a
variety of adverse outcomes, including violence.

http://survivingantidepressants.org/
Surviving Antidepressants is a peer-support group for withdrawal
syndrome.

http://fiddaman.blogspot.co.uk/
Run by UK antidepressant campaigner Bob Fiddaman. Related, in the
main, to GlaxoSmithKline's activities and Seroxat.

http://davidhealy.org/blog/
Psychiatrist, psychopharmacologist, scientist, author. Blog that is updated daily and offers reader debate.

http://rxisk.org/
RxISK is a free, independent drug-safety website to help you weigh the benefits of any medication against its potential dangers.

http://cepuk.org
Council for Evidence-Based Psychiatry 'exists to communicate evidence of the potentially harmful effects of psychiatric drugs to the people and institutions in the UK that can make a difference'.

http://www.antidepressantsfacts.com
Features research, articles, studies and personal experiences relating to antidepressants.

http://www.comingoff.com
Up-to-date information about psychiatric medication and the withdrawal process. The site has been created by people who have gone through it themselves and come out the other side.

http://www.mind.org.uk
Leading mental-health charity in England and Wales, working 'to create a better life for people with experience of mental distress'.

http://www.mind.org.uk/information-support/drugs-and-treatments/antidepressants-a-z/overview/#.VzTxar6o2iw
For a list of antidepressants currently used in the UK giving their generic names and their most common trade names in the UK.

THE PILL THAT STEALS LIVES

www.mhra.gov.uk
The government's Medicines and Healthcare Products Regulatory Agency, where you are supposed to report adverse drug reactions.

www.april.org.uk
UK charity giving a voice to patients and those bereaved due to adverse drug reactions or severe withdrawal effects.

http://missd.co
Medication-Induced Suicide Prevention and Education Foundation in Memory of Stewart Dolin is a non-profit organisation dedicated to honouring the memory of Stewart Dolin and other victims of akathisia by raising awareness of akathisia.

www.cochrane.org
A global independent network of researchers, professionals, patients, carers and people interested in health. Contributors from more than 130 countries work together to provide research and information that is free from commercial sponsorship.

www.alltrials.net
Campaigning group dedicated to getting all drug trials published.

www.madinamerica.com
Provides news of psychiatric research, original journalism articles, and a forum for an international group of writers.

survivingantidepressants.org
A site for peer support, discussion, and documentation of withdrawal and withdrawal syndrome caused by psychiatric drugs, specifically antidepressants.

http://www.seroxatusergroup.org.uk
Set up by UK patients using the GlaxoSmithKline medication Seroxat
to provide support and advice to users of the medication and to their
families and friends.

www.antidepressant-tragedies.co.uk
This website is dedicated to sharing information about suicidal
actions and thoughts caused by antidepressants.

http://actionpddwordpress.org
Action on Prescribed Drug Dependence (Scotland). Campaigning
group seeking recognition of the suffering experienced by patients
dependent on sleeping pills, tranquillisers, antidepressants and
painkillers.

www.thepillthatsteals.com
Set up by the author to help people publicise their stories. There is a
'Stolen Lives' section where people can upload a short synopsis about
a life that has been stolen, either permanently or temporarily, by
antidepressant and antipsychotic medication.